Volume 8

Econometrics Exams

Economics Reading Lists, Course Outlines, Exams, Puzzles & Problems

eno river press

Compiled by Edward Tower, September 1995
Duke University & The University of Auckland

NOTE TO USERS AND POTENTIAL CONTRIBUTORS

These teaching materials are drawn from both undergraduate and graduate programs at 105 major colleges and universities. They are designed to widen the horizons of individual professors and curriculum committees. Some include suggestions for term-paper topics, and many of the reading lists are useful guides for students seeking both topics and references for term papers and theses. Thus, they should enable faculty members to advise students more effectively and efficiently. They will also be useful to prospective graduate students seeking more detailed information about various graduate programs and to librarians responsible for acquisitions in economics. Finally, they may interest researchers and administrators who wish to know more about how their own work and the work of their department is being received by the profession.

The exams, puzzles and problems include both undergraduate and graduate exams contributed by economics departments and individual professors. They should be especially useful to professors making up exams and problem sets and to students studying for Ph.D. exams. They may also serve as the focus for study groups.

From time to time, we will reprint updated and expanded versions. Therefore, we welcome new or updated teaching materials, particularly those which complement material in this collection or cover areas we missed. Potential contributors should contact Ed Tower, Economics Department, Box 90097, Duke University, Durham, North Carolina 27708-0097, U.S.A., **tower@econ.duke.edu**

While Eno River Press has copyrighted the entire collection, authors of the various parts retain the right to reproduce and assign the reproduction of their own materials as they choose. Thus, anyone wishing to reproduce particular materials should contact their author. Similarly, those wishing to make verbatim use of departmental examinations, except as teaching materials for one's own class, should contact the department chair concerned.

Associate Compilers for this series are:
Ömer Gökçekuş, Visiting Lecturer, Duke University
Chao Jing, Graduate Instructor, University of Colorado
Wells D. Tower, Senior at Wesleyan University

Dan Tower helped produce the volumes with creativity and energy. Nancy Hurtgen and Tom Hurtgen advised on many aspects of the project. Members of the Duke Economics Department have been helpful from the inception of the project, and belated thanks go to Allen C. Kelley, who suggested in 1980 the usefulness of collecting syllabi.

Eno River Press
115 Stoneridge Drive
Chapel Hill, North Carolina 27514-9737
U.S.A.
Fax & Phone: (919) 967-8246

ISBN for the volume: 0-88024-188-8
ISBN for the series: 0-88024-160-8
Library of Congress Catalog Number: 95-061333

ECONOMETRICS EXAMS

Contents

***

U = Undergraduate G = Graduate
RE = Reading List with Exams, Problems &/ or Term Paper Topics

UCLA: Economics G
Four Hours

ECONOMETRICS
COMPREHENSIVE EXAMINATION
FALL 1994

There are two sections to the examination.

All candidates must do 2 questions from Part One and 3 from Part Two

Part One

There are three questions. You must do two. Each question has the same number of points.

1. Consider the following simple linear regression model

$$y_i = \alpha + \beta x_i + u_i, \quad i = 1, \cdots, n,$$

where u_i and x_i are independently distributed of each other, $u_i \sim N(0, \sigma_i^2)$. You have data on y and x. Explain how to estimate α and β and their standard errors for each of the following cases.

(a) $u_i = \rho u_{i-1} + e_i$, $i = -\infty, \cdots, -1, 0, 1, \cdots, \infty$, with e_i being i.i.d. $N(0, \sigma_e^2)$.

(b) $E(u_i u_j) = 0 \; \forall i \neq j$ and $\sigma_i^2 = \exp(\delta_0 + \delta_1 x_i)$, δ_0 and δ_1 are unknown.

(c) $E(u_i u_j) = 0 \; \forall i \neq j$ but σ_i^2's are completely unknown.

(d) σ_i^2's are completely unknown and u_i's are serially correlated up to a finite order, say L (Here, L is assumed to be much smaller than n.).

(e) $E(u_i u_j) = 0 \; \forall i \neq j$. $\sigma_i^2 = \sigma^2$ (constant) $\forall i = 1, \cdots, n$. Now assume that u_i and x_i are correlated. But, you observe an instrumental variable z_i such that $E(u_i z_i) = 0$ and $|E(x_i z_i)| > 0$.

(f) $E(u_i u_j) = 0 \; \forall i \neq j$. σ_i^2's are completely unknown. Again, assume that u_i and x_i are correlated. But, you observe an instrumental variable z_i such that $E(u_i z_i) = 0$ and $|E(x_i z_i)| > 0$.

(g) $E(u_i u_j) = 0 \; \forall i \neq j$. $\sigma_i^2 = \sigma^2$ (constant) $\forall i = 1, \cdots, n$. Assume that u_i and x_i are correlated. But, you observe two instrumental variables $w_i \neq z_i$ such that $E(u_i z_i) = 0$, $|E(x_i z_i)| > 0$, $E(u_i w_i) = 0$, and $|E(x_i w_i)| > 0$.

NOTE: Your score will be positively related to the efficiency of the estimator you are proposing.

2. Let $\{X_i : i = 1, 2, \ldots N\}$ be the sequence of random variables generated by (independently) rolling a six sided die N times. Thus if the 4 is face up on the ith roll, $X_i = 4$.

(a) Propose estimators for the probability of each side of the die turning up.

(b) Explain the difference between the Weak Law of Large Numbers and the Strong Law of Large Numbers by examining the limiting behavior of estimated probabilities as $N \to \infty$.

(c) Propose a test for a fair die (i.e. each side is equally likely).

3. Give very brief, succinct definitions, sufficient to demonstrate your clear understanding of the following concepts:

(a) increasing hazard rate (positive duration dependence)

(b) Box-Cox transformation

(c) Gauss-Newton method

(d) Akaike's information criterion

(e) Hausman-type test

(f) cointegration

(g) Heckman's selectivity correction

(h) translog specification

(i) error-components specification

(j) Tobit specification

Part Two

There are six questions. You must do three. Each question has the same number of points.

1. Let duration variable T_i have the following proportional hazard rate

$$h_i(t) = h_0(t)\exp(x_i\beta), \quad i = 1, \cdots, n,$$

with x_i being known constants.

(a) When $h_0(t) = \lambda$ (a constant), compute the expected value of T_i assuming that x_i is constant over time.

(b) When $h_0(t) = \lambda\alpha t^{\alpha-1}$ and when T_i is continuously observed, explain how you would estimate (α, β) and its variance-covariance matrix.

(c) When $h_0(t)$ is not parametrically specified and when T_i is continuously observed, explain how you would estimate β and its variance-covariance matrix.

(d) If $h_0(t)$ is not parametrically specified and if T_i is available up to intervals $I_1 = (0,1], I_2 = (1,2], I_3 = (2,\infty)$ how could you estimate β and its variance-covariance matrix. Explain.

(e) Let us say that you are still facing the same situation as in (d) above. How could you test the *proportionality* assumption. Explain.

(f) As you include more and more explanatory variables, what do you expect to happen to the estimated pattern of the baseline hazard function $h_0(t)$? Explain.

2. You want to analyze automobile purchase behavior of households using a *sample of households that in fact have purchased* a car during a certain period of time (Assume that observations are independent.). Obviously, there are other households in the *population* that have not spent at all on automobile purchase during the same observation period. You have a sample of households ($i = 1, \cdots, n$) with data on the amount of money spent on car purchase (y_i), and on various household characteristics (x_i) such as its income, occupation of the head of the household, family size, year of existing car. To describe this behavior, assume that a household realizes the desired amount when the desired amount is positive ($y_i = y_i^*$ if $y_i^* > 0$) where $y_i^* = x_i\beta + u_i$ denotes the desired amount of money spent on car purchase with u_i being independently and identically distributed according to a normal distribution with mean zero and unknown variance σ^2. Note that you observe neither y_i nor x_i when $y_i^* \leq 0$.

(a) Write down the likelihood function for your sample.

(b) Is a two-step Heckman type estimation feasible? Discuss.

(c) Suggest a non-linear least squares estimator.

(d) Indicate how you obtain the asymptotic variance-covariance matrix of the estimator defined in (c) above. Is White's idea of obtaining heteroscedasticity consistent variance-covariance matrix estimator applicable here?

(e) How could you improve on the non-linear least squares estimator you defined in (c). Explain.

(f) Discuss whether you can estimate β without assuming the normality of the error terms.

3. (a) Find the autocovariance function, the autocorrelation function and the spectral density function of the MA(2) process:

$$Y_t = \mu + \epsilon_t + 0.8\epsilon_{t-1} + 0.5\epsilon_{t-2},$$

with ϵ_t IID, mean zero and variance 2.

(b) For the AR(2) process with the same innovation seqence as the MA(2)

$$Y_t - 1.4Y_{t-1} + .9Y_{t-2} = \epsilon_t,$$

find,

i. the roots m_1, m_2 of the associated polynomial $m^2 - 1.4m + 0.9 = 0$,

ii. the autocorrelation function,

iii. the spectral density function.

4. (a) Discuss in a univariate time series analysis why the presence of a unit root can drastically affect the accuracy of long run forecasts.

(b) Describe the Dickey-Fuller test for a unit root in an AR(1) model. Why are standard t-ratio tables not valid for inference under the null of a unit root?

5. Explain how the loss function used in Generalized Method of Moments (GMM) differs from that used in least squares estimation. Show how in the linear regression model with homoscedastic independent errors, GMM and ordinary least squares produce the same parameter estimates for the conditional expectation function.

6. PROBLEM:

U.S. President Bill Clinton promised middle-class tax cuts during his presidential campaign, but was unable to deliver on this promise due to the severity of the federal budget deficit. Suppose you are retained by a consortium of charitable organizations to forecast the likely consequences for charitable donations of the variety of tax proposals anticipated from each of the two major U.S. political parties during the 1996 Presidential campaign.

AVAILABLE DATA:

You will have access to survey data from a national mail survey of 3000 US households. The survey asks respondents to itemize their charitable contributions by type of charity for the previous year and collects the usual complement of household sociodemographic characteristics (including 14 income brackets). The survey also collected information on political contributions and on donations to major religious organizations. The survey was conducted by an experienced market research firm, and the response rate was 52%. Zip codes for non-respondents were retained.

CHALLENGE:

Are the available data likely to be adequate to the task of addressing this research question? What problems would you anticipate with these data, and what other information might you need to collect? What are likely to be the properties of the endogenous variable(s) and will special estimators be necessary? What sort of an econometric specification would you propose to estimate, with which software, and what particular parameters would be crucial to your analysis? What particular hypotheses might you test, and how would you accomplish the required "forecasting" effort?

UNIVERSITY OF CALIFORNIA, LOS ANGELES
Department of Economics

Comprehensive Examination

Fall 1993 | Aoki, Cameron, Pesaran, Ryu

ECONOMETRICS

INSTRUCTIONS: Please do ALL THREE (3) questions in section A and TWO (2) of the four questions in section B. You have four hours to complete this examination. If you find it necessary to make assumptions in order to proceed with an answer, make these assumptions explicit.

SECTION A:

A.1. You draw a random sample of n observations ($i = 1, \cdots, n$) to study returns to schooling and to union membership. Consider the following regression equation:

$$\log w_i = x_i'\beta + \gamma_1 S_i + \gamma_2 D_i + \epsilon_i,$$

where x_i' is a row vector of socio-economic variables, w_i wage rate, S_i schooling year, and D_i union status dummy which takes value one for union members. You strongly believe that unmeasured factors affecting schooling choice and union membership also affect wage rates.

(1) Discuss how you can estimate returns to schooling (γ_1) and returns to union membership (γ_2). You need to discuss at least two estimation methods, and comment on their relative merits.

(2) Now you have two instrumental variables z_{1i} and z_{2i} which are expected to be correlated with S_i and D_i, respectively, but not with ϵ_i. Assuming that ϵ_i is i.i.d. with mean zero and variance σ^2, obtain the GMM (generalized method of moments) estimator of $(\beta' : \gamma_1 : \gamma_2)'$. Also, obtain its variance-covariance matrix consistently.

(3) How would your answer to the above question (2) be changed if you have an additional instrumental variable z_{3i}?

(4) How would your answer to (2) be changed if ϵ_i are independent but heteroscedastic.

(5) How would your answer to (2) be changed if ϵ_i follows an MA(2) process, a moving average process of order two.

A.2 Suppose you are interested in studying the Economics of the Family, in particular, child-custody arrangements after marital separations or divorces. You are particularly interested in modelling the determinants of child custody (joint, paternal, maternal), legal or informal alimony and child-support arrangements (present, absent), and father's and mother's gross labor earnings (annual, in thousands of dollars). Suppose these variables are all jointly determined, since child custody may influence earning ability and earning ability may influence custody.

In the past, mothers were most frequently awarded custody. In addition, mother's earnings were substantially less. Suppose you are particularly interested in assessing the effects of greater prevalence of joint and paternal custody on mother's earnings. You have a large data set on individual families wherein parents are either separated or divorced.

Given the nature of the variables involved, what type of model would you specify and how would you estimate it? What additional data would your model require? What specific hypotheses would you wish to formulate and how would you go about testing them? Be sure to identify which software would be appropriate for your estimation problem and what commands you might employ.

A.3. In the October 13 edition of the Los Angeles Times, there was a lengthy article on tax loopholes. Among other things, the reporter drew attention to large tax incentives for recycling equipment, asserting that casual empiricism suggested that virtually no firm that purchased recycling equipment seemed to know about the tax incentives until after the equipment had been purchased. Suppose you have been retained by the State of California to evaluate the effectiveness of these recycling tax incentives. The State wishes to know by how much these purchases would be reduced if the tax incentives were eliminated. They have provided you with a budget of $100,000 (a tiny fraction of the foregone tax revenues due to these incentives). How would you design a study to answer this question? Precisely what data would you collect and how? What type of econometric specification would be appropriate? What software would you anticipate using and why? Be sure to identify by name any likely pathologies in the data you might collect and pinpoint state-of-the-art econometric approaches to dealing with these.

SECTION B: (Choose 2 of these questions)

B.1. Dubin and McFadden (Econometrica 1984) jointly estimated the water-heat/space-heat choice and electricity consumption. Let V_w and V_s be indirect utilities from water-heat and space-heat, respectively. And let Y_w and Y_s be the electricity consumption amounts when a randomly selected household is forced to use water-heat system and space-heat system, respectively. Let

$$\begin{aligned} V_w &= z_w' \alpha_w + v_w \\ V_s &= z_s' \alpha_s + v_s \\ y_w &= x_w' \beta_w + u_w \\ y_s &= x_s' \beta_s + u_s \\ \text{with} \quad u_w &= \gamma_{ww} v_w + \gamma_{ws} v_s + \epsilon_w \\ u_s &= \gamma_{sw} v_w + \gamma_{ss} v_s + \epsilon_s. \end{aligned}$$

Assume that v_w and v_s are independent with the same distribution function $F(v) = \exp[-\exp(-v)]$, and that (ϵ_w, ϵ_s) is independent of (v_w, v_s) with zero means. Households are supposed to choose the heating system yielding the higher indirect utility. We observe for each household i $(i = 1, \cdots, n)$ in the sample (i) which heating system it has chosen, and (ii) how much electricity it has used.

(a) Discuss what kind of identifying restrictions you need to estimate parameters in the above model.

(b) Discuss how to estimate each parameter in the model consistently using a binary choice model and a two-step method (Hint on the two-step method: use

$$\begin{aligned} E(v_w \mid v_s - v_w < z_w' \alpha_w - z_s' \alpha_s) &= \lambda - \log P; \\ E(v_s \mid v_s - v_w < z_w' \alpha_w - z_s' \alpha_s) &= \lambda + \frac{1-P}{P} \log(1-P), \end{aligned}$$

where $\lambda = 0.577$ is the Euler's constant and

$$P = Pr(V_w > V_s) = \frac{\exp(z_w' \alpha_w)}{\exp(z_w' \alpha_w) + \exp(z_s' \alpha_s)}$$

B.2. Consider the bivariate first-order vector autoregressive model

$$\begin{bmatrix} x_t \\ y_t \end{bmatrix} = \begin{bmatrix} a_{11} & a_{12} \\ a_{21} & a_{22} \end{bmatrix} \begin{bmatrix} x_{t-1} \\ y_{t-1} \end{bmatrix} + \begin{bmatrix} \epsilon_{1t} \\ \epsilon_{2t} \end{bmatrix}$$

or, in matrix notation

$$\underline{w}_t = A\ \underline{w}_{t-1} + \underline{\epsilon}_t, \qquad \underline{\epsilon}_t \sim (0,\Sigma)$$

where $\Sigma = (\sigma_{ij})$ is a 2 x 2 nonsingular matrix.

(a) Assuming $|a_{22}| < 1$, derive the following univariate representation for $\{x_t\}$, and show that in general this is an ARMA(2,1) process. (L is the lag operator)

$$[\ 1-(a_{11} + a_{22} + a_{12}a_{21})L + a_{11}a_{22}L^2]\ X_t = a_{12}\epsilon_{2t} + (1 - a_{22}L)\epsilon_{1t}$$

(b) Let Ω_t be the information set at time t which contains all the observations on current and past values of x_t and y_t, i.e. $\Omega_t = (x_t, x_{t-1}, \ldots;\ y_t, y_{t-1} \ldots)$. Discuss the conditions under which the one step ahead forecast of x_t defined by $E(x_t | \Omega_{t-1})$ based on the bivariate VAR model outperforms the one step ahead forecast of x_t based on the univariate representation (2), in the mean square error sense.

(c) Suppose now that x_t and y_t are I(1) variables. Derive the condition under which x_t and y_t are cointegrated.

B.3. You want to analyze the tenure duration of CEOs (chief executive officers) in large U.S. companies using a random sample of n CEOs ($i = 1, \cdots, n$). As an economist, you expect that if a firm's abnormal return in the stock market is higher then the CEO's tenure duration will be longer. Let T_i denote the ith CEO's tenure, and x_i the corresponding firm's average abnormal return during ith CEO's tenure period, and other variables such as firm size, unionization ratio, and the CEO age. To see whether your intuition works, you model the tenure termination hazard rate as follows:

$$h_i(t) = h_0(t)e^{x_i\beta}, \ i = 1, \cdots, n \qquad (*).$$

(1) What is the expected sign of the coefficient of firm's abnormal return in the above hazard specification (*)? Explain.

(2) If $h_0(t)$ is known up to a finite number of parameters and if you observe T_i continuously, what will be the most efficient estimator of β. How to obtain its variance-covariance matrix estimate. Explain.

(3) If $h_0(t)$ is not parametrically specified and if you observe T_i continuously, how could you estimate β and its variance-covariance matrix. Explain.

(4) If $h_0(t)$ is not parametrically specified and if T_i is only available up to intervals $I_1 = (0, 1], I_2 = (1, 2], I_3 = (2, \infty)$ (in other words, you only know whether tenures end in the first three years, or in the second three years, or they last more than six years), how could you estimate β and its variance-covariance matrix. Explain.

(5) Under the setting as in (4) above, how could you test whether the baseline hazard rate is constant, that is, whether $h_0(t) = h_0$ for some constant h_0?

(6) As you add more and more explanatory variables, what do you expect to happen to the estimated pattern of the baseline hazard function $h_0(t)$? Explain.

(6) You want to test the proportionality assumption on the effect of abnormal return on the tenure termination hazard rate. The reason is as follows: at the beginning of the tenure period, board of directors is relatively hostile toward new CEOs. Therefore, performance matters a lot. On the other hand, later in the tenure period, most of the board members are appointed by the incumbent CEO and thus the CEO's position is relatively safe. In this later stage, CEO's performance does not matter much in determinating his turnover. In light of this argument, how could you change your model under situation (4) above. How could you test the proportionality assumption in (*) against the above non-proportionality scenario. Explain.

B.4. Consider the first-difference stationary m-vector process

$$\Delta x_t = A(L)\epsilon_t \quad \text{with } \epsilon_t \sim (0,\Sigma)$$

where

$$A(L) = A_0 + A_1 L + A_2 L^2 + \dots$$

and L is the lag operator.

(a) Show that

$$Var(x_{t+n} \mid \Omega_{t-1}) - Var(x_{t+n-1} \mid \Omega_{t-1}) = B_n \Sigma B_n'$$

where Var(.|) stands for the conditional variance operator and

$$B_n = A_0 + A_1 + \dots + A_n.$$

(b) Suppose that $z_t = \beta' x_t$ represents a cointegrating relation where β is an m x 1 vector. Show that

$$Var(z_{t+n} \mid \Omega_{t-1}) - Var(z_{t+n-1} \mid \Omega_{t-1}) = \beta' B_n \Sigma B_n' \beta$$

and hence or otherwise prove that the effects of shocks to x_t are not persistent as far as the cointegrating relation $z_t = \beta' x_t$ is concerned.

(c) Discuss the relevance of the result in (b) for the analysis of the speed of convergence of cointegrating relations to equilibrium.

UNIVERSITY OF CALIFORNIA, LOS ANGELES
Department of Economics

Comprehensive Examination -- Econometrics

September, 1992

Instructions: Answer THREE of the four general questions in Part A (questions 1, 2, 3, and 4) and choose ONE of Parts B (microeconometrics) and C (macroeconometrics). All questions have equal weight. You have four hours to complete this examination. Budget your time carefully. If, for some reason, the information provided in the question seems incomplete, make plausible assumptions (state them clearly) and answer to the best of your ability.

PART A (Answer <u>THREE</u> questions)

1. Simultaneous equations. (All parts weighted equally.)

a.) The usual simultaneous-equation model applies to

$$y_1 = \alpha_1 + \alpha_2 x_1 + u_1 \qquad (1)$$

$$y_2 = \alpha_3 y_1 + \alpha_4 x_2 + u_2 \qquad (2)$$

Under what specific assumptions would ordinary least squares techniques used on equation (2) alone be sufficient to estimate α_3 and α_4 consistently?

b.) The following two least squares regressions were obtained for a sample of 100 observations on these four variables:

$$\hat{y}_1 = -9x_1 + 3x_2$$

$$\hat{y}_2 = 3x_1 + x_2$$

As completely as you can, calculate estimates of the α parameters.

c.) Explain your options for estimation if the second equation in this model was modified to be:

$$y_2 = \alpha_3 y_1^2 + \alpha_4 x_2 + u_2 \qquad (2')$$

d.) Explain your options for estimation if the original specification applies but the variable y_1 is a dummy variable, taking on only the values of 0 or 1.

e.) How would you modify your estimation method if the original specification applies and all variables are continuous, but the raw data for these variables consist of 25 time-series observations for each of 4 cross-sectional entities?

PART A., continued.

2. Suppose you wish to estimate the parameters of the CES production function. The model is:

$$\ln Y = \ln \gamma - (\nu/\rho) \ln [\, \delta K^{-\rho} + (1 - \delta) L^{-\rho} \,] + \epsilon$$

a.) Suppose that you have access only to OLS estimation methods. Recall that a linear Taylor series approximation to $h(x,\beta)$ at a particular value for the parameter vector, β^0, is given by:

$$h(x,\beta) = h(x,\beta^0) + \Sigma_k\, \partial h(x,\beta)/\partial\beta_k \,\Big|_{\beta=\beta^0} \; (\beta_k - \beta_k^0).$$

Derive a linearized version of this model based on a Taylor-series expansion around the point $\rho = 0$. Explain carefully how you would recover point estimates of the parameters γ, ν, ρ, and δ.

b.) Now explain how you could use only derivative formulas and OLS estimation algorithms to attain non-linear least squares point estimates for this CES production function.

c.) How would you compute an estimate of the asymptotic covariance matrix for these parameter estimates?

3. Suppose spills at oil wells are known to follow a Poisson distribution:

$$f(n|\lambda) = e^{-\lambda}\lambda^n/n! \qquad n = 0,1,2,\ldots; \qquad \lambda > 0,$$

where λ is the expected number of spills at a given well and n is the actual number. Let m_j be the number of wells which had j spills.

a.) Suppose all wells are observed. Given $m_0, m_1, m_2, \ldots$, find an estimate of λ, and its standard error.

b.) Suppose wells without spills are not observed. Given $m_1, m_2, \ldots$, find estimates of m_0 and λ, and their covariance matrix.

c.) Suppose there are two types of wells: modernized and original. Suggest a method of estimating the effect of modernization on the frequency of spills.

PART A., continued.

4. The following table contains data on median income of blacks and whites by schooling level and also the median schooling by income level. Controlling for schooling, whites are better paid than blacks which suggests discrimination. But controlling for income, whites are better educated which suggests the reverse. Comment on the usefulness of these data for inferences about discrimination in the labor market. What additional information would be useful in drawing inferences about discrimination from these data? Develop a model which would indicate and measure the extent of discrimination and indicate how you would use the additional information in your model.

TABLE 1
Income and Education (1959)
Males (25+) Years of Age

(A)
Median Income by Schooling
Schooling (Years)

					High School		College	
	None	1-4	5-7	8	1-3	4	1-3	4+
White	1569	1962	3240	3981	5013	5529	6104	7779
Non-white	1042	1565	2353	2900	3253	3735	4029	4840

(B)
Median Schooling by Income
Income ($1,000's)

	None	0-1	1-2	2-3	3-4	4-5	5-6	6-7	7-9	10+
White	8.4	8.0	8.4	8.7	9.5	10.5	11.4	12.1	12.4	14.0
Non-white	6.9	5.1	6.5	7.8	8.7	9.3	10.4	11.2	12.1	12.8

Source: *U.S. Census of Population 1960* (vol. 1. Pt. 1, Table 223). United States Census Bureau, 1960. Hashimoto and Kochin, *Economic Inquiry*.

Choose ONE of either Part B or Part C. You will receive credit for answers to the questions in only one section.

PART B

5. Consider a foreigner who faces the decision whether to stay in his home country or to migrate to the United States. If this foreigner stays in his home country, he would earn

$$\ln W_{HOME} = X\beta_{HOME} + \epsilon_{HOME};$$

If he migrates to the United States, he would earn

$$\ln W_{U.S.} = X\beta_{U.S.} + \epsilon_{U.S.},$$

where X is a vector of individual specific covariates. He will migrate to the United States if the difference in log-wages exceeds the log-transaction cost C. Assuming that you have data on X and $W_{U.S.}$ only for those who migrated, explain how you could estimate the model. Specify assumptions you need and explain which parameters can be identified.

6. Consider a simple proportional hazard model with the hazard rate of death given by:

$$\lambda(t,x) = h_0(t)\, e^{\beta x},$$

where x is a single covariate. Explain how to estimate the model efficiently in each of the following cases:

a.) The baseline hazard $h_0(\cdot)$ is not parametrically specified; you observe n completed spells of duration $(x_1, t_1),\ldots,(x_n, t_n)$ and N-n censored spells of duration $(x_{n+1}, t_{n+1}),\ldots,(x_N, t_N)$.

b.) The baseline hazard $h_0(\cdot)$ is parametrically specified as $h_0(t) = \alpha t^{\alpha-1}$, $\alpha > 0$; observations are given as in (a.) above.

c.) The baseline hazard $h_0(\cdot)$ is not parametrically specified; observations are available only up to intervals: n individuals with covariates $x_1,\ldots,x_n$ (respectively) are known to have died during $t \in [0, 2)$ years and N-n individuals with covariates $x_{n+1},\ldots,x_N$ (respectively) are known to have lived longer than 2 years.

d.) The baseline hazard is given by $h_0(t) = \alpha t^{\alpha-1}$, $\alpha > 0$; observations are given as in (c.) above.

PART C

7. Consider the model:

$$y_t = \beta x_t + u_t, \qquad u_t = d_t\, u_{t-1} + \epsilon_t, \qquad t = \ldots -2, -1, 0, 1, 2, \ldots,$$

where the ϵ_t's are independently distributed with mean 0 and variance σ^2; the d_t's are independently distributed Bernoulli random variables which take value 1 with probability p and value 0 with probability 1-p, $0 \le p \le 1$. Assume that the ϵ_t's and the d_t's are mutually independent.

a.) Define wide sense (second-order, or covariance) stationarity.

b.) State the condition for wide-sense (second-order, or covariance) stationarity of u_t in terms of p. Comment on this condition.

c.) Under the condition of second-order stationarity, compute (i.) the variance of u_t; (ii.) the autocorrelation between u_t and u_{t-1}; and (iii.) the autocorrelation between u_t and u_{t-2}.

d.) Under the stationarity conditions, explain how to estimate the model.

8. a.) You desire to estimate the parameters of the following model:

$$y_t = \alpha + \beta\, x_t + \gamma\, y_{t-1} + \delta\, y_{t-2} + \epsilon_t$$

$$\epsilon_t = \rho\, \epsilon_{t-1} + u_t$$

Is there any problem with ordinary least squares? What method do you recommend?

b.) Show how to estimate a polynomial distributed lag model with lag of six periods and a third-order polynomial, using restricted least squares.

c.) Suppose you wish to fit a polynomial distributed lag model of the form:

$$\text{Investment}_t = \alpha + \beta\, \Sigma_i\, \delta_i\, \text{Profit}_{t-i} + \epsilon_i$$

Explain how you would go about determining an appropriate lag length and polynomial degree.

d.) Expand the rational lag model:

$$y_t = \frac{0.6 + 2L}{1 - 0.6L + 0.5\, L^2}\, x_t + \epsilon_t$$

What are the coefficients on x_t, x_{t-1}, x_{t-2}, x_{t-3} and x_{t-4}? (continued)

e.) Describe how to estimate the parameters of the model:

$$y_t = \alpha + \beta \frac{x_t}{1 - \gamma L} + \delta \frac{z_t}{1 - \phi L} + \epsilon_t$$

where ϵ_t is a serially uncorrelated, homoscedastic, classical disturbance.

f.) Discuss briefly:

i.) Shiller's smoothness prior

ii.) infinite lag models

Ph.D. Qualifying Examination — Fall 1991
UCLA Department of Economics

ECONOMETRICS

TIME: 4 hrs.

Instructions: Answer **ALL FOUR** questions in Part A. Answer **ANY TWO** questions in Part B. All questions have equal weight. Budget your time to average 40 minutes per question.

PART A

1. Explain briefly and succinctly **ALL 8** of the following:

(a) White's heteroscedasticity consistent covariance estimator
(b) Probability integral transformation
(c) Random effects models
(d) Generalized method of moments
(e) Semi-parametric estimation
(f) ARCH models
(g) Bootstrap
(h) Least absolute deviations (LAD) estimator

---

2. Recently the Federal Reserve Board announced a reduction of the prime interest rate to 5% per annum, an action that was interpreted by market analysts as a stimulant to a sluggish economy. Suppose that a Wall Street investment firm hires you to determine if this reduction in the prime rate can be expected to increase the future level of GNP. Suppose that you have access to monthly data on the growth rate of GNP(G), the rate of unemployment (U), the total number employed (E), the prime interest rate (r_0), a short term interest rate (r_1), a long term interest rate (r_2), and the inflation rate (π). As a first attempt to answer this question, an analyst at the firm had estimated the following regression.

$$G_t = \alpha + \beta_1 U_t + \beta_2 r_{0t} + \beta_3 r_t + \beta_4 r_{2t} + \beta_5 \pi_t + \beta_6 E_t$$

using monthly data and reported to the management of the firm that the prime rate (r_0) is not statistically significant.

(a) Comment on the work done by this analyst. List specifically any errors in the work.

(b) Suggest how you would analyze these data to help answer the question posed by the firm.

---

3. Models of spatial correlation have much in common with timewise autocorrelation. Discuss how they differ. Consider a model of agricultural innovation in an agrarian economy. Suppose you wish to model the determinants of whether a small farmer adopts a high-yield variety of seed ($d_i = 1$) or not ($d_i = 0$). Assume that you have a census of all $i = 1,\ldots,n$ farmers in the region. Assume that the farmer's latent expected profits from the innovation are a function of farm household attributes, X_i, as well as the latent expected profits from innovation by farmers who are adjacent neighbors. "Adjacency" is captured by a (n×n) matrix of ones and zeros (A_{ij}) where a one is entered if any pair of farms (i,j) is adjacent.

(a) Specify a functional form for farmer i's latent profits;

(b) Formulate a spatial analog of "habit-persistence" in the time-series analysis of discrete choice data (specify your assumptions);

(c) if the errors in (a) are i.i.d., what problems will afflict the errors in (b)?

(d) Derive a variance-normalized version of the model in (b);

(e) As a practical matter, what steps would you take in estimating the parameters of the original model.

---

4. Consider the following multiple regression model

$$y = X^*\beta + \epsilon,$$

where y is an n×1 vector of dependent variables, X* is an unobserved n×k matrix of data on a set of k true explanatory variables, β is k×1 parameter vector, and ϵ is an n×1 error vector. We are concerned about whether or not an observed n×k data matrix X is measuring X* with error. Let Z be an n×k data matrix on k instrumental variables which are correlated with X, but not correlated with the suspected measurement error. Also assume that both X and Z have full column rank.

(a) Sketch the main idea of Hausman's (Econometrica, 1978) specification test.

(b) Explain and write down the procedure whereby Hausman's specification testing idea can be implemented to test the existence of measurement error in X (a good answer would be to check every condition or logic of Hausman's specification test procedure).

PART B

5. Assume that a data vector y is distributed normally with mean $X\beta$ and covariance $\sigma^2 I$, where X is an observable matrix. Assume further that the vector β is normally distributed with mean 0 and covariance V.

(a) If σ^2 is known, find the following distributions:
  (i) The conditional distribution of β given y.
  (ii) The marginal distribution of y.

(b) What roles do the distributions (i) and (ii) play in a Bayesian analysis of regression?

(c) Indicate graphically the set of posterior means corresponding to the following families of prior distributions.
  (i) V proportional to the identity matrix.
  (ii) V diagonal
  (iii) V positive definite
  (iv) $V_* < V < V^*$ for given matrices V_* and V^*.

(d) To the best of your recollection, give the theorems applicable to your answers to question (c).

(e) How does your answer to (a) change if σ^2 is uncertain?

6(a) Show that the Kaplan-Meier estimator of the distribution (of a positive random variable) reduces to the empirical distribution function when there are no right censored observations (i.e., all observations are complete).

(b) You are hired as a consultant to a Bank which is planning to take over a branch of another bank called BCCI (whose assets have been recently taken over by the government). The management gives you data on 300,000 bank accounts which existed at this BCCI branch (and some still exist) between 1965 and 1991. The data consist of account characteristics such as year account began, whether it is currently active and if not the year it ended, annual interest rate paid and the year end balance of each account. Also available are associated covariates like interest rates on alternative assets (e.g., government bonds), annual inflation rate, leading indicators for the economy, and information on the individuals or commercial enterprises which held the account.

The management needs several pieces of information to calculate an appropriate bid for the takeover. Give an appropriate specification for a model which allows you to address the following questions:

  (i) What is the expected lifetime of an account which always maintains a certain minimum balance?
  (ii) How much longer do commercial accounts last over personal accounts?
  (iii) What is the impact of interest rates paid as well as the impact of returns on alternative assets on the average life of the accounts?

(iv) Briefly explain how you would conduct a Bayesian sensitivity analysis of your results.

---

7. A researcher is interested in study the wage differential between union and non-union members.

(a) He/she ran an ordinary least squares regression for the following wage equation:

$$\ln w_i = x_i\beta + \alpha d_i + \epsilon_i \qquad (1)$$

where i indices individuals, w_i is the observed wage rate, x_i is a set of nonstochastic explanatory variables, d_i is a union status dummy variable taking value 1 if individual i is a union member and 0 otherwise, and β, α are unknown parameter values. What is the researcher going to measure through the estimate of α? What might be a serious problem in the inference procedure?

(b) Now the research changed the setup as follows:

$$\begin{aligned} \ln w_{ui} &= x_i\beta_u + \epsilon_{ui}, \\ \ln w_{ni} &= x_i\beta_n + \epsilon_{ni}, \end{aligned} \qquad (2)$$

where the upper equation describes the union wage determination while the lower one describes the non-union wage determination. Explain the difference between this setup (b) and the previous one (a).

(c) Assume that a worker chooses union status according to the union and non-union wage differential, that is, worker i will be a union member if $\ln w_{ui} > \ln w_{ni}$, and a non-union member otherwise. (Use the setup in (b)). Also assume that $(\epsilon_{ui}, \epsilon_{ni})$ are i.i.d. across i, and are jointly normally distributed with mean vector $(0,0)$ and variances σ_u^2 and σ_n^2, respectively, and zero covariance. Write down the procedure by which the research could identify and estimate all the parameters in model (b), β_u, β_n, σ_u^2 and σ_n^2, using a two-step procedure. (HINT: When (u_1, u_2) is jointly normally distributed with mean vector $(0,0)$ and variances σ_1^2 and σ_2^2, respectively, and covariance σ_{12}, we have $E(u_1 | u_2 > -z) = \frac{\sigma_{12}}{\sigma_2} \cdot \frac{\phi(z/\sigma_2)}{\Phi(z/\sigma_2)}$, where ϕ, Φ are the p.d.f. and c.d.f, respectively, of standardized normal random variables.)

---

8. Consider the distributed lag model

$$y_t = \sum_{i=0}^{m} a_i x_{t-i} + \epsilon_t$$

where $\epsilon_t \sim$ i.i.d. (0,1), and x_t follows the AR(1) process

$$x_t = \rho x_{t-1} + u_t,$$

where $u_t \sim$ i.i.d. (0,1) is distributed independently of ϵ_t.

(a) Find the long-run response of y_t to a unit change in x_t, in the case where $|\rho| < 1$.

(b) Suppose that the long run response defined in (a) was estimated by regressing y_t against x_t. Find the inconsistency of this estimator for different values of ρ.

(c) Consider now the unit root case where $\rho = 1$, and carry out the exercises in (a) and (b) for this case.

(d) Hence or otherwise discuss the effect of dynamic misspecifications for the estimation of long run responses in linear distributed lag models.

Ph.D. Qualifying Examination
UCLA Department of Economics

Fall 1990

Econometrics

Time: 4 hours

Instructions: Answer ALL 3 of the questions in Part A. Answer ONE question in Part B.

Part A

Answer ALL 3 questions in Part A.

1. Explain briefly ALL of the following:

    1. Adaptive expectations
    2. Instrumental variables estimators
    3. Principal components
    4. Pre-test bias
    5. Box-Cox transformation
    6. Tobit models
    7. Heckman two-stage estimation method
    8. Lagrange multiplier tests
    9. Least absolute deviation estimation
    10. Random coefficient models

2. The n_i independent observations $(x_{i1}, x_{i2}, \ldots, x_{i,n_i})$ are drawn from a probability distribution with density function

$$f_i(x) = \lambda_i e^{-\lambda_i x} \quad x \geq 0, \quad i = 1, 2.$$

(i) Show that the maximum likelihood estimator of λ_i is equal to $1/\bar{x}_i$ where $\bar{x}_i$ is the average of the n_i observations.

(ii) Show that the critical region of a likelihood ratio test of the null hypothesis that $\lambda_1 = \lambda_2$ against the alternative that $\lambda_1 \neq \lambda_2$ depends only on the ratio $\bar{x}_1/\bar{x}_2$.

(iii) In the case where $n_1 = n_2 = 1$, show that the following region of acceptance

$$\frac{\alpha}{2-\alpha} \leq \frac{x_2}{x_1} \leq \frac{2-\alpha}{\alpha}$$

defines a test of size α of $\lambda_1 = \lambda_2$ against $\lambda_1 \neq \lambda_2$.

3. Consider the general linear first-difference stationary process

$$\Delta y_t = \mu + A(L)\,\epsilon_t, \qquad (1)$$

where Δ is the first difference operator,

$$A(L) = a_0 + a_1 L + a_2 L^2 + \ldots,$$

is a polynomial in the lag operator L, ($Ly_t = y_{t-1}$), and μ is scalar constant. The ϵ_t are mean zero, serially uncorrelated shocks with common variance σ_ϵ^2.

i. Derive the conditions under which (1) reduces to the trend-stationary model

$$y_t = \lambda t + B(L)\,\epsilon_t. \qquad (2)$$

ii. Given the observations ($y_1, y_2, \ldots, y_n$), discuss alternative methods of testing (1) against (2) and vice-versa.

iii. What is meant by "persistence" of shocks in time-series models? How useful do you think is the concept of "persistence" for an understanding of cyclical fluctuations in the U.S. real GNP?

iv. Describe and discuss the alternative methods proposed in the literature for the estimation of "persistence" measures.

3

Part B

Answer ONE question in Part B.

1. **Bayesian Testing for Unit Roots**

Suppose that the data are generated by an autoregressive process

$$y_t = \alpha + \beta y_{t-1} + \epsilon_t , \ t = 1, 2, \ldots, n,$$

where ϵ_t is a sequence of i.i.d. normal random variables with mean zero and variance σ^2.

1) a) State an assumption that allows one to treat the initial value y_0 as if it were a fixed constant, even though it is selected randomly.

b) Suppose that although observations commence at time 0, it is known that the process started at time $t = -p$ with $y_{-p} = 0$ for some finite $p \geq 1$. Should y_0 be treated as a fixed constant? If not, how should the data be analyzed if p is known?

c) Suppose that you are willing to act as if this process had been going on forever. How should you treat the first observation y_0?

2) Draw a figure to represent a prior distribution that captures the opinion that β is (a) probably close to one; (b) probably strictly less than one; and (c) possibly equal to one. Form an explicit probability distribution that has this shape.

3) Using a "diffuse" prior distribuiton for β and σ^2 and using also the assumption that y_0 is a fixed constant, describe how you would test the hypotheses: $H_1 : \beta = 1$, $H_2 : \beta \geq 1$, $H_3 : \beta > 1$.

4) Using a "diffuse" prior distribution for σ^2 and the prior distribution described in (2) for β and using also the assumption that y_0 is a fixed constant, describe how you would test the hypotheses: $H_1 : \beta = 1$, $H_2 \; \beta \geq 1$, $H_3 : \beta > 1$. Write down the formulas with enough clarity that they could be turned over to a computer programmer.

2. <u>Duration Models</u>

i) Consider the following observations on duration of a particular event:

$$t_1, t_2, t_3^+, t_4^+, t_5, t_6, t_7^+, t_8, \ldots, t_n$$

where "+" denotes that the observation is right-censored.
Explain how you would calculate the Kaplan-Meier estimate of the distribution function. Briefly outline a method for calculating an approximate confidence band for such an estimate.

ii) You are asked by a corporation to examine the Schumpeterian hypothesis that large firms adopt a new technology (say, computers) faster than smaller size firms. The data set contains information on 3-digit SIC codes, size and other characteristics of the firm for each year and whether a particular firm adopted computers in a given year.
Explain an estimation strategy for evaluating this hypothesis. Examine in detail the estimation and specification issues involved.

UNIVERSITY OF CHICAGO

G

EMPIRICAL METHODS PRELIMINARY EXAMINATION

Summer Quarter 1994

Problem 1. (20 minutes)

For each of the following estimators, explain (I) to what model it applies, (ii) the idea behind the estimator, and (iii) its asymptotic properties (do not prove these, but state what the important assumptions are).

a. Powell's symmetrically trimmed least squares estimator.
b. Robinson's estimator of the partially linear regression model.
c. Manski's maximum score estimator.
d. Powell's censored least absolute deviations estimator.

Problem 2. (20 minutes)

For the Linear Exponential Family density f(X^t, θ) exp φ(Y^t, μ(W^t,θ)), where

$$\phi(Y_t, \mu(W_t, \theta)) = a(\mu(W_t\theta)) + b(Y_t) + Y_t' c(\mu(W_t, \theta)),$$

$$\int_{R^l} \exp[\phi(y, \mu)] d\eta_t(y) = 1,$$

$$\int_{R^l} y \exp[\phi(y, \mu)] d\eta_t(y) = \mu,$$

X^t ≡ Y^t ,Z^t ≡ Y_t ,W_t . Y_t is lx1 vector and θ is qx1 vector.

a. Can you interpret the QMLE, θ_n hat as a GMM estimator which solves min M_n (θ)'J_n $^{-}$ M_n (θ)? If not, why not? If so, write down the formulas for M_n and J_n $^{-}$.

b. Denote $r_t(\theta) \equiv Y_t - \mu(W_t, \theta)$. Show that the "best" set of instruments has the following form:

$$h_t^*(W_t) = E[\partial r_t(X^t, \theta_o)/\partial\theta | W_t]\Sigma_t^{-1}$$

where

$$\Sigma_t = E[r_t(\theta_o)r_t(\theta_o)'|W_t].$$

Write Σ_t^{-1} in terms of $a(\cdot)$, $b(\cdot)$ and $c(\cdot)$.

Problem 3 (40 minutes)

Suppose you want to estimate the mean of a population by quasi-maximum likelihood methods, using the Cauchy density $f(x, \theta) = [\pi(1 + (x - \theta)^2)]^{-1}$.

a. Assume only that $E(X_t) = \theta_o$ is finite such that $|\theta_o| < K < \infty$ and prove that the $QMLE$, $\hat{\theta}_n$ is consistent for θ^*, the solution to $\max E[\log f(X_t, \theta)]$. How do you interpret θ^*? (Hint: assume that $\theta \in [-K, K]$).

b. Verify that the assumption in (a) is also sufficient for the asymptotic normality of the $QMLE$, and give the formula for the asymptotic covariance matrix, and a consistent covariance estimator.

c. For which distributions does $\theta^* = \theta_o$? How could you use the *i.i.d.* observations to test the hypothesis that the population sampled is truly Cauchy? Give a test statistic that tends to zero *a.s.* when the population is truly Cauchy, but will tend elsewhere for a relevant class of alternatives.

Problem 4. (40 minutes)

The conditional density of y given x is assumed to exist and is denoted by

$$f(y|x, \theta)$$

where θ is a vector of unknown parameters. The associated CDF of y is $F(y|x, \theta)$. Here F and f are known functions. The objective of this problem is to derive a χ^2–goodness of fit test.

Assume that you have access to i.i.d. observations of (y, x), and that θ is estimated by $\hat{\theta}$ satisfying a set of "moment" or "first order" conditions of the form

$$\frac{1}{n}\sum \psi(y_i, x, \hat{\theta}) = o_p(n^{-1/2}).$$

2

Assume that J intervals are selected in advance:

$$C_1 = (-\infty, c_1), C_2 = [c_1, c_2), \ldots, C_J = [c_{J-1}, \infty)$$

with $-\infty < c_1 < c_2 < \cdots < c_{J-1} < \infty$. Let $c_0 = -\infty$ and $c_J = \infty$.

In answering the following questions be as specific as you can. Do not worry too much about details. But you should try to convince the reader that you could fill in the details, given sufficient time and access to your personal library.

a. You are interested in testing whether $P(y \in C_j|x) = F(c_{j+1}|x, \theta) - F(c_j|x, \theta)$. How would you do that? (Hint: One way (but not the only way) to think about this is to define a vector of parameters $\mu = (\mu_1, \mu_2, \ldots, \mu_J)$ by $\mu_j = E[1\{y \in C_j\} - (F(c_{j+1}|x, \theta) - F(c_j|x, \theta))]$, and then test $\mu = 0$.)

b. Suppose that it is (practically) impossible to calculate F, but it is easy to generate data from $F(\cdot|x, \theta)$ for given values of x and θ. How could you modify the test in (a) in such a way that you would not have to calculate F?

Problem 5. (60 minutes)

Consider the following linear model:

$$y_t{}' \alpha_o = u_t$$

where the coefficient vector α_o has k components and

$$E(u_t | z_{t-1}) = 0.$$

Assume that $\{(y_t, z_{t-1})\}$ is stationary and ergodic with finite second moments and that the matrix

$$E(z_{t-1} y_t') \equiv d_o$$

has rank $k - 1$. Finally, suppose that $\{(1/\sqrt{T}) \sum_{t=1}^{T} z_{t-1} u_t : T = 1, 2, \ldots\}$ converges in distribution to a normally distributed random vector with mean zero and covariance matrix V.

a. Show that the coefficient vector α_o is only identified up to scale. In other words the direction of α_o is identified but not its magnitude.

3

Suppose that z_{t-1} has at least k components and that its second moment matrix is nonsingular. Characterize the limiting distribution of the following two alternative GMM estimators of α_o up to scale. Both use the inverse of the sample second moment estimator of z_{t-1} as weighting matrix. One normalizes the first entry of α_o to be one and the other normalizes the norm of α_o to be one.

b. Characterize the limiting distribution of both GMM estimators.

c. Show that one of the two estimators is a two-stage least squares estimator and specify which one.

d. Do the two implied estimates of direction agree? (Do the estimates agree up to scale?) Explain.

e. Under what set of circumstances will the weighting matrix used for these two estimators be asymptotically efficient.

EMPIRICAL METHODS PRELIMINARY EXAMINATION - 1993

There are three hours of questions. The suggested time allocation is given for each question. You have an extra hour for reading, thinking and organizing your answers.

Write the following information on your examination paper:

your code number at the top of the left-hand corner;
the number of the pages at the top right-hand corner;
the name of the examination at the top of each page.

Write in black ink.

1. (20 Minutes) Consider the following problem in inference. The sample size is two, and random sampling is assumed. The data generating model is

$$P_\theta(x_i = \theta - 1) = P_\theta(x_i = \theta + 1) = \frac{1}{2}; i = 1, 2$$

Is

$$c(x_1, x_2) = \begin{cases} \{\frac{1}{2}(x_1 + x_2)\} & \text{if } x_1 \neq x_2 \\ \{x_1 - 1\} & \text{if } x_1 = x_2 \end{cases}$$

a 75% confidence set? Can you get a smaller size 75% set? Justify your answers. If $x_1 \neq x_2$, what can you say about θ and what degree of "confidence" do you have in your statement. How much would you be willing to bet on θ in this situation? (Suppose you are risk-averse.)

2. (60 Minutes) Let $\hat{\beta}$ be the OLS estimator of β in

$$y = X\beta + \epsilon$$

where y is T by 1, $\epsilon \sim N(0, \Sigma)$, $\Sigma = \sigma^2 I$, X is fixed, non-stochastic, T by k matrix, and $(X'X)$ is nonsingular. Let

$$H_o : R\beta = r$$

where R is m by k of rank m.

a. Prove:

(i) $R\hat{\beta}$ has a multivariate normal distribution.

(ii) $R\hat{\beta}$ is independent of $(y - X\hat{\beta})'(y - X\hat{\beta})$.

(iii) Construct a test statistic for the hypothesis H_o and consider the power function for the alternative:

$$H_a : R\beta = r + \Delta i$$

where Δ is a scalar and i is a prespecifed vector. Write out the non-centrality parameter and the distribution of the test statistic under the alternative.

(iv) As $T \to \infty$ characterize the power function for the test; now consider a test when $\Delta = \frac{\delta}{\sqrt{T}}$. (You obviously base tests on $\sqrt{T}(R\hat{\beta} - r)$).

b. Show how to construct a $1-\alpha$ confidence interval for any linear function $\eta'\beta$ so that the overall probability for the class is exactly $1-\alpha$. Use your result to devise a size α test that $\beta = 0$ (componentwise) and that any linear combination of β is also zero. In the context of estimating a Cobb-Douglas production function, is this an interesting hypothesis? Explain.

c. For the prior specified below, how would you use Bayesian methods to determine whether or not to include the last variable, x_k, in the model? Would Bayesian "testing" lead to a sharp "include - exclude" criterion? Assume X is independent of $\beta, \epsilon, \sigma^2$,

$$f(\beta, \frac{1}{\sigma^2}) = f_N(\beta|\beta^*, \sigma^2(N^*)^{-1}) f_\gamma(\frac{1}{\sigma^2}|(s^*)^2, v^*)$$

where f_γ is gamma with parameters $(s^*)^2$ and v^*; f_N is normal with mean β^* and covariance $\sigma^2(N^*)^{-1}$. Show how the posterior mean has a GLS-like interpretation (pooling sample and prior information).

3. (50 Minutes) Suppose one has the following model

$$y_i = g(d_i, x_i) + \epsilon_i$$

where $E[\epsilon_i|x_i, z_i] = 0$ and the endogenous random variable d_i takes on two values 0 and 1. Assume that we observe independent and identically distributed vector of (x_i, y_i, z_i, d_i) for $i = 1, 2, 3, \ldots$.

a. If we collect i's whose $d_i = 0$ and use kernel regression estimator for $g(0, x_i)$, is the estimator consistent for $g(0, x_i)$? Explain your answer.

b. Calculate $E[y_i|x_i, z_i]$, and using your answer describe a way to estimate $g(0, x_i)$ and $g(1, x_i)$ consistently, and in route provide an identification condition.

4. (50 Minutes) Consider the following estimation problem. Suppose that there is a parameter vector (α_o, β_o) to be estimated and that the information available for estimating these parameters is summarized by the following two sets of moment conditions:

$$(*) \qquad E\rho_1(y_t, \alpha_o) = 0$$

$$(**) \qquad E\rho_2(y_t, \alpha_o, \beta_o) = 0.$$

Imagine that β_o is the parameter of interest, and for convenience, we will suppose that it is a scalar. Since the second set of moment conditions entails α_o, to use this moment condition for identifying and estimating β_o requires estimation of α_o.

For notational convenience, construct a function ρ by stacking ρ_1 and ρ_2:

$$\rho(y, \alpha, \beta) = \begin{pmatrix} \rho_1(y, \alpha) \\ \rho_2(y, \alpha, \beta) \end{pmatrix}.$$

We presume that a central limit approximation of the form:

$$(1/\sqrt{T}) \sum_{t=1}^{T} \rho(y_t, \alpha_o, \beta_o) \xrightarrow{D} N(0, V)$$

applies where V is a positive-definite matrix. Consider the following two approaches to estimation. One approach is to estimate (α_o, β_o) simultaneously using both sets of moment conditions (*) and (**). The other approach is sequential (two-step), whereby α_o is estimated first using moment conditions (*), and then β_o is estimated using moment conditions (**) and the initial estimator of α_o. In analyzing the asymptotic properties of these estimators you are free to make the appropriate identification and smoothness restrictions.

a. Under what restrictions on V and/or the derivatives of ρ will the resulting two estimators be asymptotically equivalent?

b. Under what restrictions will the two-step estimator have the same limiting distribution as a one-step (infeasible) estimator that imposes the true value α_o when using moment conditions (**) to estimate β_o?

c. Under what restrictions will the two-step estimator be less efficient than the infeasible estimator mentioned in part b. Under these restrictions what can be said about standard errors for the two-step estimator constructed ignoring the initial stage estimation?

d. Why might the two-step estimator be valuable to use in practice in circumstances when it is less efficient asymptotically than the simultaneous estimator?

Empirical Methods Prelim

Buchinsky, Hansen, Heckman

Summer 1992

You have **FOUR HOURS TO COMPLETE THIS EXAM**, and there are **THREE HOURS** worth of questions to answer. You are given an extra hour to read over the questions or proofread your answers.

1. (30 minutes) Consider the following binary choice model

$$(*) \qquad Pr(d_i = 1 \mid x_i) = \frac{\exp(x_i\beta)}{1 + \exp(x_i\beta)} \qquad i = 1,\ldots,I$$

Assume x_i is iid (wrt i) $E(x_i x_i') = \Sigma_x$ is positive definite $\|\beta\| \leq c < \infty$.

a) Prove that as $I \to \infty$, plim $\hat{\beta} \to \beta$ where $\hat{\beta}$ is the MLE and

$$I^{1/2}(\hat{\beta} - \beta) \sim N(0, \Sigma_\beta).$$

(Define Σ_β).

b) Prove that if

$$\hat{\epsilon}_i = \left[d_i - \frac{\exp(x_i\hat{\beta})}{1 + \exp(x_i\hat{\beta})}\right]$$

then

$$\frac{1}{I}\sum_{i=1}^{I} x_i'\hat{\epsilon}_i = 0$$

Thus if x_i contains a constant, the mean of the logit residuals is zero.

c) Compare the asymptotic distribution of

$$\tilde{\beta} = \underset{\beta}{argmax} \sum_{i=1}^{I} \left[d_i - \frac{\exp(x_i\beta)}{1 + \exp(x_i\beta)} \right]^2$$

with $\hat{\beta}$. Can you develop a "GLS" like adaptation of $\tilde{\beta}$ to make it more efficient?

d) Is the estimator β^* consistent? Let

$$\beta^* = \underset{\beta}{argmax} \sum_{i=1}^{I} \left[d_i - \frac{\exp(x_i\beta)}{1 + \exp(x_i\beta)} \right]^2 w_i(\beta),$$

$$w_i(\beta_i) = \left[\frac{\exp(x_i\beta)}{1 + \exp(x_i\beta)} \cdot \frac{1}{1 + \exp(x_i\beta)} \right]^{-1}$$

and the weight (as a function of β^* and $w_i(\beta)$ are determined simultaneously?

2. (40 minutes) Consider the following regression model:

$$y_i = x_i'\beta_0 + u_{0i} \quad (i = 1,..,n),$$

where $Quant_\theta(y_i \mid x_i) = x_i'\beta_\theta$, $u_{\theta i} \equiv y_i - Quant_\theta(y_i \mid x_i)$, x_i is a k × 1 vector with $x_{1i} \equiv 1$ for all i = 1,....,n, and β_θ is a k × 1 vector of unknown parameters.

a) The bootstrap estimator of Var($\hat{\beta}_\theta$) (for bootstrap sample of size m = n) is given by

$$\hat{Var}(\hat{\beta}_\theta) = \frac{1}{n} \sum_{j=1}^{B} (\hat{\beta}_\theta^{(j)} - \hat{\beta}_\theta)(\hat{\beta}_\theta^{(j)} - \hat{\beta}_\theta)',$$

where $\hat{\beta}_\theta^{(j)}$ (j = 1,....B) are the B bootstrap estimates, and $\hat{\beta}_\theta$ is the estimate for β_θ from the original data.

Consider an alternative method for computation of the bootstrap estimate: (i) for each draw of bootstrap sample, $(y^{(j)}, X^{(j)})$, compute $\tilde{y}^{(j)} = y^{(j)} - X^{(j)}\hat{\beta}_\theta$; (ii) compute the bootstrap estimate $\tilde{\beta}_\theta^{(j)}$ from a quantile regression of $\tilde{y}^{(j)}$ on $X^{(j)}$; and (iii) compute

$$\hat{Var}(\hat{\beta}_\theta) = \frac{1}{n} \sum_{j=1}^{B} \tilde{\beta}_\theta^{(j)} \tilde{\beta}_\theta^{(j)\prime}.$$

Aside from the machine precision, would the two methods yield, numerically, the same estimates for Var ($\hat{\beta}_\theta$)? Justify your answer as precisely as possible.

b) Consider the following model of heteroskedasticity:

$$y_i = x_i'\beta + \sigma(x_i)\,\epsilon_i,$$

where $\sigma(x_i) = (1 + \gamma' x_i)$ and $\text{Quant}_\theta(\epsilon_i \mid x_i) = Q_\theta$. What does this specification imply for the quantile regression model? That is, if we write $y_i = x_i'\beta_\theta + u_{\theta i}$, what is β_θ and what is $u_{\theta i}$? Is $\text{Quant}_\theta(u_{\theta i} \mid x_i) = 0$?

c) Assuming that the heteroskedastic model in (b) is correct, how would two estimates at two different quantiles, θ_1 and θ_2 ($0 < \theta_1 < \theta_2 < 1$), compare to each other? How would you test your hypothesized relationship?

d) Suppose that $\text{Quant}_\theta(u_{\theta i} \mid x_i) \neq 0$, but there exists a random vector z_i such that $\text{Quant}_\theta(u_{\theta i} \mid z_i) = 0$. Would you expect that an estimator $\hat{\beta}_\theta$, which solves

$$\frac{1}{n}\sum_{i=1}^{n}(\theta - 1/2 + 1/2 sgn(y_i - x_i'\hat{\beta}_\theta))z_i = 0,$$

is a consistent estimator for β_θ? Indicate why or why not? (Be brief).

3. (35 minutes)

Consider the following panel data model:

(1) $$y_{it} = \alpha_i + \beta z_{it} + u_{it}, \quad (i = 1,\ldots,N;\ t = 1,\ldots,T)$$

where α_i is a fixed individual's parameter, and $u_i = (u_{i1},\ldots,u_{iT})' \sim$ i.i.d. $(0, \Sigma_u)$.

The variable z_{it} is not directly observed. Instead we observe only an erroneous measure of z_{it}:

(2) $$x_{it} = z_{it} + v_{it},$$

where v_{it} is independent of z_{it}, and $v_i = (v_{i1},\ldots,v_{iT})' \sim$ i.i.d. $(0, \Sigma_v)$.

(a) Show that a least-squares regression carried out for the transformed model

4

would not yield a consistent estimator for β. For a fixed T would the results change if we use deviation from the individual's means, i.e.,

$$y_{it} - \bar{y}_i = \beta(x_{it} - \bar{x}_i) + u_{it} - \bar{u}_i,$$

(where $\bar{y}_i = (1/T)\sum_{t=1}^{T} y_{it}$ and $\bar{x}_i = (1/T)\sum_{t=1}^{T} x_{it}$)? Explain.

b) What restrictions on Σ_v and Σ_u does one need to impose in order to be able to obtain a consistent estimator for β, using only within-sample data? (T fixed and N going to infinity).

c) Suppose now that the model also includes a lagged dependent variable, so that it is given by

(3) $$y_{it} = \alpha_i + \gamma y_{i,t-1} + \beta z_{it} + u_{it} \quad (i = 1,\ldots,N;\ t = 1,\ldots,T),$$

and $\Sigma_v = \mathrm{diag}(\sigma_v^2,\ldots,\sigma_v^2)$.

Determine whether or not there exists a consistent estimator for β. T fixed and N going to infinity. If you answer that there is such an estimator, explain how to obtain it. Otherwise, explain why one does not exist.

d) Assume now that the model in equation (1) applies, but α_i is not a fixed-effect parameter. Instead, assume that α_i is a correlated random-effect:

$$\alpha_i = \delta' x_i + w_i,$$

where $E(\alpha_i \mid x_i) = \delta' x_i$. Assume that $\Sigma_v = \mathrm{diag}(\sigma_v^2,\ldots,\sigma_v^2)$ and $\Sigma_u = \mathrm{diag}(\sigma_u^2,\ldots,\sigma_u^2)$. Can you provide a consistent estimator for β? Assume T fixed and N going to infinity. Be very explicit in your answer.

4. (15 minutes) Consider the following periodic autoregression sometimes used as a model of seasonality:

$$y_{t+1} = \lambda_t y_t + \gamma_t w_{t+1}$$

where $\{w_t\}$ is a sequence of independent and identically normally distributed random variables with mean zero and variance 1. The coefficient sequence $\{(\lambda_t, \gamma_t)\}$ is periodic with period two and $|\lambda_t| < 1$.

a) Can this process be viewed as being stationary? Please explain.

b) Imagine running an autoregression of y_{t+1} on y_t ignoring the seasonality. What is the probability limit of the ordinary least squares estimator?

5. (60 minutes) Consider the following nonlinear econometric equation:

$$\phi(y_i, x_i, \beta_0) = e_i$$

where $E(e_i \mid x_i) = 0$, e_i has a finite second moment, β_0 is a k-dimensional parameter vector, ϕ is a "smooth" function of β specified a *priori*, and $\{(y_i, x_i)\}$ is a sequence of independent and identically distributed random vectors.

a) Show how to construct an infinite number of unconditional moment conditions to be used to estimate the parameter vector β_0.

b) Suppose you make an *ad hoc* selection of k of those moment conditions. Give a condition for *global* identification of the parameter vector using these moment conditions. Also, provide a *local* identification condition.

c) Provide a characterization of the asymptotic distribution for an estimator constructed using k moment conditions that satisfy both the identification conditions you proposed in part b.

d) Imagine forming a whole family of such generalized method of moments estimators where each estimator is associated with an alternative collection of moment conditions. Does this class of estimators have an efficiency bound? If so, provide a characterization of it.

EMPIRICAL ECONOMICS PRELIM

SUMMER 1991

You have **FOUR HOURS** TO COMPLETE THIS EXAM, and there are **THREE HOURS** worth of questions to answer. You are given an extra hour to read over the questions or proofread your answers.

PART I: Answer Two of the following three questions!

1. (15 minutes) In a certain population, $y = \alpha + \beta z + u$ and $x = z + v$, where z, u, and v are (unobserved) independent random variables, with $E(z) = \mu$, $E(u) = 0 = E(v)$.

In random sampling from that population, only x and y are observed. Let $\hat{y} = a + b x$ and $\hat{x} = c + d y$ denote the sample least-squares linear regression of y on x, and of x on y, respectively. Show that $\text{plim } b \le \beta \le \text{plim } (1/d)$.

2. (15 minutes) Let $\{y_t : t=0,1,...\}$ be a stochastic process with increments that are stationary, ergodic and have finite second moments. Suppose the increment process has a moving-average representation of the form:

$$y_t - y_{t-1} = \alpha(L)w_t$$

where $\{w_t\}$ is a stationary and ergodic n-dimensional martingale difference sequence and $\alpha(z)$ is a 1 by n vector function of z with power series expansion:

$$\alpha(z) = \sum_{j=0}^{\infty} \alpha_j z^j \quad \text{where} \quad \sum_{j=0}^{\infty} j|\alpha_j| < \infty.$$

Show that there exists a permanent-transitory decomposition of $\{y_t\}$:

$$y_t = p_t + \tau_t$$

where $\{p_t\}$ is a martingale and $\{\tau_t\}$ is a stationary, ergodic process with finite second moments. When displaying the existence of this decomposition, charactize the coefficients of the moving-average representation for the transitory component $\{\tau_t\}$. Is this decomposition unique? Can the variance of $\{p_t - p_{t-1}\}$ be identified? If so, how?

3. (15 minutes) Consider the GEV model

$$G(Y) = (a_1 Y_1^{1-\sigma} + a_2 Y_2^{1-\sigma})^{\frac{1}{1-\sigma}} + Y_3 , \qquad a_1, a_2 > 0$$

where the probability of choice j conditioned on Y is

$$P_j = Y_j(\partial G/\partial Y_j)/G(Y) \quad j = 1,2,3.$$

If $\sigma > 1$, verify that choice probabilities are statistically well-defined but there is no random utility representation. What is the interpretation of the model if $\sigma = 1$? Write out the social surplus function for the model with $\sigma < 1$.

PART II: Answer Two of the following three questions!

4. (30 minutes) For the simple linear model

$$y_t = \beta_o x_t + u_t , \qquad t = 1, \ldots, T,$$

suppose you wish to test the null hypothesis H_o: $E(x_t u_t) = 0$, under the maintained hypothesis $E(z_t u_t) = 0$, where y_t, x_t, and z_t are scalar observable random variables and β_o is an unobservable coefficient. To simplify calculations, assume that all variables have mean zero ($E(x_t) = E(z_t) = E(u_t) = 0$), and that, under the null hypothesis, the errors are homoskedastic ($E(u_t^2 | x_t, z_t) = \sigma_u^2$).

Consider the following two approaches for testing this hypothesis:

(i) Estimate β_o by the IV estimator $\tilde{\beta} \equiv (z'y)/(z'x)$, where x, y, and z are T-dimensional vectors of observed variables. Then, using the residual vector $\tilde{u} \equiv y - \tilde{\beta}x$, check whether the sample covariance of x and $\tilde{u}$ is significantly different from zero using $S_1 \equiv (x'\tilde{u})/\sqrt{T}$.

(ii) Check whether the IV estimator $\tilde{\beta}$ is significantly different from the least squares estimator $\hat{\beta} \equiv (x'y)/(x'x)$, using $S_2 \equiv \sqrt{T}\,(\hat{\beta} - \tilde{\beta})$.

For either of these two approaches, a consistent estimator of the unknown variance σ_u^2 is given by $s_u^2 \equiv (\tilde{u}'\tilde{u})/T$.

A. Show that the ratio of S_1 to S_2 does not depend upon the dependent variable y_t, and that (suitably normalized) test statistics for each of these approaches are algebraically identical.

B. Derive the limiting distribution of this (suitably normalized) test statistic under the sequence of local alternative hypotheses $H_{A,T}$: $u_t = x_t(\delta_o/\sqrt{T}) + v_t$, where δ_o is an arbitrary scalar and v_t is independent of x_t.

5. (30 minutes) Consider the following problem. Let $(X_1,\ldots,X_N)$ be a random sample from a normal model with mean μ variance σ^2. Let the prior probability that $\mu = \mu_0$ be c. For $\mu \in [L,U]\backslash\mu_0$ the prior is uniform, for some L,U with $-\infty < L < U < \infty$.

a. Verify that the posterior probability that $\mu = \mu_0$ is

$$\bar{c} = c \exp[-N(\bar{X} - \mu_0)^2/2\sigma^2]/k$$

where $k = c \exp[-N(\bar{X} - \mu_0)^2/2\sigma^2]$

$$+ (1-c) \int_I \exp[-\mu(\bar{X} - \mu)^2/2\sigma^2]d\mu$$

b. Suppose $\bar{X}$ is such that when performing a significance test of size α for $H_0 : \mu = \mu_0$, you reject marginally, i.e. $\bar{X} = \mu_0 + \lambda_\alpha \sigma/\sqrt{N}$. Find the posterior probability that $\mu = \mu_0$.

c. Show that as $N \to \infty$, $\bar{c} \to 1$. Hence, $\bar{X}$ is statistically significantly different from μ_0 but the posterior probability favoring μ_0 goes towards unity.

d. Interpret this result. Is this a paradox?

6. (30 minutes) Consider the nonparametric regression model

$$y_t = g(x_t) + u_t, \quad t = 1, \ldots, T,$$

where y_t and x_t are jointly continuously distributed with finite variances, joint density function $f_{y,x}(y, x)$, marginals $f_y(y)$ and $f_x(x)$, and with $E[u_t | x_t] = 0$ (i.e., $g(x_t) = E[y_t | x_t]$) and $E[u_t^2 | x_t] = \sigma^2$. Furthermore, f_x and g_x are Lipschitz continuous, i.e., $|f_x(a)-f_x(b)| \le f_0|a-b|$ and $|g(a)-g(b)| \le g_0|a-b|$ for some f_0 and g_0. An estimator for the value of $g(x)$ at a fixed point $x = x_0$ is the uniform kernel estimator

$$\hat{g}(x_0) \equiv \left[\frac{1}{T}\sum_{t=1}^{T} w_{tn} y_t\right] \cdot \left[\frac{1}{T}\sum_{t=1}^{T} w_{tn}\right]^{-1}, \text{ where}$$

$$w_{tn} \equiv (h_T)^{-1} \cdot 1(|x_t - x_o| \le h_T/2),$$

and h_T is a nonrandom bandwidth sequence.

Suppose u_t and x_s are independent for all t and s, x_t is i.i.d., $f_x(x_o) > 0$, and u_t is weakly stationary with autocovariance sequence $\gamma_u(s) \equiv \mathrm{Cov}(y_t, y_{t-s})$ that is absolutely summable, i.e.,

$$\sum_{s=0}^{\infty} |\gamma(s)| < \infty.$$

Find conditions on the bandwidth sequence h_T under which $\hat{g}(x_o)$ is (weakly) consistent. Try to make your assumptions as weak (general) as possible.

PART III: Answer **Two** of the following three questions!

7. (45 minutes) Consider the discrete choice model

$$d = 1 \quad \text{iff} \quad X\beta + U \ge 0$$
$$= 0 \quad \text{otherwise}$$

X is a 1 x k vector of observables ;

U is a random variable which is absolutely continuous with respect to Lebesgue measure; and

$E(U) = 0$, $E(U^2) = \sigma^2 < \infty$.

Establish the following propositions as rigorously as you can. (Show why or why not true);

a. If U is independent of X and the density of U is known (up to scale parameter σ), β is identified up to the scale parameter if, with probability one, X is of "full rank" i.e. with probability one, it is not contained in a subspace of less than k in dimension.

b. $E(U|X) = 0$ does not suffice to identify β; (Assume density of U is not known, even up to a scale parameter).

c. If Median $(U|X) = 0$, for all X, β is identified (up to scale parameter σ); moreover the distribution of U is identified. (Assume X is of full rank).

d. Same as (c) except that now we insist that at least one coordinate of X (conditional on other coordinates) is absolutely continuous with respect to Lebesgue measure.

e. Devise an estimator that exploits all information in (d) (and in the statement of model) and briefly indicate how you would verify consistency.

8. (45 minutes) Suppose you are interested in the effects of individual-specific explanatory variables on the duration of individual unemployment. You are given a random sample of observations on the duration of unemployment spells, y_i, which you will use as the dependent variable in your analysis. Also, for each observation, you are given a vector of explanatory variables, x_i, which do not vary during the duration of the unemployment spell (x_i includes sociodemographic indicator variables, education level and work experience at the beginning of the unemployment spell, etc.).

Two additional features of the sample must be taken into consideration. First, there are two ways unemployment spells can end: either the individual finds a new job (which includes being rehired by her former employer), or the individual leaves the labor market. The data include an indicator variable d_i, which takes the value 1 if the individual finds a job and 0 if she leaves the labor market.

Second, the dependent variable is only measured in monthly intervals, i.e., $y_i = 1$ if unemployment lasted less than (or equal to) one month, $y_i = 2$ if unemployment lasted between one and two months, etc. Hence, there is a difference between the "true" unemployment duration (which is a continuous random variable) and the observed "grouped" dependent variable.

Propose a model for analysis of these data, and discuss how you would estimate the parameters of interest. Be as specific as possible about the algebraic form of the model and the assumptions you make on any error terms. Be sure your analysis accounts for the discreteness of the dependent variable and the two distinct sources of exit from unemployment.

9. (45 minutes) Consider the following *two step* estimation problem. Suppose that a k_1-dimensional parameter vector β_{o1} is estimated using the moment conditions:

$$Ef_{1t}(\beta_{o1}) = 0$$

Let $\{b_{1T} : T \geq 1\}$ denote the resulting estimator. This initial estimator is used in a second scalar moment condition:

$$Ef_{2t}(\beta_{o1}, \beta_{o2}) = 0$$

to construct an estimator $\{b_{2T} : T\geq 1\}$ of the scalar parameter β_{o2}. The composite random function $\{f_t\}$ is stationary and ergodic sequence of random functions where $f_t(\beta_o)' = [f_{1t}(\beta_{o1})', f_{2t}(\beta_o)]$. In addition, $\left\{(1/\sqrt{T}) \sum_{t=1}^{T} f_t(\beta_o) : T\geq 1\right\}$ converges in distribution to a normally distributed random vector with mean zero and covariance matrix $V = \begin{bmatrix} V_{11} & V_{12} \\ V_{21} & V_{22} \end{bmatrix}$.

a. Derive the asymptotic distribution of $\{b_{1T} : T\geq 1\}$ and $\{b_{2T} : T\geq 1\}$. You are free to impose the appropriate rank and smoothness conditions when deriving this distribution.

b. Compare the asymptotic variance of $\{b_{2T} : T\geq 1\}$ to the variance asymptotic of a pseudo estimator $\{\hat{b}_{2T} : T\geq 1\}$ obtained when the true value of the parameter β_{1o} is used in the second stage estimator. Under what set of circumstances will the asymptotic variances agree? Is it possible for the the asymptotic variance of $\{\hat{b}_{2T} : T\geq 1\}$ to be larger than the asymptotic variance of $\{b_{2T} : T\geq 1\}$? If so, when will this occur?

University of Chicago
ECONOMETRICS
Preliminary Examination for the Ph.D. and the A.M. Degree
Summer Quarter 1994

Part I

State whether each of the following statements is ***true, false*** or ***uncertain*** and provide precise explanations of your answers.

I.1 There is no difference between observed and expected information (expected information is sometimes called "Fisher information").

I.2 Use of fixed or stochastic regressors (explain how these regressors differ) makes no difference in classical or sampling theory and Bayesian inference in the regression model.

I.3 Given that γ is the shrinkage parameter of the ridge regression estimator, the bias of the estimator becomes larger as γ increases in value.

I.4 The method of scoring is an algorithm used to estimate parameters of nonlinear models iteratively that uses the inverse of the expectation of the Hessian matrix, or the negative of the inverse of the information matrix as the positive definite direction matrix.

I.5 For an AR(1) process, $y_t = \rho y_{t-1} + \varepsilon_t$, $t = 1, 2, ..., T$, with y_0 given, it is impossible to get a ***finite sample*** Bayesian or non-Bayesian test of the hypothesis $\rho = 1$ versus $\rho \neq 1$ because when $\rho = 1$, the unit root case, the process is non-stationary.

I.6 In the case that a structural coefficient $\gamma = \pi_1/\pi_2$, where π_1 and π_2 are reduced form coefficients, the estimator $\hat{\gamma} = \hat{\pi}_1/\hat{\pi}_2$, where $\hat{\pi}_1$ and $\hat{\pi}_2$ are least squares estimators of π_1 and π_2, respectively, is better in a mean-squared error sense than a Bayesian posterior mean or median of γ derived using a diffuse prior for the parameters.

Part II

Answer *two, and only two,* of the following questions.

II.1 Consider a standard binary probit model,

$$y_i = \begin{cases} 1 \text{ with probability } \Phi(x_i'\beta) \\ 0 \text{ with probability } 1-\Phi(x_i'\beta) \end{cases} \qquad i = 1, 2, ..., n.$$

1. Write down the regression function, (E[y | x]) for this problem and indicate how this model could be estimated by nonlinear least squares (NLS). Compare the NLS and maximum likelihood (ML) estimators for this model.

2. Now consider the possibility that there are some misclassified data for the y variable, that is some responses are 1's when they should be 0's and vice versa. We model the misclassification as follows.

   The distribution of $y_i \mid y_i^*$ is:

   $$y_i = zy_i^* + (1-z)(1-y_i^*)$$

   where $z_i = 1$ with prob π, and $z_i = 0$ with prob $1-\pi$ (π is the probability of misclassification) and the distribution of $y_i^* \mid x_i$ is:

   $$y_i^* = 1 \text{ with prob } \Phi(x_i'\beta) \text{ and } y_i^* = 0 \text{ with prob } (1-\Phi(x_i'\beta))$$

   a. Compute $E[y_i \mid x_i]$.

   b. Explain why the standard MLE of β is inconsistent in this problem.

   c. Outline a nonlinear least squares approach to estimating π and β.

   d. Write down the likelihood function for the probit model with misclassification.

   e. Explain why π and β are identified in the probit model and not in the linear probability model ($y = x\beta + \varepsilon$).

II.2 Consider the following nonlinear model:

$$f(x_t, \theta) = \theta_0 + \theta_1 x_t + \theta_2 \log(\theta_1 x_t) \qquad (1.1)$$

$$t = 1, ..., T$$

$$y_t = f(x_t, \theta) + e_t; \quad e_t \sim IN(0, \sigma_e^2) \qquad (1.2)$$

1. What are the objective function $S(\theta)$ of the nonlinear least squares estimator and the "normal equations" with respect to θ?

2. Let $Z(\theta) \equiv \partial f(x, \theta)/\partial\theta$. Derive an explicit expression for $Z(\theta)$ and form: $Z(\theta)'Z(\theta)$. Is this a p.d. matrix?

3. Write down the explicit expression $Z(\theta)'[y - f(x, \theta)]$ and provide the n-th step of the Gauss-Newton algorithm.

4. Assume $\hat{\theta}$ to be the value that globally optimizes $S(\theta)$. Write down the form of the estimate for σ_e^2, $\hat{\sigma}_e^2$.

II.3 Consider the following autoregressive model of order two, AR(2), for the output growth rate of an economy, $y_t = \alpha + \beta_1 y_{t-1} + \beta_2 y_{t-2} + u_t$, $t = 1, 2, ..., T$. Assume that the u_t's have been independently drawn from a normal distribution with mean zero and variance σ^2 and that y_0 and y_{-1} are given.

1. Provide both maximum likelihood and Bayes' estimates of the parameters of this model and explain their properties and justifications.

2. Derive the roots of this AR(2) process and explain their properties and implications for the output growth rate process. Then indicate how to compute the posterior probability that the two roots are complex conjugate roots. What are the period and amplitude of the oscillatory component and how can posterior densities for them be computed?

3. Given a prior density for α, β_1, β_2 and σ, how can its implications for the properties of the roots and oscillatory components be determined?

Part III

Answer *two, and only two* of the following questions.

III.1 Consider the following SEM structural model

$$\underset{(T\times N)(N\times N)}{Y \quad \Gamma} = \underset{(T\times K)(K\times N)}{X \quad B} + \underset{(T\times N)}{U}, \tag{3.1}$$

and

$$E[U] = 0; \qquad E\left[\frac{U'U}{T}\right] = \Sigma \tag{3.2}$$

1. **Is it possible to estimate Γ and B in (3.1) with no restrictions on Γ, B, and Σ? If not, explain why.**

2. **Show that when all the structural equations are just identified, the 3SLS estimator for the reduced form parameters reduces to the 2SLS estimator.**

3. **For a two-equation (N=2) identified system, explain why "systems" estimators such as FIML and 3SLS are more precise in large samples than "single-equation" estimators such as LIML, 2SLS and other members of the k-class. Provide a comparison of alternative estimators' large sample covariance matrices and briefly discuss estimators' finite sample properties.**

III.2 Let $\underset{(T\times 1)}{y} = \underset{(T\times k)(k\times 1)}{X \quad \beta_0} + \underset{(T\times 1)}{e}$ with $e \sim IN(0, \sigma_0^2 I_T)$

and $\underset{T\to\infty}{\text{plim}}\ X'X/T = \Omega$ where Ω is positive definite.

1. **Prove that the maximum likelihood estimators for β_0 and σ_0^2 are consistent being careful to state all your assumptions.**

2. **If the variables in X are correlated with the elements of e and if Z is a T×r matrix ($r \geq k$) of r instrumental variables that are correlated with the variables in X but not with e, prove that the 2SLS estimator of $\theta_0' = (\beta_0' \ \sigma_0^2)$ is a special case of the GMM estimator for θ_0.**

3. Derive the large sample properties of the 2SLS estimator in part 2 of this question explaining all needed assumptions. Is the 2SLS estimator optimal in finite samples?

III.3 Let
$$\underset{T\times 1}{y_1} = \underset{T\times m_1}{Y_1}\;\underset{m_1\times 1}{\gamma_1} + \underset{T\times k_1}{X_1}\;\underset{k_1\times 1}{\beta_1} + \underset{T\times 1}{u_1}$$

be the first equation, assumed identified of a structural model and let the unrestricted reduced form equations be $(y_1 \vdots Y_1) = X(\underline{\pi}_1 \vdots \Pi_1) + (\underline{v}_1 \vdots V_1)$, with $\underset{T\times k}{X} = (\underset{T\times k_1}{X_1} \vdots \underset{T\times k_0}{X_0})$. Assume that the rows of $(\underline{v}_1 \vdots V_1)$ have been independently drawn from a MVN$(\underline{0}, \Omega)$, where Ω is positive definite symmetric.

1. Show that $X\pi_1 = X\Pi_1\gamma_1 + X_1\beta_1 = \bar{Z}_1\delta_1$, with $\bar{Z}_1 = (X\Pi_1 \vdots X_1)$ and $\delta_1' = (\gamma_1' \vdots \beta_1')$, are restrictions on the reduced form parameters π_1 and Π_1. How do these restrictions affect the estimation of γ_1 and β_1 in the case of "just" and "over-identification"?

2. If a posterior density for $(\pi_1\ \Pi_1)$ is available that has finite first and second moments, show how it can be employed to derive optimal point estimates of δ_1 relative to the following loss functions where $\hat{\delta}_1$ is some estimate:

   (a) $L_1 = (y_1 - \bar{Z}_1\hat{\delta}_1)'(y - \bar{Z}_1\hat{\delta}_1)$

   (b) $L_2 = (\underline{\delta}_1 - \hat{\delta}_1)'\bar{Z}_1'\bar{Z}_1(\delta_1 - \hat{\delta}_1)$

   $= (X\pi_1 - \bar{Z}_1\hat{\delta}_1)'(X\pi_1 - \bar{Z}_1\hat{\delta}_1)$

   and

   (c) $L_3 = wL_1 + (1-w)L_2 \qquad 0 \le w \le 1$

3. Explain how the Gibbs Sampler can be employed to compute finite sample posterior densities given that diffuse priors are employed for the parameters of the system $y_1 = Y_1\gamma_1 + X_1\beta_1 + u_1$ and $Y_1 = X\Pi_1 + V_1$. Give various procedures for checking the convergence of the Gibbs Sampler.

Part IV

Answer *two, and only two* of the following questions.

IV.1 Consider the following production function for a firm:

$$\ln y_t + \theta y_t = \alpha + \beta_1 \ln L_t + \beta_2 \ln K_t + u_t \qquad t = 1, 2, ..., T$$

where y_t, L_t and K_t are output, labor input and capital input, respectively in period t and u_t is a disturbance term.

1. For any given value of u_t, say $u_t = 0$, what are the properties of this production function? How do the values of θ and $\beta_1 + \beta_2$ affect the behavior of returns to scale and the shape of the long-run average cost function?

2. Given data on y_t, L_t and K_t and u_t's that are NID(0, σ^2), write down the likelihood function, show how to calculate ML estimates and explain their properties. How would you compute and interpret a 90% confidence interval for θ? How would you test the hypothesis $\theta = 0$ and compute the power of your test?

3. Using a diffuse prior density for the parameters, explain how to obtain the marginal posterior density for θ and how to construct a 90% Bayesian interval. Provide an interpretation of this interval and contrast its interpretation with that of the sampling theory interval. Will these two intervals be of the same length?

IV.2 Consider the following model for a firm's quarterly dividend payments. For quarter t, the firm can change or not change its dividend rate. To represent this discrete choice, let $y_t = 1$ represent a dividend change and $y_t = 0$ no dividend change with probabilities P_t and $1\text{-}P_t$, respectively for t = 1, 2, ..., T. Further, let the value of P_t = $P_t = P_t(g_t)$, where $g_t = D^*_t - D_{t-1}$, the gap between the actual dividend rate, D_{t-1} and the desired or target rate, D^*_t. Assume that $D^*_t = kE_t$, where k is a parameter and E_t is the firm's quarterly earnings. Thus

$$y_t = \begin{cases} 1 & P_t(g_t) \\ 0 & 1-P_t(g_t) \end{cases}$$

1. What is a reasonable form for the function $P_t(g_t)$? Given your choice, formulate a likelihood function under the assumption that the y_t's are independent. How would you use ML and Bayesian methods to analyze your model and to make probability statements about the probability of a dividend change in a future period, say T+1?

2. If in addition to your model for y_t, suppose that you have the following model for the amount of dividend rate change, $D_t - D_{t-1}$, ***given that*** a ***dividend change is made***,

$$\begin{aligned} D_t - D_{t-1} &= \beta(D_t^* - D_{t-1}) + \varepsilon_t \\ &= \beta(kE_t - D_{t-1}) + \varepsilon_t \end{aligned} \qquad t = 1, 2, \ldots, T$$

with the ε_t's NID(0, σ^2). How would you use this model and the dichotomous model for dividend change to predict (1) whether a dividend change will be made next period, say in T+1, and (2) how much the change will be?

IV.3 There has been much controversy about how to determine whether x affects y or y affects x or whether a two-way interaction is present. For example, x might be income and y health status. Or x might be advertising expenditure of a firm and y the firm's sales. Suppose that the following model for x and y is assumed to hold:

$$\begin{aligned} y_t &= \beta_{10} + \gamma_{12}x_t + \beta_{11}z_{1t} + \beta_{12}z_{2t} + u_{1t} \\ x_t &= \beta_{20} + \gamma_{21}x_t + \beta_{23}z_{3t} + \beta_{24}z_{4t} + u_{2t} \end{aligned} \qquad t = 1, 2, \ldots, T$$

where z_{1t}, z_{2t}, z_{3t} and z_{4t} are exogenous variables, and (u_{1t}, u_{2t}) are disturbance terms assumed NID(0, Σ), where Σ is a 2×2 positive definite symmetric matrix.

1. How would you analyze the above system to determine whether $x \rightarrow y$ or $y \rightarrow x$ or $x \leftrightarrow y$? Provide explicit procedures in your answer.

2. What role would predictive analyses play in your assessment of alternative hypotheses?
3. Since the competing hypotheses' validity is uncertain, what would you compute to quantify this uncertainty?

- 7 -

University of Chicago
ECONOMETRICS
Preliminary Examination for the Ph.D. and the A.M. Degree
Summer Quarter 1993

Part I

(1 hour)

I.1 For each of the following statements, indicate whether it is ***true***, ***false*** or ***uncertain*** and provide an explanation of your answer.

a. If there are no cross-equation correlations between the disturbances in a linear simultaneous equation model, equation-by-equation estimation by least squares provides consistent coefficient estimators.

b. Using a diffuse prior density for an autoregressive model's parameters, given initial conditions and past data, t = 1, 2, ..., T, a 90% Bayesian predictive interval (define) for the dependent variable in period T+1 is exact while the usual non-Bayesian 90% prediction interval is approximate and has a completely different interpretation.

c. If some vector observations are incomplete, that is observations are missing for some of the elements of the vector, dropping such incomplete observations in an analysis will only inflate the standard errors of parameter estimates.

d. Parameters are either identified or not identified and thus they can not be "over-identified" or "just-identified".

e. In a linear autoregressive model, that is a model with one or more lagged dependent variables in it and auto-correlated errors, least squares estimation of coefficients is inappropriate because it produces biased estimators.

f. Since shrinkage estimators for parameters of regression models are biased, they are clearly not optimal Gauss-Markov estimators and the Gauss-Markov theorem can be used to show that shrinkage estimators are inadmissible.

g. If two-stage least squares (2SLS) cannot be applied to estimate parameters of a linear simultaneous equation model because of a lack of instruments, one can estimate the model's parameters by the limited information maximum likelihood (LIML) method or by a Bayesian method at the cost of a distributional assumption and introduction of a prior density with the latter method.

Part II.

(1 hour)
Answer *two,* and *only two* of the following questions, II.1-II.3.

II.1 Consider the following structural model of female labor supply:

$$W_{ri} = X'_{1i}\,\beta_1 + u_{1i} \tag{1}$$

$$W_{0i} = X'_{2i}\,\beta_2 + u_{2i} \tag{2}$$

$$\begin{aligned} H_i &= \delta(W_{0i} - W_{ri}) \text{ if } W_{0i} > W_{ri}, \\ &= 0 \qquad\qquad \text{otherwise.} \end{aligned} \tag{3}$$

$i = 1, 2, \ldots, N$. (u_{1i}, u_{2i}) are iid bivariate normal with zero means, variances and covariance $(\sigma_1^2, \sigma_2^2, \sigma_{12})$. The other variables are:

W_{ri}: (unobserved) reservation wage.
W_{0i}: offered market wage (positive for working women, 0 for non-working women).
H_i: working hours.
X_{1i}, X_{2i}: vectors of demographic variables.
(β_1, β_2) (both vectors) and $(\delta, \sigma_1^2, \sigma_2^2, \sigma_{12})$ (all scalars) are structural parameters with unknown values.

a. Derive the reduced form labor supply equation. Coupled with the wage offer equation, this constitutes a two-equation reduced form system. List the reduced form parameters.

b. Show that the least square estimator of β_2 in the wage offer equation, obtained by using the observations for working women in the sample, is biased.

c. Describe a two-step procedure for consistent estimation of β_2.

d. Write down the log likelihood function of the reduced form system and discuss the identification problem as it relates to estimating the structural parameters from the reduced form parameter estimates.

e. The following demographic variables are available in the sample:

WA = age,
WE = years of schooling,
K6 = number of kids below 6,
PRIN = property income,
UN = unemployment rate in the county of residence,
CIT = 1 if resident of large city, 0 otherwise
RACE = 1 if white, 0 otherwise.

Give examples in specifying X_{1i} and X_{2i} for which the structural parameters are under-identified, just-identified and over-identified.

Note: If (x_1, x_2) is bivariate normal with mean (μ_1, μ_2), variances and covariance $(\sigma_1^2, \sigma_2^2, \sigma_{12})$, the following formulas hold:

$$E(x_1 \mid x_2 < c) = -\sigma_{12}\phi(z)/\Phi(z),$$

$$E(x_1 \mid x_2 \geq c) = \sigma_{12}\phi(z)/(1 - \Phi(z)), \; z = (c - \mu_2)/\sigma_2. \tag{4}$$

II.2 a. Given quarterly observations on a corporation's regular dividend payment, D_t, and its earnings, E_t, $t = 1, 2, .., T$, an investigator used least squares to estimate Lintner's dividend equation,

$$D_t - D_{t-1} = b(D_t^* - D_{t-1}) + u_t \tag{5}$$

with D_t^*, the target dividend, assumed given by $D_t^* = kE_t$, where k = payout rate. The estimation results produced an estimate of b equal to .30. With such a value for b, how many quarters will it take to eliminate 90% of the gap between D_t^* and D_{t-1}? Comment on the reasonableness of this result.

b. The investigator noticed that for a number of quarters, $D_t - D_{t-1} = 0$. How will such zero observations affect the estimation of b in the above Lintner equation? What are the properties of the estimates of b and k (explain how k can be estimated) when many values of the dependent variable are exactly equal to zero?

c. Consider the following equation for the probability of a dividend change in the t'th quarter:

$$P_t = 1 - c\,\exp\{-a(kE_t - D_{t-1})^2\} \qquad t = 1, 2, \ldots, T \qquad (6)$$

with c and a assumed positive. After explaining the properties of this function, show how it can be used in analyzing the quarterly data on dividend change and no dividend change; that is provide assumptions needed to formulate a likelihood function and indicate how to estimate the parameters c, a and k. If c is estimated to be different from one, say .90, what is the estimate of the probability of a dividend change given that $kE_t - D_{t-1} = 0$?

d. Explain how to use equations (1) and (2) in the analysis of the quarterly dividend data to obtain estimates of the parameters in these equations (hint: Apply (1) just to quarters in which there was a non-zero dividend change.) How will the estimation of b be affected relative to the result obtained in part a? Finally, indicate how you would forecast the corporation's dividend change, $D_{T+1} - D_T$, for a future quarter, T+1, and obtain a measure of precision for your forecast.

II.3 Let (t_i, x_i), i = 1, 2, ..., N, be an iid sample of duration times and the corresponding vector of covariates.

a. Prove that the hazard function is time invariant if and only if the duration time follows an exponential distribution.

b. If the hazard function for individual i is specified as $\exp(-x_i'\beta)$, show that the logarithm of t_i follows a linear regression. Discuss the statistical properties of the disturbance terms.

c. Characterize the efficiency loss in using least square, instead of maximum likelihood, in estimating the slope parameters in (b).

d. Give some examples in which the assumption of time invariant hazard may be too restrictive; suggest more appropriate specifications.

e. Compare the above "hazard function" approach with a "regression" approach that involves regressing t_i or $\ln t_i$ on the covariates, x_i.

Part III.

(1 hour)

Answer *two*, and *only two* of the following questions, III.1-III.3.

III.1 The consumption CAPM asset pricing model for n assets with possibly different maturities implies the following Euler equations:

$$E_t[\beta^{m_i} x_{t+m_i}^{-\alpha} r_{it+m_i}] = 1, \qquad i = 1, 2, \ldots, n, \quad t = 1, 2, \ldots, T \tag{7}$$

where

x_t = real per capita consumption growth at time t,
r_{it} = real gross return of asset i at time t,
m_i = maturity of asset i,
$0 < \beta < 1$ and $\alpha > 0$ are parameters with unknown values.

a. Describe an instrumental variables procedure for estimating α and β. Discuss the choice of appropriate instruments.

b. Show that there are testable over-identifying restrictions under certain conditions. Describe how one may test these restrictions.

c. Show that, under appropriate assumptions, the set of Euler equations imply a log-linear vector autoregression system with testable parameter restrictions.

d. Describe a Bayesian procedure for analyzing the model in (c).

III.2 Let $\ln L_T(\alpha)$ be the log likelihood function for a sample $\{y_i\}$ of size T, where the parameter vector $\alpha \in R^k$ satisfies the constraints $\alpha = g(\beta)$, $\beta \in R^m$, $m < k$, $g(\cdot)$ is a known, differentiable function.

(i) Show that the constrained MLE of α (with suitable scaling and centering) has a singular asymptotic normal distribution, i.e. its asymptotic covariance matrix is singular.

(ii) Verify that the unconstrained MLE is asymptotically inefficient relative to the constrained MLE.

(iii) Another estimation method is the minimum distance method. It has two steps. The first step is to derive the unconstrained MLE α^*. The second step is to estimate the equation $\alpha^* = g(\beta) + w$, $w = \alpha^* - \alpha$, by nonlinear GLS, i.e. solve for β^* from $\min_\beta (\alpha^* - g(\beta))'\Omega^{-1}(\alpha^* - g(\beta))$ where Ω is the asymptotic covariance matrix of $T^{1/2}(\alpha^* - \alpha)$.

(a) Show that the minimum distance estimator β^* has the same asymptotic distribution as the constrained MLE of β.

(b) Show that $(\alpha^* - g(\beta^*))'\Omega^{-1}(\alpha^* - g(\beta^*))$ is asymptotically chi-square. Derive the degrees of freedom.

III.3 Consider the first equation, assumed identified, of a simultaneous equation model,

$$y_1 = Y_1 \gamma_1 + X_1 \beta_1 + u_1 \tag{8}$$

with associated reduced form equations,

$$(y_1\ Y_1) = X(\pi_1\ \Pi_1) + (v_1\ V_1) \quad \text{or } Y = X\Pi + V \tag{9}$$

a. With standard normal assumptions regarding the disturbance terms and a diffuse prior density for the parameters, explain how to compute the exact posterior density for the structural coefficients by numerical integration and by Gibbs Sampling techniques. Indicate how recently derived convergence criteria can be employed to check the convergence of the Gibbs Sampling procedure.

b. Show how to derive and compute finite sample, optimal Bayesian point estimates for coefficients in the above structural equation and compare them to various sampling theory estimates. Compare alternative loss functions and for a given loss function, compute posterior expected losses for an optimal estimate and for various alternative estimates, say, ordinary least squares and two-stage least squares estimates.

c. How can the one-step ahead predictive density for y be computed and used to obtain a prediction interval and an optimal point prediction?

Part IV.

(1 hour)

Answer *two*, and *only two* of the following questions, IV.1-IV.3.

IV.1 (Monte-Carlo integration) In Bayesian analyses we are interested in computing integrals of the form

$$I = \frac{1}{c}\int g(\theta)p(\theta)d\theta, \; c = \int p(\theta)d\theta. \tag{10}$$

where $p(\theta) = f(\text{data} \mid \theta)\pi(\theta)$, the product of a likelihood function and a (possibly improper) prior density; c is the normalizing constant. For instance I is the posterior mean if $g(\theta) = \theta$.

a. Show that if we can draw iid sample values, θ_i, i = 1, 2, ..., N, directly from the posterior density, the Monte-Carlo sample mean

$$I_N = \frac{1}{N}\sum_{i=1}^{N} g(\theta_i) \tag{11}$$

is a consistent, asymptotically normal estimator of the quantity of interest I, under suitable regularity conditions. Display an estimate of the asymptotic variance which can be used for measuring numerical accuracy.

b. If it is difficult to sample directly from the posterior, we may sample from an importance function and the Monte-Carlo estimator is

$$I_{N^*} = \frac{\sum_{i=1}^{N} g(\theta_i)w(\theta_i)}{\sum_{i=1}^{N} w(\theta_i)} \tag{12}$$

where $w(\theta) = p(\theta)/h(\theta)$, $h(\cdot)$ is the importance function; for instance $h(\cdot)$ may be a multivariate Student-t density with suitably chosen mean, covariance matrix and degrees of freedom parameter. Prove that, under suitable regularity conditions, the Monte-Carlo estimator I_N. is consistent and asymptotically normal. Display an estimate of the asymptotic variance which can be used for measuring numerical accuracy.

c. In view of the asymptotic results in (b), discuss issues in choosing the importance function $h(\cdot)$.

IV.2 Consider the following autoregressive-leading indicator (ARLI) model:

$$y_t = \alpha + \beta_1 y_{t-1} + \beta_2 y_{t-2} + \beta_3 x_{1t-1} + \beta_4 x_{2t-1} + u_t, \qquad t = 1,2,\ldots T \qquad (13)$$

where x_{1t} and x_{2t} are leading indicator variables, the u_t's have been independently drawn from a $N(0, \sigma^2)$ distribution and the initial values of the variables are given.

a. If a relationship such as that above is available for each of N countries, or regions, or firms, explain what shrinkage estimation and prediction techniques are and under what conditions they are likely to increase the precision of estimation and prediction.

b. Given a prior density for the parameters of the relation (13), explain how you would establish its implications, analytically or numerically, for the properties of the roots of the autoregressive process, that is the probability that they are complex conjugate, and if so, the implications for the amplitude and period of the oscillatory component. Similarly, given a posterior density for the parameters, say in the multivariate Student-t form, how can it be used analytically or numerically to make inferences about the properties of the roots of the process?

c. After showing how to derive the predictive density function for y_{T+1}, show how it can be employed to make an optimal decision with respect to making a choice between forecasting that $y_{T+1} > y_T$ or $y_{T+1} < y_T$ using a symmetric or asymmetric loss structure.

IV.3 After providing an explanation of the standard specifying assumptions for the following "seemingly unrelated regression" (SUR) model, $y_i = X_i \beta_i + u_i$, $i = 1,2,\ldots,M$, answer the following questions.

a. Assuming that the β_i's have the same dimension, how would you test the hypothesis that they are all equal to a common vector, θ, versus the alternative that they are not equal to a common vector using non-Bayesian and Bayesian approaches? Are there large sample connections between the two approaches and how can the use of P-values for the large sample chi-squared statistic be given a Bayesian interpretation using the Schwarz approximation?

b. If the same data are to be used to investigate the hypothesis of equality and to estimate the regression coefficients, what is an optimal Bayesian pre-test estimate relative to quadratic loss for this problem? How would you solve the "pre-test estimation" problem in a non-Bayesian approach?

c. What is the mixed predictive density for a future vector of dependent variables, its mean and dispersion given that posterior probabilities associated with the two hypotheses regarding the regression coefficients are available?

University of Chicago
ECONOMETRICS
Preliminary Examination for the Ph.D. and the A.M. Degree
Summer Quarter 1992

Part I

Indicate whether the following statements are *true, false* or *uncertain* and in each case explain your answers.

I.1 Haavelmo's maximum likelihood estimator of the marginal propensity to consume, β in his model $c_t = \alpha + \beta y_t + u_t$ and $y_t = c_t + z_t$, $t = 1,2,...,T$ where c_t, y_t and z_t are per capita consumption, income and autonomous spending, respectively, and the u_t's are $NID(0, \sigma^2)$ disturbance terms is inadmissible (define) relative to a squared error loss function for finite T.

I.2 Since we do not have to estimate an unconstrained model to calculate the efficient score test statistic, the score test is ideal if we are not sure about the unconstrained model.

I.3 It is irrational and contrary to Muth's rational expectations hypothesis for an economic agent to employ a biased predictor.

I.4 The maximum likelihood estimator has minimum asymptotic variance among all consistent and asymptotic normal estimators.

I.5 The P-value (define) associated with a sampling theory test statistic is conceptually and algebraically unrelated to the posterior probability associated with the null hypothesis being tested.

I.6 If the disturbances in a simultaneous equation model have no cross-equation contemporaneous correlation, a single-equation method of estimation such as the 2SLS method is fully efficient.

Part II.

Answer *two,* and *only two* of the following questions.

II.1 Consider the following errors in the variables model:

$$y_t = x_t^* \beta + u_t,$$

$$x_t = x_t^* + v_t,$$

$t = 1,2,\ldots,T$. (u_t, v_t, x_t^*) are unobservable but known to be iid, trivariate normal with zero mean and a diagonal covariance matrix $\mathrm{diag}(\sigma_u^2, \sigma_v^2, \sigma_*^2)$. The unknown parameters to be estimated are σ_u^2, σ_v^2, σ_*^2, and β.

a. Write down the likelihood function.

b. Provide a method of moments (instrumental variable) interpretation of the maximum likelihood estimation procedure, and thereby demonstrate that none of the four parameters is identified without further information.

c. Suppose that a third variable z_t is known to be correlated with x_t^* but is independent of u_t and v_t. Demonstrate that the moment equations you found in (b) can now be augmented to provide consistent estimates of the four parameters.

d. Suppose that there are two variables (z_{1t}, z_{2t}) that have the properties of z_t in (c). Show that the extra information implies a more efficient method of moments estimator than (c).

e. Show that (d) also implies a model specification test.

II.2 Consider the linear multiple regression model (MRM), $\underset{\sim}{y} = X\underset{\sim}{\beta} + \underset{\sim}{u}$, where $\underset{\sim}{y}$ is an $n\times 1$ vector of observations on the dependent variable, X is an $n\times k$ matrix of observations on k independent variables, $\underset{\sim}{\beta}$ is a $k\times 1$ vector of parameters and $\underset{\sim}{u}$ is an $n\times 1$ vector of error terms. After explaining carefully the usual assumptions for the MRM, explain an economic or business example in which any *two* of the usual assumptions may not be appropriate and then answer the following questions.

a. What are the consequences of the two departures from usual assumptions, individually and jointly, for the properties of the least squares estimator of $\underset{\sim}{\beta}$?

b. What procedures would you use to determine whether one, both or neither of your two possible departures from standard assumptions are present?

c. How would you estimate β and predict a future value of the dependent variable taking into account that you have used the data to evaluate your two possible departures from standard assumptions?

II.3 (Discrete choice) We are to study the decision of high school graduates as to whether or not they go to college and, if they do, to which college they go. Assume that each student has $k > 2$ possible colleges from which to choose. For each student i, $i = 1,2,\ldots,n$, we observe z_i (family income and level of parents' education) and x_i^j (the quality index and the cost of the jth college), $j = 1,2,\ldots,k$. We also observe for every student in the sample whether he/she went to college and, if the student did, his/her college choice.

a. Display the (multinomial) probit and logit formulations of this problem.

b. The logistic formulation is often criticized by many as having the "independence from irrelevant alternative" (IIA) property. Explain and illustrate the criticism in the current context.

c. Suggest a generalized extreme value (GEV) formulation of the problem. Compare and contrast your model with the probit and logit formulations.

Part III.

Answer *two*, and *only two* of the following questions.

III.1 A researcher attempts to estimate the demand elasticity of a product using the following regression:

$$q_t = \alpha_0 + \alpha_1 p_t + \varepsilon_t, \qquad t = 1,2,\ldots,T, \tag{2}$$

where q_t and p_t are the logarithm of the observed quantity and price respectively. The researcher is satisfied with the estimation result because the least square estimate of α_1 turns out to be negative and the associated t-statistic is large.

a. Marshallian supply-demand analysis suggests that the researcher's procedure is fundamentally flawed, unless special assumptions have been made. Explain.

b. It is known that material cost w_t is a major component of the cost of production but has no effect on consumer demand. Explain how one may use this information to estimate the desired demand elasticity.

c. In addition to (b), it is also known that consumer demand is related to aggregate income I_t and aggregate advertising expenditure A_t, but these two variables have no effect on supply. Suggest a procedure that provides a more efficient estimate than that put forward in (b). Justify your answer.

III.2 Consider the first equation of a linear structural econometric model $\underset{\sim}{y}_1 = Y_1\underset{\sim}{\gamma}_1 + X_1\underset{\sim}{\beta}_1 + \underset{\sim}{u}_1$ and the reduced form equations $(\underset{\sim}{y}_1 \ \vdots \ Y_1 \ \vdots \ Y_0) = X(\underset{\sim}{\pi}_1 \ \vdots \ \Pi_1 \ \vdots \ \Pi_0) + (\underset{\sim}{v}_1 \ \vdots \ V_1 \ \vdots \ V_0)$, where $X = (X_1 \ \vdots \ X_0)$. After explaining the usual normality assumptions made for the reduced form matrix of error terms, indicate what these assumptions imply for the distribution of $\underset{\sim}{u}_1$. Then answer the following questions.

a. Given your normality assumption, what does it mean to say that $\underset{\sim}{\gamma}_1$ and $\underset{\sim}{\beta}_1$ are identified? What is the necessary and sufficient condition for these parameters to be identified? Can this condition be tested?

b. Are there any estimates of $\underset{\sim}{\gamma}_1$ and $\underset{\sim}{\beta}_1$ that have a finite sample justification? Explain what they are and comment on their properties (be sure to consider the maximum likelihood estimate along with others).

c. Compare Bayesian and non-Bayesian techniques for determining whether some or all of the variables in Y_1 are exogenous. After commenting on how such pre-tests affect standard errors and other properties of estimators, indicate a formal Bayesian procedure for integrating pre-testing and estimation.

III.3 Given a regression equation for each of m firms, $\underset{\sim}{y}_i = X_i\underset{\sim}{\beta}_i + \underset{\sim}{u}_i$, $i = 1,2,\ldots,m$, where $\underset{\sim}{y}_i$ is an $n\times 1$ vector of observations on the i'th firm's dependent variable, X_i is an $n\times k$ given matrix of rank k, $\underset{\sim}{\beta}_i$ is a $k\times 1$ vector of parameters and $\underset{\sim}{u}_i$ is an $n\times 1$ vector of error terms. Assume that $(\underset{\sim}{u}_1, \underset{\sim}{u}_2, \underset{\sim}{u}_3, \ldots, \underset{\sim}{u}_m)$ has been drawn from a zero-mean multivariate normal distribution with covariance matrix, $\Omega = \Sigma \otimes I_n$, where Σ is an $m\times m$ positive definite symmetric matrix. After explaining the implications of assuming $\Omega = \Sigma \otimes I_n$, answer the following questions.

a. What is an asymptotically efficient estimator of the $\underset{\sim}{\beta}_i$'s and what do "asymptotically efficient" and "asymptotically unbiased" mean?

b. Using a diffuse prior density for the $\underset{\sim}{\beta}_i$'s and Σ, derive the conditional posterior density for the $\underset{\sim}{\beta}_i$'s given Σ and for Σ given the $\underset{\sim}{\beta}_i$'s and comment on their properties. How can these conditional densities be employed to compute the marginal posterior distributions of the $\underset{\sim}{\beta}_i$'s and of the elements of Σ by use of the "Gibbs' Sampler"?

c. Explain how to analyze the above equation system with the added assumption $\underset{\sim}{\beta}_i = \underset{\sim}{\theta} + \underset{\sim}{v}_i$, $i = 1,2,\ldots,m$ with the $\underset{\sim}{v}_i$'s $NID(\underset{\sim}{0}, \tau^2 I_k)$ and distributed independently of the $\underset{\sim}{u}_i$'s.

Part IV.

Answer *all* of the following questions.

IV.1 For a first-order normal autoregression, $y_t = \rho y_{t-1} + \varepsilon_t$, $t = 1,2,\ldots,T$ with y_0 given and the ε_t's NID$(0,\sigma^2)$, derive the posterior odds for the two hypotheses, H_0: $\rho = 1$ and $0 < \sigma < \infty$ and H_1: $\rho \neq 1$ and $0 < \sigma < \infty$, using a normal prior density for ρ given σ under H_1 and a diffuse prior density for σ under both H_0 and H_1. What are the salient properties of the posterior odds expression? How can the posterior odds be employed to choose between H_0 nd H_1 in such a way as to minimize expected loss? Derive an optimal point prediction of y_{T+1} with respect to a squared predictive error loss function, $L(y_{T+1}, \tilde{y}_{T+1}) = (y_{T+1} - \tilde{y}_{T+1})^2$, that reflects uncertainty about H_0 and H_1. Last, under H_1 and its associated prior density, explain how to compute the joint predictive density for y_{T+1} and y_{T+2} and explain its properties. Compare the above results with results provided by non-Bayesian methods for analyzing this "unit-root" problem.

IV.2 After explaining why Stein "shrinkage" estimation and prediction techniques are important in econometrics, analyze a particular econometric problem and show in what ways "shrinkage" techniques have or can improve on results yielded by alternative estimation and prediction methods.

Part I.

University of Chicago
ECONOMETRICS
Preliminary Examination for the Ph.D. and the A.M. Degree
Summer Quarter 1991

For each of the following statements, indicate whether it is *true, false* or *uncertain* and provide precise explanations of your answers.

I.1 The least squares estimator of the slope coefficients in the normal linear regression model is inadmissible relative to quadratic loss but is admissible in the class of linear estimators relative to quadratic loss.

I.2 Although we cannot apply 2SLS to estimate parameters of an under-identified equation in a simultaneous equation model, other methods such as LIML and GMM can be applied to obtain consistent parameter estimates.

I.3 The maximum likelihood estimator for the regression parameters in a seemingly unrelated regression system is the same as the equation-by-equation least squares estimator if the regression errors are normally distributed with a diagonal contemporaneous covariance matrix.

I.4 The Cobb-Douglas production function is inappropriate for use in econometrics because its associated average cost function is not U-shaped.

I.5 Never use ordinary least squares to estimate coefficients of a simultaneous equation model because it is not optimal in any sense in finite samples and produces inconsistent and/or asymptotically inefficient estimates.

I.6 While Bayesians can make probability statements about parameters' possible values given observed data, non-Bayesians cannot and do not make such probability statements and thus non-Bayesian or sampling theory probability statements are useless.

Part II.

Answer *two,* and *only two* of the following questions.

II.1 Consider the Friedman consumption function model for panel data:

$$y_{it} = \alpha + \beta x^*_{it} + \varepsilon_{it}$$

$$x_{it} = x^*_{it} + v_i,$$

$i = 1,2,\dots,N$ (individuals), $t = 1,2,\dots,T$ (time), ε_{it} iid $(0,\sigma^2)$, v_i iid $(0,\phi^2)$, $E(\varepsilon_{it}v_j) = 0$ for all i, j and t. y_{it}, x_{it} and x^*_{it} are consumption expenditure, measured personal income and (unobserved) permanent income respectively. v_i captures individual heterogeneity and measurement errors. Interest centers on the marginal propensity to consume β.

a. Show that a pooled regression of y_{it} on a constant and x_{it} gives inconsistent estimates.

b. Denote group means (across individuals) by $\bar{y}_t = \sum_{i=1}^{N} y_{it}/N$ and $\bar{x}_t = \sum_{i=1}^{N} x_{it}/N$ and prove that the Wald-Friedman group-means estimator, for $T = 2$, $\hat{\beta} = (\bar{y}_2-\bar{y}_1)/(\bar{x}_2-\bar{x}_1)$ consistently estimates β as $N \to \infty$. Suggest a consistent estimator for α.

c. Show that the Wald-Friedman estimator is an instrumental variables estimator with two categorical instruments, $z^1_{it} = 1$ *if* $t = 1$, 0 otherwise, and $z^2_{it} = 1 - z^1_{it}$. Suggest a test to evaluate the null hypothesis $\alpha = 0$.

d. Generalize the Wald-Friedman estimator for $T > 2$.

II.2 A marketing researcher reports to you that he has fit a multinomial logit model to purchase data on a panel of N households observed over T periods. There are m choice alternatives. The logit choice probabilities for purchase of good i are a function of only the log of the price for that good, $\Pr(i) = F(\alpha_i + \beta_p \ln(\text{Price}_i))$.

a. Write down the form of the multinomial choice probabilities and the likelihood for the data.

b. What has the marketer implicitly assumed about the distribution of purchases across time and across households?

The marketer computes elasticities of choice probabilities with respect to price. He notes that the cross-elasticities are not symmetric. On the basis of this observation, he claims that price theory is wrong.

c. Derive the expression for the cross-price elasticities. Explain explicitly how to test symmetry.

d. Explain why even if the marketer is right that the elasticities are not symmetric, he is wrong about price theory [hint: the answer to this question is based on economic not statistical reasoning].

II.3 Some econometricians have argued that "variable-returns-to-scale" production functions are more reasonable and provide better explanations of firm behavior than production functions which have returns-to-scale equal to some fixed value. After discussing evidence and analysis bearing on this issue, derive the returns to scale function and average cost function associated with the following production function: $\log V + \theta V = \beta_0 + \beta_1 \log L + \beta_2 \log K$, where V = output, L = labor input, K = capital input and θ and the β's are parameters. Then answer the following questions:

a. Given data on V, L, and K for a sample of firms in a given year, how would you use them to estimate θ and the β's? Carefully discuss your specifying assumptions.

b. How would you test the hypothesis $\theta = 0$ using non-Bayesian and Bayesian approaches?

c. If β_0 is not a constant but varies from firm to firm, explain what type of data and assumptions would be needed to estimate the β_{0i}'s, θ, β_1 and β_2 and how to perform the needed calculations.

Part III

Answer *two*, and *only two* of the following questions.

III.1 Suppose the data are an iid sample from the exponential family of distributions:

$$p(x \mid \theta) \propto c(\theta) \exp\{q(\theta)' t(x)\} h(x)$$

here θ is a kx1 vector and t(x) is a function from R^n to R^k, $p(x \mid \theta)$ is the joint density of the data.

a. Show that t(x) is a sufficient statistic.

b. Write down the form of the natural conjugate prior for this family.

c. Show that the posterior density based on the natural conjugate prior is unimodal.

d. Explain how the fact that the prior in part b is a natural conjugate prior can be used to help assess the hyperparameters of the prior.

III.2 Consider the following two models for y_t, the logarithm of real GNP in year t, t = 1,2,...,T,

$$y_t = \alpha + \beta_1 y_{t-1} + \gamma t + u_t \quad (1)$$

$$y_t = \alpha + \beta_1 y_{t-1} + \beta_2 y_{t-2} + \gamma t + u_t \quad (2)$$

where y_0, and y_{-1} are given, the u_t's are assumed NID(0,σ^2) and α, β_1, β_2, and γ are parameters with unknown values.

a. An agnostic says that neither (1) nor (2) is the appropriate model since y_t follows a random walk with drift, that is $\beta_1 = 1$, $\beta_2 = 0$ and $\gamma = 0$. Explain what you would compute in Bayesian and non-Bayesian approaches to evaluate this agnostic's view and explain your views with respect to the adequacy of (1) or (2).

b. If (2) is considered to be an appropriate model for the observations, explain how to compute a posterior probability that the process contains an oscillatory component. Indicate how to compute posterior distributions for the period and amplitude of the oscillatory component, conditional on its presence.

c. From (1), using a diffuse prior density for the parameters, derive the joint predictive density for the future observations, y_{T+1} and y_{T+2} and explain how to use a Monte Carlo approach to evaluate it and the marginal predictive densities of y_{T+1} and y_{T+2}. How would you compute the value of $\Pr\{y_{T+2} > y_{T+1} > y_T \mid D_T\}$, where D_T denotes given data and prior information available at time T?

III.3 Consider a nonlinear regression model with endogenous regressors: $y_t = f(x_t', \beta) + u_t$, u_t iid zero mean, variance σ^2, t = 1,2,...,T. x_t is a k-vector containing endogenous variables. z_t is a vector of q instruments. The nonlinear two-stage least square (NL2SLS) or generalized methods of moment (GMM) estimator is defined as

$$\hat{\beta} = \arg\min_\beta h(\beta)'Z(Z'Z)^{-1}Z'h(\beta),$$

where $h(\beta)$ is a T-vector with the t'th element equal to $y_t - f(x_t', \beta)$, Z is T by q with the t'th row equal to z_t'. Show that

a. If the model is under-identified (q < k), the NL2SLS is ill-defined. In particular, demonstrate that there exists a continuum of minimizers to the defining minimization problem.

b. If the model is just-identified (q = k), all q sample orthogonality conditions are identically zero, i.e.

$$\frac{1}{T}\sum_{t=1}^{T} z_t\hat{u}_t = 0,$$

where $\hat{u}_t = y_t - f(x_t',\beta)$.

c. If the model is over-identified ($q > k$), demonstrate that T times R^2 from an auxiliary regression of NL2SLS residuals on the instruments provides a specification test of over-identifying restrictions.

Part IV

Answer *two*, and *only two* of the following questions.

IV.1 Consider the following standard normal linear regression model:

$$\underline{y} = X\underline{\beta} + \underline{u}$$

where $\underline{y}' = (y_1, y_2, \ldots, y_n)$, X is an nxk nonstochastic matrix, $\underline{\beta}$ is a kx1 vector of regression coefficients and $\underline{u}$ is an nx1 vector of disturbances which are assumed to be independently drawn from a normal distribution with mean zero and variance σ^2 which has an unknown value.

a. Explain a natural conjugate prior density for $\underline{\beta}$ and σ and show how it can be used to obtain a posterior density for $\underline{\beta}$ and σ even in the case of multicollinearity, that is when $X'X$ is a singular matrix. What is the posterior mean for $\underline{\beta}$ and how is it related to a ridge regression estimate of $\underline{\beta}$?

b. It is usually stated that the posterior mean for $\underline{\beta}$, derived in part a is optimal relative to a quadratic loss function. What does this statement mean? Does the ridge regression estimate enjoy similar optimality properties relative to a quadratic loss function?

c. Show that the posterior mean of $\underline{\beta}$ and the ridge regression estimate of $\underline{\beta}$, viewed as estimators are biased. What justifies the use of biased estimators?

d. Consider the following "balanced" loss function:

$$L_B(\hat{\underline{\beta}},\underline{\beta}) = w(\underline{y}-X\hat{\underline{\beta}})'(\underline{y}-X\hat{\underline{\beta}}) + (1-w)(\hat{\underline{\beta}}-\underline{\beta})'X'X(\hat{\underline{\beta}}-\underline{\beta})$$

where $\hat{\underline{\beta}}$ is some estimate of $\underline{\beta}$ and $0 < w < 1$, with w's value given. Given a posterior density for $\underline{\beta}$ with mean $\bar{\underline{\beta}}$, say that based on a natural conjugate prior distribution as in part a, use it to take the expectation of $L_B(\tilde{\beta},\beta)$ and to obtain the value of $\tilde{\beta}$, say $\tilde{\beta}^*$, that minimizes posterior expected loss. How would you prove that $\tilde{\beta}^*$ is admissible? Is $\tilde{\beta}^*$, viewed as an estimator less biased than $\tilde{\beta}$, the posterior mean derived in part a? How does the bias depend on the value of w?

IV.2 (a) Consider the following ARMA(2,1) process:

$$X_t - 2.5X_{t-1} + X_{t-2} = \varepsilon_t + 4\varepsilon_{t-1}, \quad \varepsilon_t \text{ iid } N(0,\sigma^2).$$

Calculate the spectral density.

(b) Show that there exists another ARMA(2,1) process (with different AR and MA parameters) with a spectral density proportional to the one you found in (a) and that both processes have exactly the same autocorrelation structures.

(c) For an ARMA(p,q) model with unknown parameters, discuss and suggest suitable identification conditions.

IV.3 Consider the problem of computing the posterior mean of a vector of model parameters, θ:

$$E[\theta] = \int \theta\, p(\theta)\, \ell(\theta \mid D)\, d\theta / \int p(\theta)\, \ell(\theta \mid D)$$

or

$$E[\theta] = N/D$$

where $p(\theta)$ is a prior density and $\ell(\theta \mid D)$ is a likelihood function.

Tierney and Kadane approximate both the numerator and denominator using separate Laplace approximations. A Laplace approximation to the integral, $I = \int f(x)\,dx$, is developed by writing f(x) as exp(lnf(x)) and expanding lnf(x) in a second order Taylor series. Using the second order Taylor series, the integral can be approximated as the normalizing constant of a multivariate normal density.

a. Derive the Laplace approximations for N and D.

b. Suppose that a uniform prior is used. Describe how standard quasi-Newton algorithms can be used to implement the Laplace approximations. Be specific about how to compute the gradients and hessians.

UNIVERSITY OF CHICAGO

Econometrics

Part I. Preliminary Examination for the Ph.D. and the A.M. Degrees

Summer Quarter, 1990

Consider *six (6), and only six (6)* of the following statements. Are they true, false or uncertain? In each case, provide analysis to explain and support your answer.

I.1 Omitting a relevant explanatory variable in a regression equation will always introduce bias in estimation of the remaining coefficients and of the disturbance term variance.

I.2 If a sequence of random vectors, $\{X_n, n = 1,2,...\}$ converges in distribution to a random vector X, then X_n also converges to X in distribution component-wise. The converse is not true unless X is normally distributed.

I.3 In connection with the standard normal linear multiple regression model, the least squares coefficient estimator and the unbiased error term variance estimators are inadmissible estimators relative to squared error and asymmetric LINEX loss functions.

I.4 In the context of the linear simultaneous equation model, the full information maximum likelihood (FIML) estimator is always more efficient than the limited information maximum likelihood (LIML) and two and three stage least squares estimators.

I.5 Bayesian and non-Bayesian prediction intervals (define) have the same interpretation and are always numerically the same in applications.

I.6 Stein shrinkage techniques cannot be applied to the seemingly unrelated regression (SUR) model because in the SUR model equations' disturbance terms are contemporaneously correlated.

I.7 The Wald, Lagrange Multiplier and likelihood ratio tests are equivalent and thus it doesn't matter which is used in practice in testing hypotheses about regression coefficients' values.

I.8 It is impossible to analyze three hypotheses, e.g. $\beta = 0$, $\beta > 0$ and $\beta < 0$ where β is a regression coefficient, in the Neyman-Pearson framework whereas it is possible to do so in the Bayesian framework.

Part II. (90 minutes)

Answer *two (2), and only two (2)* of the following questions in this part.

II.1 Consider the linear regression model,

$$y_t = \beta_0 + \beta_1 x_{1t} + \beta_2 x_{2t} + \varepsilon_t, \qquad t = 1,2,\ldots,T \tag{1}$$

and suppose that interest is centered on the following hypothesis:

$$H_0: \beta_1 + \beta_2 = 1$$

(a) Suggest and give justifications for a statistical procedure to test the hypothesis H_0 under the following alternative conditions:

(1) The disturbance vector $\varepsilon = (\varepsilon_1, \varepsilon_2, \ldots, \varepsilon_T)'$ is normally distributed with a zero mean vector and covariance matrix, $\sigma^2\Sigma$, where Σ is a known positive definite matrix, i.e., $N(\mathbf{0}, \sigma^2\Sigma)$.

(2) The distribution of ε is unknown but the sample size is very large.

(b) Using a diffuse prior density for the parameters and the normality assumption regarding ε in (1) above, explain how to compute the posterior probability that $\beta_1 + \beta_2 > 1$, $\beta_1 + \beta_2 < 1$ and $0.90 < \beta_1 + \beta_2 < 1.10$.

II.2 Consider the model

$$y = X_1\beta_1 + X_2\beta_2 + \varepsilon \tag{2}$$

where **y** and ε are Tx1 vectors, X_1 and X_2 are non-stochastic Txk_1 and Txk_2 matrices with $(X_1 \vdots X_2)$ of full column rank, and β_1 and β_2 are regression coefficient vectors with unknown values. The elements of ε are assumed to be iid with zero means and common variance σ^2.

(a) What statistical procedure or procedures can be used to evaluate the hypothesis that β_1 does not have a constant value within the sample period? What are the properties of your suggested procedure or procedures?

(b) Suppose that y is related to X_1 and X_2 nonlinearly, that is

$$y = f(X_1, X_2, \beta_1, \beta_2) + \varepsilon$$

where f has a known nonlinear form and ε has the properties stated above. What is the generalization of the procedure or procedures that you suggested in (a)? State clearly any additional assumptions that are required to justify your generalization and indicate properties of your generalized procedure.

(c) If β_1 in (2) is not constant but time-varying, formulate a time-varying parameter model and given a distribution on the initial state, show how to compute posterior and predictive densities recursively.

II.3 Consider a binary logit model:

$$Y_i = \begin{cases} 1 \text{ with probability } P_i \\ 0 \text{ with probability } 1\text{-}P_i \end{cases}$$

where $P_i = \exp(x_i'\beta)/[1 + \exp(x_i'\beta)]$, where x_i is a vector of non-stochastic input variables and β is a vector of parameters. Assume that the Y_i's $i = 1,2,...,n$ are independent and that the nxk matrix X, of which x_i' is the i'th row, is of full column rank. Then

(a) Compute the Hessian of the log-likelihood function.

(b) Prove that the log-likelihood is globally concave.

(c) If the log-likelihood is concave, does that imply that there exists a unique maximum likelihood estimate?

(d) What is the difference between observed and expected information in this model?

(e) Is your result in (d) dependent on the logit form of the probability locus? Would it hold true for models of the general form: $P_i = F(x_i'\beta)$, where F is a cumulative distribution function?

II.4 Consider the following autoregressive-leading indicator (ARLI) model:

$$y_t = \alpha_0 + \alpha_1 y_{t-1} + \alpha_2 y_{t-2} + \beta_1 x_{i,t-1} + \beta_2 x_{2,t-1} + \varepsilon_t \qquad t = 1,2,\ldots,T$$

Assume that the ε_t's are normally and independently distributed, each with zero mean and variance σ^2, that initial values of y_t and x_{1t} and x_{2t} are given and that x_{1t} and x_{2t} are exogenous variables, observed $t = 1,2,\ldots,T$.

(a) With a diffuse prior density for the parameters derive the joint predictive density for y_{T+1} and y_{T+2} given $x_{1,T+1}$ and $x_{2,T+1}$ and comment on its properties. Explain how to compute the marginal predictive density for y_{T+2}. If $x_{1,T+1}$ and $x_{2,T+1}$ have unknown values, what could be done to cope with this problem?

(b) Provide a definition of a turning point in the y-series and explain how to compute the probability of a downturn or an upturn in the y-process.

Explain how to make a decision to forecast a downturn in the y-process in a formal Bayesian decision theoretic framework.

(c) How can an investigator use Bayesian methods to explore properties of the roots of the AR(2) part of the above ARLI model? Conditional on the roots being imaginary, derive posterior densities for the amplitude and period of the oscillatory component.

Part III. (90 minutes)

Answer *two (2) and only two (2)* of the following questions in this part.

III.1 Consider an identified equation of a linear simultaneous equation model, say the first,

$$y_1 = Y_1\gamma_1 + X_1\beta_1 + u_1$$

where y_1 and Y_1 are a Tx1 vector and a Txm_1 matrix of observations on endogenous variables, X_1 is a Txk_1 matrix of observations on k_1 predetermined variables, γ_1 and β_1 are m_1x1 and k_1x1 vectors of structural parameters and u_1 is Tx1 vector of disturbance terms. Let

$$(y_1 \vdots Y_1) = X(\pi_1 \vdots \Pi_1) + (v_1 \vdots V_1)$$

be the reduced form equations for y_1 and Y_1 where $X = (X_1 \vdots X_0)$ is a Txk matrix of full column rank and π_1 is a kx1 vector and Π_1 a kxm_1 matrix of reduced form coefficients and $V \equiv (v_1 \vdots V_1)$ is a Tx$(m_1$+1) matrix of reduced form disturbances. Assume that the rows of V are normally and independently distributed with zero mean vector and positive definite symmetric covariance matrix Ω.

(a) Show that the first structural equation, shown above, can be expressed as

$$\begin{aligned} y_1 &= X_1\Pi_1\gamma_1 + X_1\beta_1 + v_1 \\ &= Z_1\delta_1 + v_1 \end{aligned}$$

and that

$$X\pi_1 = Z_1\delta_1$$

with $Z_1 = (X\Pi_1 \vdots X_1)$ and $\delta_1' = (\gamma_1' \ \beta_1')$. Then discuss properties of the following loss functions:

(i) $L(\delta_1,\hat{\delta}_1) = (\hat{\delta}_1-\delta_1)'Z_1'Z_1(\hat{\delta}_1-\delta_1)$

(ii) $L(\delta_1,\hat{\delta}_1) = (y_1-Z_1\hat{\delta}_1)'(y_1-Z_1\hat{\delta}_1)$

(iii) $L(\delta_1,\hat{\delta}_1) = (y_1-Z_1\hat{\delta}_1)'(y_1-Z_1\hat{\delta}_1) + c(\hat{\delta}_1-\delta_1)'Z_1'Z_1(\hat{\delta}_1-\delta_1)$

where $\hat{\delta}_1$ is some estimate of δ_1 and c in (iii) is a given non-negative constant.

(b) Introduce a prior density for (π_1,Π_1,Ω) and use it along with the likelihood function for the above reduced form equations to derive a marginal posterior density for (π_1,Π_1). Discuss its properties.

(c) Show how a posterior density for (π_1,Π_1) can be used to obtain optimal point estimates for δ_1 using the loss functions in (i)-(iii) above. Discuss properties of these estimates.

III.2 Consider the following simultaneous equation model

$$\sum_{i=1}^{3} y_{ti}\beta_{ij} + \sum_{i=1}^{4} x_{ti}\gamma_{ij} = u_{tj} \qquad \begin{array}{l} t = 1,2,\ldots,T \\ j = 1,2,3 \end{array}$$

The following a priori restrictions are imposed on the system: (1) $\beta_{31} = \beta_{21} = 0$, (2) $\gamma_{32} = \gamma_{42} = 0$, (3) $\beta_{13} = \gamma_{33} = \gamma_{43} = 0$, and (4) $\beta_{11} = \beta_{22} = \beta_{33} = 1$.

(a) Determine which equations satisfy the rank condition.

(b) For each identified equation, determine whether one can find an estimator which is asymptotically more efficient than the limited information maximum likelihood estimator.

(c) Discuss the large sample properties of full information maximum likelihood and Bayesian estimators for the parameters of the above system under the assumption that the system is properly specified to have Gaussian or normal disturbance terms and under the following conditions:

(i) The disturbances are non-normally distributed.

(ii) Some identifying restrictions are incorrect.

III.3 Consider the standard errors-in-variables problem:

$$y_i = \alpha + \beta x_i^* + \varepsilon_i \qquad i = 1,2,\ldots,n$$
$$x_i = x_i^* + v_i$$

with the ε_i's and v_i's zero mean normally and independently distributed error terms with common variances, σ_ε^2 and σ_v^2, respectively.

(a) Suppose that we wish to test the hypothesis $\beta = 0$ using a t-statistic based on the least squares estimator of β, β_{LS}, namely

$$t = (\beta_{LS} - 0)/s_{\beta_{LS}}$$

where $s_{\beta_{LS}}$ = the usual standard error of the least squares estimator, β_{LS}. Can we use the univariate Student-t tables to select a critical value? In particular, is the significance level or probability of a type I error affected by the errors-in-the variables problem?

(b) How is the power of the test described in part (a) affected by the errors-in-variables problem?

(c) If $\alpha = 0$, as in Friedman's consumption model, give a proof, with needed assumptions, that β_{LS} is an inconsistent estimator for β. Further assuming that $Ex_i^* = \mu_x$ for all i, use the method of moments to obtain an estimator for β and establish its properties.

(d) If the x_i^*'s are non-stochastic, suggest an instrumental variable estimator which is consistent and asymptotically normal under suitable regularity conditions. Prove that your estimator is consistent and asymptotically normally distributed stating clearly assumptions needed in your proofs. Compare your instrumental variable estimator to the maximum likelihood estimator for β.

III.4 Sets of regression equations are frequently encountered in the analysis of panel data in econometrics. Provide an example of such an application including a *complete* specification of a model and explanation of the underlying economic problem. Then answer the following questions:

(a) How would you test the hypothesis that individuals in the panel have the same regression coefficient vectors?

(b) If individuals' coefficient vectors are not far different in value, how can this information be exploited to obtain "improved" estimators and predictors. In what sense, or senses, are the estimators and predictors improved?

(c) What assumptions can be made to reduce the number of parameters in the disturbance covariance matrix and how would you estimate the system with such restrictions imposed on the disturbance covariance matrix? Provide derivations of the properties of your coefficient estimator.

(d) What economically motivated hypotheses are of interest in the application that you have chosen and indicate how you would proceed to evaluate them.

III.5 Consider two time series processes,

$$y_{1t} = \varepsilon_{1t} \qquad \varepsilon_{1t} \sim iid\ N(0,\sigma_1^2)$$
$$y_{2t} = \rho y_{2t-1} + \varepsilon_{2t} \qquad \varepsilon_{2t} \sim iid\ N(0,\sigma_2^2)$$

(a) What is the ARMA representation of the series, z_t, formed by the sum of y_{1t} and y_{2t}? Assume that ε_{1t} and ε_{2t} are independent.

(b) Relate the standard parameterization of the ARMA representation of the z_t series to the three parameters, ρ, σ_1, and σ_2. Assume that ε_{1t} and ε_{2t} are independent.

(c) Given a sample of the z_t series, are the three parameters, ρ, σ_1, and σ_2 identified?

(d) Suppose $\text{cov}(\varepsilon_{1t},\varepsilon_{2t}) \neq 0$, how does this change your answer in (c)?

(e) Which of the following two procedures will give better forecasts of z_t: (i) forecast z_t from the ARMA process for it, and (ii) forecast y_{1t} and y_{2t}, separately and use the sum of the forecasts as a forecast of z_t?

Part I. Answer question 1 and either 2 or 3.

1. The first assumption of the classical, normal linear regression model is that $E(y|\mathbf{x})$ is a linear function of $\mathbf{x}$, apart from an additive random error. Here y is a scalar (the random variable whose variation is to be explained) and $\mathbf{x}$ is a $K \times 1$ vector of exogenous variables.

a. Express the model in equation form, adding your own notation for parameters and errors as needed. Indicate the sample size by your notation.

b. What assumption is made concerning the correlation between the errors and $\mathbf{x}$? What is the result of a violation of that assumption?

c. Apart from being normally distributed, what assumptions are made about the errors? For each assumption you have indicated, what is the result of a violation of that assumption?

d. Discuss least squares estimators if the assumption of normality of errors cannot be maintained. That is, what can be said about the optimality of least squares estimators, and what do we know about the distribution of test statistics? Does the Gauss-Markov theorem rely on normality? What, if any, additional assumptions are necessary in this (nonnormal) situation?

Choose one of the following two questions.

2. The distribution of linear and quadratic forms plays an important role in econometrics. Suppose ϵ is an $n \times 1$ multinormally distributed random vector with variance-covariance matrix $\Omega = \{\omega_{ij}\}$. Indicate what distribution each of the quantities in a. through c. below has, and show why it has that distribution.

a. ϵ_i/ω_{ii} ;

b. $\Omega^{-1/2}\epsilon$, where $\Omega^{-1/2}$ is the matrix such that $\Omega^{-1/2}\,\Omega^{-1/2} = \Omega^{-1}$;

c. $\epsilon'\Omega^{-1}\epsilon$.

3. An estimator sometimes employed when the data are characterized by multicollinearity is the *ridge estimator*, defined as

$$\hat{\beta} = (X'X + kI)^{-1}X'y \quad ,$$

where k is a constant (> 0) chosen by the analyst. Of course if $k = 0$ the ridge estimator is equivalent to the least squares estimator, b.

a. Find the expectation and variance of $\hat{\beta}$.

b. Show that $V(b) - V(\hat{\beta})$ is a positive semidefinite matrix. Hint: Write $X'X = C\Lambda C'$, where Λ is diagonal and $CC' = C'C = I$, and note that $kI = kCC' = C(kI)C'$. Recall that $(AB)^{-1} = B^{-1}A^{-1}$, and if $D = \{ d_i \}$ is diagonal, then $D^{-1} = \{ 1/d_i \}$.

c. Taking into consideration your results from parts a. and b., when would you prefer $\hat{\beta}$ to b? Why is preferring $\hat{\beta}$ to b *not* a violation of the Gauss-Markov theorem?

Part II. Answer two of the following three questions.

1. Suppose you have data for T years on each of N firms suitable for the estimation of investment demand functions. Assume there are contemporaneous correlations among the errors across firms,

$$E(\epsilon_{it}\epsilon_{jt}) = \sigma_{ij}$$

and that the error variances differ across firms,

$$E(\epsilon_{it}) = \sigma^2_i = \sigma_{ii}$$

but there is no temporal autocorrelation.

Present the GLS models appropriate for estimating the investment functions (a) assuming structural equivalence across the firms; (b) assuming the production functions differ across firms. For each case explain how all unknown parameters can be estimated.

2. The generalized normal regression model is given by

$$y = X\beta + \epsilon \qquad E(\epsilon\epsilon') = \sigma^2\Omega,$$

where X is nxk, Ω is a known nxn positive definite matrix, and β (kx1) and σ^2 are unknown parameters. The joint p.d.f for ϵ (nx1) is

$$f(\epsilon) = (2\pi)^{-n/2} \mid \sigma^2\Omega \mid ^{-1/2}\exp\{-1/2[\epsilon'(\sigma^2\Omega)^{-1}\epsilon]\}$$

A. Present the likelihood function and derive the maximum likelihood estimators for β and σ^2 and the information matrix.

B. Present two important properties of the information matrix (or its inverse) and explain how these properties relate to the asymptotic efficiency of the maximum likelihood estimators.

3. Variations on two-stage least squares estimation are to be applied to the equation

$$y_{t1} = \beta_1 + \beta_2 y_{t2} + \beta_3 y_{t3} + \beta_4 x_{t1} + \beta_5 x_{t2} + \epsilon_{t1}$$

where, the y_{tj} are jointly dependent, x_{ti} are predetermined, and the additional predetermined variables in the other equations of the model are x_{t3}, x_{t4}, and x_{t5}.

a. Present explicitly (showing all variables in the regressions) the two stages of the standard two-stage least squares estimator of this equation.

b. Explain what happens to the two-stage least squares estimator if the list of predetermined variables in the first stage is limited to x_{t2}, x_{t3}, and x_{t4}.

c. Explain what happens to the two-stage least squares estimator if the list of predetermined variables in the first stage is limited to x_{t1}, x_{t2}, and x_{t3}.

d. Present the Hausman specification test for the hypothesis that x_{t2} is predetermined, against the alternative that it is jointly dependent. (Note: the general form of the Wald test is

$$(\delta_R - \delta_U)'[\mathrm{VarCov}(\delta_U - \delta_R)]^{-1}(\delta_R - \delta_U)$$

where δ_R and δ_U are the estimators under the null and alternative hypotheses, respectively).

Part III. Answer one of the following two questions.

1. In the regression model, $Y_i = \beta_1 + \beta_2 X_{i2} + \beta_3 X_{i3} + \epsilon_i$, the errors are hypothesized to follow a second order autoregressive process:

$$\epsilon_t = \rho_1 \epsilon_{t-1} + \rho_2 \epsilon_{t-2} \;\; u_t$$

where u_t meets classical model assumptions.

A. Describe a test appropriate for testing second order autocorrelation in this model. Present explicitly any regressions involved in the construction of this test.

B. Assuming second order autocorrelation is indicated by your test, present explicitly a method for treating the problem.

2. Suppose the three-variable regression model is suspected to have a problem of heteroscedasticity:

$$y_i = \beta_1 + \beta_2 x_i + \beta_3 z_i + \epsilon_i$$

A. If heteroscedasticity is present in a model, what happens to the properties of the least squares estimators?

B. Describe the White and Goldfeld-Quandt tests for heteroscedasticity. Explain when you might prefer one test over the other.

C. Describe the weighted least squares and White procedures for treatment of the problem, explaining when you would prefer one approach over the other.

University of Colorado at Boulder

Econometrics
January, 1995

Ph.D. Comprehensive Exam

Answer **both** questions 1 and 2.

1. True, False, or Uncertain? For each statement, give a one paragraph (approximately) explanation of your answer.

a. The Gauss-Markov theorem assures that least squares is the best estimator.

b. Estimation is made more efficient by pooling in the Seemingly Unrelated Regression (SUR) model.

c. We are always advised to correct for heteroskedasticity, even if we are unsure the problem exists, since ordinary least squares is a special case of generalized least squares.

d. The use of a maximum likelihood estimator insures efficiency, as long as the correct distributional assumption is made.

2. Consider the following simultaneous equations model:

$$y_1 = \gamma_{12}y_2 + \beta_{11}x_1 + \epsilon_1$$

$$y_2 = \gamma_{21}y_1 + \beta_{21}x_1 + \beta_{22}x_2 + \epsilon_2.$$

a. Examine the order and rank conditions for identification of each equation. Do your conclusions change if it is assumed that $E(\epsilon_1\epsilon_2) = 0$?

b. Outline the steps in the two-stage least squares (2SLS) estimation of the first equation. Present the formula for the estimator, and for the estimator of $\sigma_1^2 = \text{Var}(\epsilon_1)$.

c. Discuss the conditions necessary for the consistency and asymptotic normality of the 2SLS estimator. What is the asymptotic covariance matrix of the 2SLS estimator?

Answer **either** question 3 or 4.

3. Consider the exponential distribution as a model of the time to failure, t:

$$f(t) = (\tfrac{1}{\theta})\exp(-\tfrac{1}{\theta}t) \quad , \quad t \geq 0, \theta > 0.$$

a. Find the expression for the cumulative distribution function for t.

b. Derive the *hazard*, the instantaneous probability of failure given survival to time t^*.

c. Suppose θ is parameterized as $\theta = \beta'x$. From a sample $t_1, t_2, \ldots, t_n$ of observations on t find the maximum likelihood estimator of β.

d. Find the asymptotic distribution of your estimator in part c.

4. Consider the following index model:

$$y_i^* = \alpha + \beta d_i + \epsilon_i \quad , i = 1,\ldots,100, \quad \epsilon_i \sim N(0,\sigma^2) \text{ for all i.}$$

$$y_i = 1 \quad \text{if } y_i^* > 0 \ ,$$
$$y_i = 0 \quad \text{if } y_i^* \leq 0 \ .$$

The only regressor, d, is a dummy variable, and $\bar{y} = .44$, $\bar{d} = .48$, and $\sum y_i d_i = 16$.

a. Find the maximum likelihood estimators of α and β. (Hint: it may help to formulate the likelihood in terms of α and $\delta = \alpha + \beta$).
b. Estimate the asymptotic standard errors of your estimates.
c. Test the hypothesis that $\beta = 0$ using a likelihood ratio test.

Answer **either** question 5 or 6.

5. Carefully state and prove the Gauss-Markov theorem.

6. Derive the constrained least squares estimator, that is, the estimator that minimizes the sum of squared errors in the model

$$y = X\beta + \epsilon,$$

under the condition that $R\beta = q$. Here R is a $J \times K$ matrix of rank J and q is a $J \times 1$ vector of known constants.

Answer **either** question 7 or 8.

7. Consider the general nonlinear regression model

$$y_i = f(x_i;\beta) + \epsilon_i \quad , i = 1,\ldots,n \ .$$

where x_i is an $L \times 1$ vector of known values and β is a $K \times 1$ vector of unknown parameters. Present in detail one method of estimating the parameter vector β and its covariance matrix. (Begin with the appropriate expansion of f). Discuss one economic application of an inherently nonlinear estimation problem.

8. Consider the regression model

$$y_t = \beta y_{t-1} + \epsilon_t$$

$$\epsilon_t = \rho \epsilon_{t-1} + u_t \ .$$

It is true that $\text{plim } r = \dfrac{\beta\rho(\beta+\rho)}{1+\beta\rho}$, where $r = \dfrac{\sum_{t=2}^{T} e_t e_{t-1}}{\sum_{t=2}^{T} e_t^2}$. Use this result to show that $\text{plim } \frac{r}{b} = \beta\rho$ and $\text{plim } (b + r) = \beta + \rho$, where b is the least squares estimator of β. If you were given only the least squares regression results and the Durbin-Watson statistic, could you estimate β and ρ? If so, how? If not, why not?

University of Colorado at Boulder

ECONOMETRICS

PhD Comprehensive Examination

August, 1994

Answer both of the following questions.

1. A system of simultaneous equations may be written

$$y'_t B + x'_t \Gamma = \epsilon'_t .$$

Suppose B and Γ are both 3×3 matrices of unknown coefficients, except that the diagonal elements of B are all one.

a) Derive one method of checking the identification of this system <u>under general linear restrictions on the parameters</u>.

b) Check identification of <u>each</u> equation when

$$\beta_{21} + \beta_{31} = 0, \beta_{12} = 0, \gamma_{21} = \gamma_{32} = \gamma_{33} = 0$$

2. Consider the following nonlinear regression function.

$$y_t = x_t^\beta + u_t,$$

where u_t is independently but not identically distributed with zero mean and the heteroskedastic variance σ_t^2. Answer the following questions. (Hint: $\frac{dx_t^\beta}{d\beta} = x_t^\beta \ln x_t$).

a) How do you estimate the β? Propose a suitable estimation procedure, and be specific.

b) Derive the asymptotic distribution of above estimate, and calculate the asymptotic variance.

c) If $\sigma_t^2 = \sigma_0^2$ (homoskedastic), how does its asymptotic variance change?

d) If you want to test the nonlinear null hypothesis $h(\beta) = 0$, propose an appropriate asymptotic test statistic.

Choose one (1) of the following two (2) questions.

3. There are two random variables x_1 and x_2, which have a bivariate normal distribution such that

$$\begin{pmatrix} x_1 \\ x_2 \end{pmatrix} \sim N\left(\begin{pmatrix} \mu_1 \\ \mu_2 \end{pmatrix}, \Sigma\right), \text{ where } \Sigma = \begin{bmatrix} \sigma_1^2 & \sigma_{12} \\ \sigma_{12} & \sigma_2^2 \end{bmatrix}.$$

Bivariate normal density function of x_1 and x_2 is

$$f(x_1,x_2) = \frac{1}{2\pi} \cdot \frac{1}{\sigma_1\sigma_2\sqrt{1-\rho^2}} e^{-\frac{1}{2}q}$$

where $\rho = \dfrac{\sigma_{12}}{\sigma_1 \cdot \sigma_2}$,

$$q = \frac{1}{1-\rho^2}\left[\left(\frac{x_1-\mu_1}{\sigma_1}\right)^2 - 2\rho\left(\frac{x_1-\mu_1}{\sigma_1}\right)\left(\frac{x_2-\mu_2}{\sigma_2}\right) + \left(\frac{x_2-\mu_2}{\sigma_2}\right)^2\right].$$

Answer the following questions:

a) Derive the conditional density function of x_1 given x_2.

b) Find $E(x_1|x_2)$ and $var(x_1|x_2)$.

4. Suppose $X \sim N(\mu, \sigma^2)$, and you have a sample $x = (x_1, \ldots, x_n)'$ drawn from this distribution.

a) Derive the log- likelihood function.

b) Solve for the maximum likelihood estimators of μ and σ^2.

c) Derive the Hessian matrix of the log-likelihood function. Prove that it is diagonal with negative diagonal elements. Conclude that the solution is indeed a maximum.

d) Prove that the sample mean and variance are independent. (note: the diagonality of the Hessian indicates $\bar{x}$ and s^2 are uncorrelated. Hint: $\bar{x} = i'x/n$ and $s^2 = x'Ax/n$ where $A = I - i'i/n$, $i = (1, \ldots, 1)'$.)

Choose one (1) of the following two (2) questions.

5. The decision to migrate may be due to economic factors such as employment possibilities. The act of migrating is dichotomous.

a) Define all notation in presenting the logit and probit formulations of a model of migration.

b) Choose one (logit or probit), and derive the log-likelihood equation.

c) Interpret the coefficients of the model estimates (for example, how an increase in the wage differential would affect the probability of migration). Be explicit, using examples if necessary.

d) How is goodness-of-fit described in this model?

e) The distance one migrates (if one migrates) is also amenable to economic modeling. Present a statistical model for dealing with this type of data (the Tobit Model).

f) Indicate the log-likelihood function.

g) Why would least squares (dropping non-movers or treating them as moving zero miles) be inappropriate?

6. Consider the following censored regression model

$$y_i^* = x_i' \beta_0 + u_i \qquad E(u_i | x_i) = 0.$$

we observe $y_i = y_i^* \cdot 1(x_i' \beta_0 + u_i > 0)$, where $1(\lambda) = 1$ if λ is true and zero otherwise.

a) If u_i is normally distributed with mean 0 and the variance is σ^2, what is the proper estimation method for the unknown parameters β_0 and σ^2. Also, derive the asymptotic properties of the estimates in detail.

b) If the distribution of u_i is unknown, how would you apply the generalized method of moments (GMM) to estimate β_0. Discuss the appropriate estimation technique.

c) When the distribution of u_i is unknown, we can also apply the semi-parametric single index model to estimate the unknown parameter β_0. What is the semi-parametric single index model and how would you estimate β_0?

University of Colorado at Boulder

January 5, 1994

Comprehensive Exam in Econometrics

Directions: Answer questions: 1, 2, and 3, and <u>either</u> 4A <u>or</u> 4B. Show all work. Good luck.

1. Consider the classical normal linear regression model for n observations on K explanatory variables:

$$\mathbf{y} = \mathbf{X}\boldsymbol{\beta} + \boldsymbol{\epsilon} \quad , \tag{1}$$

where $\boldsymbol{\epsilon} \sim \mathrm{N}(\mathbf{0}, \sigma^2\mathbf{I})$. Assume that X is nonstochastic, fixed in repeated samples, and has full column rank. Suppose there are J linear restrictions on the parameters

$$\mathbf{R}\boldsymbol{\beta} = \mathbf{q} \quad , \tag{2}$$

where **R** is a J×K matrix of constants with rank J and **q** is a J×1 vector of constants. The restricted least squares estimator is the vector $\mathbf{b}^*$ that satisfies equation 2 and minimizes

$$f(\mathbf{b}^*) = (\mathbf{y} - \mathbf{X}\mathbf{b}^*)'(\mathbf{y} - \mathbf{X}\mathbf{b}^*) \quad . \tag{3}$$

a. Solve the above constrained optimization problem and show that

$$\mathbf{b}^* = \mathbf{b} - (\mathbf{X}'\mathbf{X})^{-1}\mathbf{R}'[\mathbf{R}(\mathbf{X}'\mathbf{X})^{-1}\mathbf{R}']^{-1}(\mathbf{R}\mathbf{b} - \mathbf{q}) \quad ,$$

where **b** is the ordinary (unconstrained) least squares estimator, $\mathbf{b} = (\mathbf{X}'\mathbf{X})^{-1}\mathbf{X}'\mathbf{y}$.

b. Find the variance of $\mathbf{b}^*$, and compare it to $\mathrm{V}(\mathbf{b})$.

c. Develope a test statistic to test the joint null hypothesis $\mathrm{H}_0\!:\!\mathbf{R}\boldsymbol{\beta} = \mathbf{q}$.

Suppose $\sigma^2 = 1$, $\mathbf{b} = (5 \;\; -4 \;\; 2)'$, and

$$(\mathbf{X}'\mathbf{X})^{-1} = \begin{bmatrix} 3 & 1 & 1 \\ 1 & 2 & 1 \\ 1 & 1 & 2 \end{bmatrix} .$$

d. On the basis of this information estimate $\boldsymbol{\beta}$ given you believe $\beta_1 + \beta_2 = \beta_3$.

2. Consider the model $y_i = \mu + \epsilon_i$, $i = 1,\ldots,n$. Note that this is the same as the regression of y_i on only a constant: $y_i = \mu \times 1 + \epsilon_i$, or in matrix algebra

$$y = \mu i + \epsilon \quad ,$$

where y, i, and ϵ are $n \times 1$ vectors. Suppose there is heteroskedasticity that depends upon a variable, z_i:

$$V(\epsilon_i) = \sigma^2 z_i^2 \quad .$$

a. Find the least squares estimator of μ, and its variance in this model with heteroskedasticity.

b. Find the generalized least squares estimator, and its variance.

c. Briefly discuss how you would test for heteroskedasticity in this model

3. Consider the model

$$C_t = \alpha_0 + \alpha_1 y_t + \epsilon_{1t} \tag{3.2}$$

$$I_t = \beta_0 + \beta_1 (y_t - y_{t-1}) + \epsilon_{2t} \tag{3.3}$$

$$y_t = C_t + I_t \tag{3.4}$$

where the endogenous vector at time t is given by

$$Y_t = (C_t, I_t, y_t)$$

and the disturbance terms satisfy all the standard assumptions.

a. Put this model into the form:

$$Y_t \Gamma + X_t \beta = \epsilon_t$$

and determine whether or not the rank condition for identification is satisfied for equation 3.2.

b. How would you estimate equation 3.2?

Choose either 4A or 4B.

4A. Consider the following limited dependent variable model:

$$y_{1i}^* = x_{1i}'\beta_1 + u_{1i}$$

$$y_{2i}^* = x_{2i}'\beta_2 + u_{2i}$$

$$y_i = \min(y_{1i}^*, y_{2i}^*) \ ,$$

where $u_i = (u_{1i}, u_{2i})$ has an iid bivariate normal distribution with zero mean vector and covariance matrix $\Sigma = \{\sigma_{ij}\}$. The variable y_{1i} is observed if $x_{1i}'\beta_1 + u_{1i} > 0$ and is equal to zero otherwise. If y_{1i} is observed, y_{2i} is observed if $x_{2i}'\beta_2 + u_{2i} > 0$, and is zero otherwise.

a. Sketch graph in u_{1i},u_{2i} space indicating possible data configurations (regimes).
b. Write an appropriate likelihood function for this sequential model, and propose an estimation procedure.
c. Are all parameters identified? Justify your answer.
d. Propose a two-step estimation procedure.

4B. How would you model the following situations? For each, indicate the dependent and independent variables you would use. Develop the econometric model carefully, as in both cases estimation is not straightfoward. Then discuss how you would estimate the parameters of the model. Indicate any problems with conventional or naive estimation. Carefully define all terms, and make explicit any assumptions you make. Speculate on the signs of coefficients, and discuss any policy implications or uses of the research. For one of the two situations, indicate the appropriate likelihood function for maximum likelihood estimation.

a. You have information on the earnings of adult siblings (brothers and sisters), as well as demographic information such as age, education, and experience. The siblings have all been raised in the same environment, so it is a good opportunity to specify a human capital (earnings) to estimate the returns to schooling.

b. Public utility companies offer incentives to customers to conserve energy. You have billing data (actual energy use from before and after the conservation action taken by the individual households), as well as survey data on housing characteristics for a sample of program participants as well as a sample of nonparticipants.

University of Colorado at Boulder

ECONOMETRICS **Ph.D. Comprehensive Examination**

August, 1993

Directions: Show all work. Answer question 1, either question 2 or 3, either question 4 or 5, and either question 6 or 7, for a total of four questions.

1. **(required)** Consider the classical normal linear regression model with two sets of regressors:

$$y = X_1\beta_1 + X_2\beta_2 + \epsilon,$$

where $\epsilon \sim N(0,\sigma^2 I)$. Assume that X_1 and X_2 have K_1 and K_2 columns ($K_1 + K_2 = K$), respectively, and that $X = (X_1 \vdots X_2)$ is nonstochastic, fixed in repeated samples, and has full column rank. Suppose it is known that the parameter vector satisfies the condition $R\beta = q$, where R is a $J\times K$ matrix and q is a $J\times 1$ vector of known constants. The constrained or restricted least squares estimator is:

$$b_* = b - (X'X)^{-1}R'[R(X'X)^{-1}R']^{-1}(Rb-q)$$

where $b = (b_1'\ b_2')' = (X'X)^{-1}X'y$.

a. We wish to restrict the model so that $\beta_2 = 0$. Find the appropriate R and q.

b. Prove that the restricted estimator is $\begin{bmatrix} b_{y\cdot 1} \\ 0 \end{bmatrix}$, where $b_{y\cdot 1}$ is the least squares coefficient vector in the regression of y on X_1 (the "short" regression). Hint: For any nonsingular matrix $A = (A_1 \vdots A_2)$, $A^{-1}A_1 = \begin{pmatrix} I \\ 0 \end{pmatrix}$ and $A^{-1}A_2 = \begin{pmatrix} 0 \\ I \end{pmatrix}$.

c. Prove that if the restriction is $\beta_2 = \beta_2^0$, the restricted estimator of β_1 is

$$b_1^* = (X_1'X_1)^{-1}X_1'(y - X_2\beta_2^0).$$

d. Show that the restricted coefficient vector may be written $b^* = [I - CR]b + w$, where w is not a function of b, and display C and w.

e. Show the covariance of the restricted least squares estimator is

$$\sigma^2(X'X)^{-1} - \sigma^2(X'X)^{-1}R[R(X'X)^{-1}R']^{-1}R(X'X)^{-1},$$

and that this matrix may be written

$$V(b)[V^{-1}(b) - R'V^{-1}(Rb)R]V(b).$$

f. Conclude that the restricted least squares estimator never has a larger variance-covariance matrix than the unrestricted least squares estimator. Why would we ever want to use the unrestricted least squares estimator?

Answer **either** question 2 or question 3.

2. Often in applied econometrics we deal with positive random variables (such as expenditures) that may have long (non Gaussian) right tails. An appropriate model in some cases may be the *lognormal*—assume that the natural logarithm of the dependent variable is a linear function of explanatory variables and normally distributed random error:

$$\log y_i = \beta' x_i + \epsilon_i\,, \quad \epsilon_i \sim N(0,\sigma^2)\,, \tag{1}$$

(1) Interpret β_k, the coefficient of the k-th explanatory variable.

Transformed to linearity the model of equation 1 is

$$y_i^* = \exp(\beta' x_i + \epsilon_i) = \exp(\beta' x_i) \cdot \exp(\epsilon_i)\,. \tag{2}$$

(2) Considering equation 2, discuss what the log transformation implies about the errors in a linear model.

(3) Find $E(y_i^*)$. (Hint: if $u \sim N(0,\sigma^2)$ and $v = e^u$, then $F(v) = \frac{1}{\sqrt{2\pi}\,\sigma v} e^{-\frac{1}{2}\left(\frac{\log v}{\sigma}\right)^2}$).

(4) Now suppose that this positive random variable y_i^* is not always observed. Instead, we observe y_i according to

$$y_i = \begin{cases} y_i^* & \text{if } \log y_i^* > c_i \\ 0 & \text{if } \log y_i^* \le c_i \end{cases}$$

where c_i is a known, lower threshhold. For a data on y_i, x_i, and c_i, write the log—likelihood function, and indicate from parameter estimates $\hat{\beta}$ and $\hat{\sigma}^2$ what expression you would use to estimate $\Pr(y_i^* \ge 1)$.

3. Consider the following equation system:

$$y_{1t} = \beta_{10} + \beta_{11} x_{1t} + u_{1t}$$
$$y_{2t} = \beta_{20} + \beta_{21} x_{2t} + u_{2t} \quad , \qquad t = 1,\ldots,T.$$

This is called the singular equations system if $y_{1t} + y_{2t} = 1$, $\beta_{10} + \beta_{20} = 1$, $\beta_{11} + \beta_{21} = 0$ (for $x_{1t} = x_{2t}$), and $u_{1t} + u_{2t} = 0$. Examples include the linear expenditure system and systems of share equations. Assume the errors have a first-order autoregressive structure such that

$$u_{1t} = \rho u_{1t-1} + v_{1t}$$
$$u_{2t} = \rho u_{2t-1} + v_{2t}$$

where (v_{1t}, v_{2t}) are independent of (u_{1t}, u_{2t}) and the autoregressive coefficients of (u_{1t}, u_{2t}) are the same.

(1) Calculate $\text{cov}(u_{1t}, u_{2t})$.

(2) Derive the complete structure of $E(u\,u')$, where $u' = (u_1', u_2')$ and $u_1' = (u_{11}, u_{12},\ldots,u_{1t})$.

(3) Show that least squares estimates of each equation are equivalent to the SUR-GLS estimates.

Answer **either** question 4 or question 5.

4. Consider the following censored regression equations:

$$y_{1i}^* = x_{1i}'\beta_1 + u_{1i}$$
$$y_{2i}^* = x_{2i}'\beta_2 + u_{2i}$$

where (u_{1i}, u_{2i}) have the bivariate normal distribution with mean zero and positive definite variance matrix Σ, with nonzero covariance. Latent variables y_{1i}^* and y_{2i}^* are not fully observed. Instead, y_{1i} and y_{2i} are observed such that

$$y_{1i} = y_{1i}^* \times 1(x_{1i}'\beta_1 + u_{1i} > w_{1i})$$
$$y_{2i} = y_{2i}^* \times 1(x_{2i}'\beta_2 + u_{2i} < w_{2i})$$

where (w_{1i}, w_{2i}) are observed variables. Notice here that y_{1i}^* is observed if it is greater than w_{1i} while y_{2i}^* is observed if it is less than w_{2i}.

(1) Write an appropriate log-likelihood function.
(2) Propose a suitable estimation method and discuss the possible problems of estimation.

5. The following is a simplified version of the autoregressive conditional heteroskedasticity (ARCH) model:

$$y_t = x_t'\beta_0 + \epsilon_t,$$

where x_t is a $k \times 1$ vector of exogenous (nonstochastic) variables. The disturbance term ϵ_t is iid., and the conditional moments of ϵ_t, conditioned on Ω_{t-1} (a past information set) are mean zero and variance h_t, i.e.,

$$E(\epsilon_t \mid \Omega_{t-1}) = 0, \quad \text{Var}(\epsilon_t \mid \Omega_{t-1}) = h_t = \alpha_0 + \alpha_1\epsilon_{t-1}^2.$$

We are proposing the semiparametric ARCH estimation procedure. Different from the conventional ARCh models, we do not assume the normality of the conditional distribution of ϵ_t. Instead, we will apply the generalized method of moments (GMM) estimation procedure. Answer the following questions:

(1) Assume that all the past information Ω_{t-1} is summarized in the current exogenous variable x_t. Parameters of interest are (α,β_0), where $\alpha = (\alpha_0,\alpha_1)'$. Be explicit about the minimum number of moment conditions for this problem and derive those conditions.

(2) Derive an appropriate loss function for the GMM estimation and design an optimal weighting matrix for this problem.

(3) Discuss the advantages of this procedure over the conventinal ARCH estimation procedure.

Answer either question 6 or question 7.

6. Consider the model:

(a) $y_{ti} = X_{ti}\beta_i + \epsilon_{ti}$ $\qquad i = 1,\ldots,N$
(b) $\epsilon_{ti} = \rho_i\epsilon_{t-1,i} + u_{ti}$ $\qquad t = 1,\ldots,T$

with obvious notation and:

$E[u_{ti}] = 0,\ E[u_{ti}\ u_{tj}] = \sigma_{ij}$
$E[u_{ti}u_{sj}] = 0\ \ \forall\ \ t \neq s$

(1) Express ϵ_{ti} in terms of u_{ti} and its lags and express ϵ_{tj} in terms of u_{tj} and its lags and then determine $E[\epsilon_{ti}\epsilon_{tj}]$.

(2) Express $\epsilon_{t-1,j}$ in terms of $u_{t-1,j}$ and its lags and calculate: $E[\epsilon_{t-1,j}\ \epsilon_{ti}]$.

(3) Calculate $E(\epsilon_{ti}\epsilon_{sj})$ for $s < t$.

(4) Suggest an estimator for $E(\epsilon_{ti}\epsilon_{tj})$.

7. Consider the model:

$$y_t = a + bX_t + \epsilon_t$$

where $\epsilon_t = \rho\epsilon_{t-1} + u_t$ $\quad t = 1,\ldots,T$ with $|\rho| < 1$ and X_t non-stochastic. The u_t are iid with $E(u_t) = 0$ and $E(u_t^2) = \sigma_u^2$. Suppose $\rho = 0.8$ but the researcher (you) believes $\rho = 0.5$. Finally, assume $|X_t| < M$, and $\lim_{T\to\infty} T^{-1}X'X = Q$, where Q^{-1} exists.

NOTE: X is the T×2 regressor matrix.

(1) If ρ is taken to be 0.5 and the model transformed via Cochrane-Orcutt, what is the mean and the variance of the resulting disturbance term?

(2) Let $\hat{\beta}' = [\hat{a},\hat{b}]$ be the OLS estimator of $\beta' = [a,b]$ based on the C-O transformation where ρ is assumed 0.5. Determine plim $(\hat{\beta})$.

University of Colorado at Boulder

January 4. 1993

Comprehensive Exam
Econometrics

Directions: Answer a total of four questions: 1 and 2, and one each of 3A <u>or</u> 3B, and 4A <u>or</u> 4B. Show intermediate steps. Good luck.

1. Consider the classical normal linear regression model:

$$\mathbf{y} = \mathbf{X}\beta + \epsilon \quad ,$$

where $\epsilon \sim \mathrm{N}(0, \sigma^2\mathbf{I})$. Assume that X is nonstochastic, fixed in repeated samples, and has full column rank. For the least squares estimator $\mathbf{b} = (\mathbf{X}'\mathbf{X})^{-1}\mathbf{X}'\mathbf{y}$,

a. prove that b is unbiased;

b. prove that b is consistent (carefully state any additional assumptions used in this step);

c. find the covariance matrix of b and prove that it is efficient (Gauss-Markov).

2. Consider the following regression model:

$$y_i = \mathbf{x}_i'\beta + u_i \quad ,$$

where $\mathbf{x}_i$ is a $K \times 1$ nonstochastic vector and β is a $K \times 1$ vector of unknown parameters. Assume y_i has the exponential distribution with probability density function:

$$f(y_i|\mathbf{x}_i) = (\mathbf{x}_i'\beta)^{-1}\exp\{-(\mathbf{x}_i'\beta)^{-1}y_i\} \quad . \quad y_i \geq 0.$$

a. Show that $E(y_i|\mathbf{x}_i) = \mathbf{x}_i'\beta$, and that $V(y_i|\mathbf{x}_i) = (\mathbf{x}_i'\beta)^2$.

b. Prove that that generalized least squares (GLS) estimator and the maximum likelihood (ML) estimator are the same in this model, and derive the asymptotic distribution of β. Provide an explanation of the equivalence of GLS and ML even though y_i has the exponential distribution, not the normal distribution.

Choose <u>either</u> 3A or 3B.

3A. Consider the following limited dependent variable model:

$$y_{1i}^* = x_{1i}'\beta_1 + u_{1i}$$

$$y_{2i}^* = x_{2i}'\beta_2 + u_{2i}$$

where $u_i = (u_{1i}, u_{2i})$ has an iid bivariate normal distribution with zero mean vector and covariance matrix $\Sigma = \{\sigma_{ij}\}$. The variable y_{1i} is observed if $x_{1i}'\beta_1 + u_{1i} > 0$ and is equal to zero otherwise. If y_{1i} is observed, y_{2i} is observed if $x_{2i}'\beta_2 + u_{2i} > 0$, and is zero otherwise.

a. Write an appropriate likelihood function for this sequential model, and propose an estimation procedure. (Hint: a graph in u_{1i}–u_{2i} space indicating possible data configurations (regimes) might be helpful).

b. Are all parameters identified? Justify your answer.

3B. The following model is a simplified version of the autoregressive conditional heteroskedasticity (ARCH) model (do not be intimidated—this is a straightforward maximum likelihood application):

$$y_t = x_t'\beta + \epsilon_t, \quad \epsilon_t|\Psi_{t-1} \sim N(0, h_t) \quad ,$$

$$h_t = \alpha_0 + \alpha_1\epsilon_{t-1}^2 \quad ,$$

where x_t is a $K \times 1$ vector of exogenous (nonstochastic) variables. The conditional distribution of ϵ_t, conditioned on Ψ_{t-1}, is normal with mean zero and variance h_t, i.e. $E(\epsilon_t|\Psi_{t-1}) = 0$, $V(\epsilon_t|\Psi_{t-1}) = h_t$. The conditional variance of ϵ_t is a linear function of ϵ_{t-1}^2.

a. Write a log-likelihood function to estimate $\boldsymbol{\theta} = (\boldsymbol{\alpha}', \boldsymbol{\beta}')$, where $\boldsymbol{\alpha} = (\alpha_0, \alpha_1)'$.

b. Show that the above MLE is consistent (i.e., show that the expected value of the first order conditions of the maximum likelihood function are equal to zero).

c. In ARCH maximum likelihood estimation of $\boldsymbol{\theta}$, the information matrix is block diagonal. Derive the covariance matrix of the MLE of $\boldsymbol{\alpha}$.

Choose <u>either</u> 4A or 4B:

4A. Consider the model:

$$y_t = X_t\beta + \epsilon_t \qquad \text{for } t = 1,\ldots,T$$

where $E(\epsilon_t) = 0$, ϵ_t and ϵ_s are independent for all $t \neq s$, and $E(\epsilon_t^2) = \sigma^2(\frac{t}{1+t})$. Let the T observations on the model be given as:

$$Y = X\beta + \epsilon \quad ,$$

where Y and ϵ are $T \times 1$, X is $T \times K$, and β is $K \times 1$.

a. Determine $E(\epsilon\epsilon')$.
b. Let $\hat{\epsilon} = Y - X\hat{\beta}$. Determine $\hat{\rho}$ such that $\frac{E(\hat{\epsilon}'\hat{\epsilon})}{\hat{\rho}} = \sigma^2$.

4B. Given a SUR (Seemingly Unrelated Regressions) model, where the i-th equation is given by:

$$Y_i = X_i\beta_i + u_i \quad , \quad \text{for } i = 1, 2, 3 \text{ (units)}, \quad t = 1,\ldots,T = 1, 2, 3, 4 \text{ (time)},$$

where Y_i and u_i are $T \times 1$, X_i is $T \times K_i$, and β_i is $K_i \times 1$. Assume

(i) X_i is non-stochastic, $\rho(X_i) = K_i$, for all i;
(ii) elements of $|X_i| < M$ (bounded);
(iii) $T^{-1}X_i'X_i \xrightarrow{p} Q_i$ and Q_i^{-1} exists;
(iv) $E(u_iu_i') = \sigma_{ii}I_T$; and
(v) $E(u_iu_j') = \sigma_{ij}I_T$.

Explain thoroughly how to obtain $\hat{\beta}^{SUR} = \{\hat{\beta}_i^{SUR}\}$.

Duke University

Field Examination in Statistics
January 1994

G

Six Questions, 20 points each

1. Let the discrete random variable X have the Poisson distribution with parameter $\lambda > 0$:

$$\Pr(X = x) = p(x) = \frac{\lambda^x e^{-\lambda}}{x!}, \qquad x = 0, 1, 2, \ldots,$$

1-A. Verify that $\sum_x p(x) = 1$. [Recall the infinite series expansion $e^u = \sum_{j=0}^{\infty} u^j/j!$]

1-B. Verify that the moment generating function of the Poisson distribution is

$$M(t) = e^{\lambda(e^t - 1)}$$

1-C. Working from the moment generating function in Part B., show that $E(X) = \lambda$, and $Var(X) = \lambda$.

2. Let X and Y be jointly normally distributed with means μ_1, μ_2, variances σ_1^2, σ_2^2, and covariance $\sigma_{12} = \rho\sigma_1\sigma_2$, $|\rho| < 1$.

2-A. Find constants α and β such that $Cov(X, Y - \alpha - \beta X) = 0$. What is the relationship between the random variable $U = Y - \alpha - \beta X$ and X?

2-B. Use the result from part A. to determine the conditional distribution of Y given $X = x$.

2-C. Briefly explain how to mimic the work in Parts A. and B. of this problem to determine the conditional distribution of X given $Y = y$.

3. Let $X_1, X_2, \ldots, X_n, X_{n+1}$ be a random sample from the $N(\mu, \sigma^2)$ distribution. Let $\bar{X} = \sum_{i=1}^{n} X_i/n$ and $S^2 = \sum_{i=1}^{n}(X_i - \bar{X})^2/n$.

3-A. Find c such that $c(\bar{X} - X_{n+1})/S$ follows a t distribution.

3-B. Let $\alpha \in (0, 1)$. Determine k such that $\Pr(\bar{X} - kS < X_{n+1} < \bar{X} + kS) = 1 - \alpha$. Explain why the interval $\bar{X} \pm kS$ is called a prediction interval for X_{n+1}.

4. Let $X_1, X_2, \ldots, X_n$ be a random sample from a density $f(x|\theta)$, where $\theta \in Q \subset \Re^K$. Consider the level-$\alpha$ test of the point null $H_0 : \theta = \theta_0$ against the point alternative $H_1 : \theta = \theta_1$, where θ_0 and θ_1 are distinct points in Q. Characterize the critical region of the best test under the Neyman-Pearson theory. Discuss the optimal hypothesis test (or lack thereof) if $K > 1$ and the alternative hypothesis is a region in $\Re^K$, instead of a single point.

5. Recall that $Q = \sum_{j=1}^{J} Z_j^2$ follows a $\mathcal{X}^2(J)$ distribution if Z_j are *iid* N(0,1) random variables. Suppose the $R \times 1$ random vector Y is $N(\mu, \Sigma)$, $\det(\Sigma) \neq 0$.

5-A. Sketch the argument that $(Y - \mu)'\Sigma^{-1}(Y - \mu)$ is $\mathcal{X}^2(R)$.

5-B. What is the distribution of $(Y - \nu)'\Sigma^{-1}(Y - \nu)$ if $\nu \in \Re^R$ and $\nu \neq \mu$? What can be said about the distribution of $(Y - \mu)'W^{-1}(Y - \mu)$ for some symmetric positive definite matrix $W \neq \Sigma$?

6. Let X and Y denote random variables of the continuous type with joint pdf $f(x, y)$ such that Y has mean μ_Y and positive variance σ_Y^2; let $E(Y|X = x) = \phi(x)$. Prove the Rao-Blackwell Theorem, which says that $E[\phi(X)] = \mu_Y$ and $Var[\phi(X)] \leq \sigma_Y^2$.

Duke University

Field Examination in Statistics
Spring 1993

Six Questions, 20 points each

1. Let the random variable X have the pdf

$$f(x) = \frac{2}{\sqrt{2\pi}} e^{-x^2/2},$$

for $0 < x < \infty$, and $f(x) = 0$ elsewhere. Find the mean and variance of X.

2. Let Z be N(0,1). The moment generating function of the random variable $W = Z^2$ is $M_W(t) \equiv E(e^{tW}) = (1-2t)^{-1/2}$ for $|t| < 1/2$. Now let X_1 and X_2 be independent chi-square random variables with r_1 and r_2 degrees of freedom, respectively. Derive the momeent generating function of the random variable $Y = X_1 + X_2$.

3. Let Y_1 and Y_2 be stochastically independent unbiased statistics for a scalar parameter θ. Suppose the variance of Y_1 is twice the variance of Y_2. Find constants k_1 and k_2 such that $k_1Y_1 + k_2Y_2$ is an unbiased statistic with the smallest possible variance for such a linear combination.

4. Let X and Y denote random variables of the continuous type with joint pdf $f(x,y)$ such that Y has mean μ_Y and positive variance σ_Y^2; let $E(Y|X=x) = \phi(x)$. Prove the Rao-blackwell Theorem, which says that $E[\phi(X)] = \mu_Y$ and $Var[\phi(X)] \leq \sigma_Y^2$.

5. Discuss the relationships among the follow distributions: (i) Z, the standard normal; (ii) $\chi^2(r)$, the chi-square with r degrees of freedom; (iii) $t(r)$, the t-distribution with r degrees of freedom; (iv) $F(r_1, r_2)$, the F-distribution with r_1 and r_2 degrees of freedom.

6. Let $X_1, X_2, \ldots, X_{20}$ be a random sample of size 20 from the $N(\mu, 1)$ distribution. Let $L(\mu)$ denote the likelihood function, i.e., the joint pdf of $X_1, X_2, \ldots, X_{20}$ viewed as a function of μ. The problem is to test $H_0 : \mu = 1$ against $H_1 : \mu = 0$, where the parameter space is $\mu \in \Omega = \{0, 1\}$. Let the critical region be defined by $L(1)/L(0) \leq k$.

A. Show that $L(1)/L(0) \leq k$ is equivalent to $\bar{x} \leq c$.

B. Find c so that the significance level is $\alpha = 0.05$.

C. Indicate how to compute the power function of the test.

D. Is this test procedure optimal in any sense? Explain.

Duke University

Econometrics Field Examination

(April 1995) **G**

(There are four parts, each of which carries equal weight. **Good Luck!**)

Part I. (25 points) Briefly yet precisely describe the following concepts. Exemplify their usage in economics.

I-A. Likelihood. Conditional Likelihood. Partial Likelihood. Pseudo Likelihood.

I-B. GMM.

I-C. EM algorithms.

I-D. Bootstrapping.

Part II. (25 points) Consider the Sample Selection Model.

$$y_{1i} = \alpha_1 + X_i'\beta_1 + u_i$$

$$y_{2i} = \alpha_2 + X_i'\beta_2 + v_i$$

where (u_i, v_i) are iid bivariate random variables. You observe $y_i = \max\{y_{1i}, y_{2i}\}$, $\delta_i = 1_{(y_i = y_{1i})}$, along with X_i.

II-A. Assume (u_i, v_i) is jointly normal with mean 0 and variance

$$\Sigma = \begin{pmatrix} \sigma_1^2 & \sigma_{12} \\ \sigma_{12} & \sigma_2^2 \end{pmatrix}.$$

Explain the identification of the parameters $(\alpha_1, \beta_1, \alpha_2, \beta_2, \sigma_1, \sigma_2, \sigma_{12})$ and construct a consistent estimation procedure. How do you estimate the standard error of your estimator for β_1, say.

II-B. Now suppose you do not want to impose any functional-form assumption on the distribution of (u_i, v_i), discuss the identification of (α_1, α_2).

Part III. (25 points) In economic models with panel data, there is a debate on fixed effect model (FEM) versus random effect model (REM). Write an essay on the debate. Clearly define FEM and REM, their estimation procedures, available statistical tests, etc.

Part IV. (25 points) Suppose $\{X_1, X_2, \ldots, X_n\}$ is a iid sample of size n from a truncated negative exponential distribution, whose density function is

$$f(x) = \frac{1}{\lambda} e^{-\frac{1}{\lambda}(x-\alpha)} 1_{(x \geq \alpha)}.$$

IV-A. Derive the MLE $(\hat{\lambda}, \hat{\alpha})$ for (λ, α).

IV-B. Show that $\hat{\lambda}$ and $\hat{\alpha}$ have different rate of convergence.

IV-C Use the result from B to construct estimator for the standard error of $\hat{\lambda}$.

Duke University

Econometrics Field Examination

(January 1995)

(There are four parts, each of which carries equal weight. **Good Luck!**)

Part I. (25 points) Briefly and precisely describe the following concepts.

I-A. Jensen Inequality and its role in proving consistency of the maximum likelihood estimatior.

I-B. Fundamental Probability Integral Transform and its role in numerical simulations.

I-C. Hausman's Sepcification Test.

I-D. White's hetroscedasticity robust variance estimator.

Part II. (25 points) Consider the Sample Selection Model.

$$y_{1i} = X_i'\beta_1 + u_i$$

$$y_{2i} = X_i'\beta_2 + v_i$$

where (u_i, v_i) are iid bivariate normal with mean 0 and variance

$$\Sigma = \begin{pmatrix} \sigma_1^2 & \sigma_{12} \\ \sigma_{12} & \sigma_2^2 \end{pmatrix}.$$

You observe $y_i = \max\{y_{1i}, y_{2i}\}$. along with X_i. Explain the identification of the parameters $(\beta_1, \beta_2 . \sigma_1, \sigma_2, \sigma_{12})$ and construct a consistent estimation procedure. Briefly explain why it is consistent.

Part III. (25 points)

III-A. First consider the linear regression model

$$\mathbf{y} = X\beta + \mathbf{u},$$

Suppose $E\mathbf{u} = 0$ and $E\mathbf{uu}' = P$ where P is an $(N \times N)$ othogonal projection matrix of rank $M < N$, i.e., $|P| = 0$. Suppose also $PX = X$. Show in this case the OLS estimator,

$$\hat{\beta} = (X'X)^{-1}X'\mathbf{y}$$

is *blue*. (Hint: Since P is orthogonal projection, there exists a $N \times M$ matrix Z such that $P = Z(Z'Z)^{-1}Z'$.)

III-B Next cosider the fixed-effect panel data model,

$$\mathbf{y}_i = X_i\beta + \mathbf{e}\alpha_i + \mathbf{u}_i, \qquad i = 1, ..., N \tag{1}$$

where $\mathbf{y}_i$ and $\mathbf{u}_i$ are $T \times 1$ vector, $\mathbf{e}$ a vector of unity. Premultiply (1) by $Q = I - T^{-1}\mathbf{e}\mathbf{e}'$. the $T \times T$ matrix of mean-sweeping transformation matrix. you have,

$$Q\mathbf{y}_i = QX_i\beta + Q\mathbf{u}_i, \qquad i = 1, ..., N \tag{2}$$

Explain how the result from **3.A** can be applied here to derive the *blue* estimator for β.

Part IV. (25 points) Let X be a scalar random variable with continuous probability density function $f(x)$. You are interested in a quantity called the Shannon Entropy, which is defined as

$$e_f \equiv E[-\log f(X)] = -\int f(x)\log f(x)dx.$$

Assume you have N number of independent observations: $X_1, ..., X_N$.

IV-A. Suppose you have reason to believe that $f(x)$ belongs to some parametric family, how do you estimate e_f? Construct an example.

IV-B. Suppose you do not want to assume any parametric form for $f(x)$. how do you estimate e_f?

IV-C. Suppose you are given two sets of data which represent the the economic performance under two regimes. You want to know which regime is more instable (has larger entropy), how do you construct a non-parameric testing procedure?

Duke University

Econometrics Examination, Spring 1994
Four Questions, Equal Weight

1. Consider the least-mean-distance estimator for $\theta_0 \in \Theta \subseteq \Re^p$ defined by

$$\hat{\theta} = \arg\min_{\theta \epsilon \Theta} \Big(\frac{1}{T} \sum_{t=1}^{T} g(y_t, \theta) \Big)$$

where $g : \Re^M \times R^p \rightarrow R^1$, and you may specify other regularity conditions on g as needed.

1-A. Suppose $\{y_t\}$ is *iid*, $\theta_0 = \arg\min_{\theta \epsilon \Theta}\{E[g(y_t, \theta)]\}$, and $E[g(y_t, \theta)] > E[g(y_t, \theta_0)]$ for $\theta \in \Theta$, $\theta \neq \theta_0$. Outline the asymptotic distribution theory, including consistency and asymptotic normality, for $\hat{\theta}$ in this case. Characterize the matrices defining the asymptotic covariance matrix of $\hat{\theta}$.

1-B. Continuing Part **1-A**, describe how to write the maximum likelihood estimator as a least-mean-distance estimator and discuss the form of the asymptotic covariance matrix.

1-C. Suppose we weaken the assumption in Part **1-A** to $\{y_t\}$ is strictly stationary and ergodic. For this case, outline the asymptotic distribution theory, including consistency and asymptotic normality, for $\hat{\theta}$. Characterize the matrices defining the asymptotic covariance matrix of $\hat{\theta}$.

2. Suppose y_t is generated by the nonlinear regression model

$$y_t = f(x_t, \beta_0) + u_t,$$

with error specification $u_t \sim N(0, \sigma_t^2)$, and

$$\sigma_t^2 = \alpha_0 + g(u_{t-1}, z_t, \alpha_1)$$

Here x_t and z_t are fixed sequences of observed exogenous variables, and β_0, α_0, and α_1 are unknown parameters.

2-A. Explain how you could estimate this model by maximum likelihood. Be very specific about the form of the likelihood function and the optimization problem defining the estimator.

2-B. In reference to the MLE estimation, explain in some detail how you could conduct a test of

$$H_0 : \alpha_1 = 0 \quad \text{against} \quad H_1 : \alpha_1 \neq 0$$

using each of three major methods (i) Wald; (ii) Likelihood ratio; and (iii) Lagrange multiplier.

3. Suppose the process $\{y_t\}$ is an MA(1) process

$$y_t = \mu + \epsilon_t + \alpha\epsilon_{t-1}$$

where $\{\epsilon_t\}$ is *idd* $N(0, \sigma^2)$.

3-A. Derive $c_j(\alpha, \sigma) = Cov(y_t, y_{t-j}), j = 0, \pm 1, \pm 2$ in terms of the underlying parameters.

3-B. Let $\bar{y} = (1/T)\sum_{t=1}^{T} y_t$, $\hat{c}_0 = (1/T)\sum_{t=1}^{T}(y_t - \bar{y})^2$, $\hat{c}_1 = (1/T)\sum_{t=2}^{T}(y_t - \bar{y})(y_{t-1} - \bar{y})$. Consider the estimator of μ, α, σ defined by the solution to the following system of equations

$$\begin{aligned} \mu - \bar{y} &= 0 \\ c_0(\alpha, \sigma) - \hat{c}_0 &= 0 \\ c_1(\alpha, \sigma) - \hat{c}_1 &= 0 \end{aligned}$$

Describe how to characterize this estimator as a GMM estimator and how to estimate consistently its asymptotic covariance matrix.

4. Let $\{y_t\}$ be an *iid* scalar process with *pdf* $f(y)$. Consider the kernel estimator of $f(y)$ defined by

$$\hat{f}(y) = \frac{1}{Tb_T}\sum_{t=1}^{T} K\left(\frac{y_t - y}{b_T}\right)$$

where K is a nonnegative kernel function such that $\int K(u)du = 1$, $\int uK(u)du = 0$, $\int u^2K(u)du < \infty$.

4-A. Derive directly $E[\hat{f}(y)]$ and $Var[\hat{f}(y)]$.

4-B. Cite [no formal derivation necessary] a condition on b_T that ensures $\hat{f}(y) \xrightarrow{M} f(y)$ as $T \to \infty$. Briefly interpret the condition in view of the expressions in Part **4-A.**

4-B. A kernel estimator can be normalized so as to follow a central limit theorem. Describe a construction that will accomplish this task.

Econometrics Exam

Duke University

Spring 1992

Four Questions, Equal Weight

1. Suppose the 2×1 parameter θ is estimate by maximum likelihood, $\hat{\theta} = \arg\max_{\theta \in \Theta}\{\mathcal{L}(\theta)\}$, where $\mathcal{L}(\theta)$ is the sample loglikelihood function. Suppose also that the sample size is $T = 100$, and that

$$\hat{\theta} = \begin{pmatrix} 3 \\ 2 \end{pmatrix}$$

$$\left(\frac{\partial^2 \mathcal{L}(\hat{\theta})}{\partial\theta\partial\theta'}\right)^{-1} = \begin{bmatrix} 4 & 1 \\ 1 & 1 \end{bmatrix}$$

A. Indicate how to carry out the Wald tests for the null hypotheses

$$H_0 : \theta_1 = 0, \theta_2 = 0$$

$$H_0 : \theta_1 + e^{\theta_2} = 0$$

B. Discuss how one would go about about conducting the tests defined in Part A. using the likelihood ratio (LR) and Lagrange multiplier (LM) tests.

2. Consider the basic linear regression model

$$y = X\beta + u, \qquad u \text{ is } N(0, \sigma^2 I)$$

where X is a fixed $T \times K$ matrix of full rank. Consider the null hypothesis $H_0 : R\beta = 0$, where R is a $q \times K$ matrix, $q < K$, and R is full rank.

A. Let ESS^U, denote the unrestricted residual sum of squares from applying OLS to the basic model and let ESS^R denote the minimum residual sum of squares under the restriction $R\beta = 0$. Prove that $(ESS^R - ESS^U)$ is statistically independent of ESS^U. Simplifying hint:

Think of reparameterizing the restriction so that so that $\beta = H\gamma$ along the restriction, where γ is $(K-q)\times 1$ and H is $K \times (K-q)$.

B. Consider a sequence of hypotheses defined by restrictions defined by $R_1\beta = 0, R_2\beta = 0, \ldots, R_J\beta = 0$, where R_j is $q_j \times K$, and $1 \leq q_1 < q_2 \cdots < q_J < K$ and $row(R_j) \subseteq row(R_{j+1})$ where $row(\cdot)$ denotes the row space of a matrix. In other words, the hypotheses are nested and become increasingly more restrictive as j increases. Let ESS_j denote the minimum residual sum of squares under the jth restriction. Use your result from Part A to show that

$$ESS_J = ESS_1 + \sum_{j=2}^{J} w_j,$$

where $w_j = ESS_j - ESS_{j-1}$, $j = 2, 3, \ldots, J$, and w_j is nonnegative and independent of w_{j-1}.

3. An m-estimator, $\hat{\theta}$, for a $K \times 1$ parameter vector $\theta_0 \in \Theta \subseteq \Re^K$ is defined to be a solution to K equations:

$$\sum_{t=1}^{T} \psi(z_t, \hat{\theta}) = 0,$$

where $\{z_t\}$ is a stochastic process and ψ is a $K \times 1$ vector function such that $E(\psi[z_t, \theta_0]) = 0$. In your answer below you may assume additional regularity conditions (differentiability, domination conditions, etc.) as need be. Also, you may assume that θ_0 is the only $\theta \epsilon \Theta$ satisfying $E(\psi[z_t, \theta]) = 0$.

A. Suppose $\{z_t\}$ is an *iid* process. Outline the theory showing that the asymptotic distribution theory for the m-estimator takes the form $\sqrt{T}(\hat{\theta} - \theta_0) \rightarrow^d N(0, A^{-1}BA^{-1})$, where B and A are $K \times K$ matrices. Characterize the matrices A and B.

B. Suppose $\{\psi(z_t, \theta_0)\}$ is a strictly stationary process with an MA(J) representation, $\psi(z_t, \theta_0) = C(L)\epsilon_t$, with $C(L)$ being a J-degree polynomial in the lag operator, L, $J < \infty$, and $\{\epsilon_t\}$ is a possibly conditionally heteroskedastic innovation process. Indicate how the asymptotic theory of $\sqrt{T}(\hat{\theta} - \theta_0)$ needs to be modified to subsume this case. Contrast the parameters of the asymptotic distribution (the A and B matrices) for this case with those of part A.

4. Explain three of the six following concepts. Be concise and specific.

(*i*) Augmented Dickey-Fuller test

(*ii*) Heteroskedasticity robust (HAC) variance estimation

(*iii*) Tobit estimation

(*iv*) Logistic regression

(*v*) Variance-bias tradeoff

(*vi*) kernel estimation of a density at a point

Duke University

April 1991

Econometrics Exam

Three parts, equally weighted. Answer all questions.

PART I

I-A.

Suppose we have a model $Y = X\beta + \epsilon$, where β is $K \times 1$, Y is $n \times 1$, X is $n \times K$ with rank $K < n$ and $\epsilon \sim N(0, \sigma^2 I)$. We posit a null hypothesis:

$$H_0/R\beta = r,$$

where R, r are known, R is $m \times K$ with rank $m < K$. We test the null using the appropriate test statistic and if the appropriate test statistic is greater than a critical value, c, we reject the null. If the test statistic is less than or equal to c, we accept the null.

$$\text{Let } \beta^* = \begin{cases} b = (X'X)^{-1}X'Y & \text{if } u > c \\ \tilde{\beta} = b - (X'X)^{-1}R[R(X'X)^{-1}R']^{-1}[Rb - r] & \text{if } u \leq c, \end{cases}$$

where u is the appropriate test statistic, c is a critical value depending on desired type one error. Note that $\tilde{\beta}$ is the constrained least squares estimator (constrained by the null hypothesis).

1. What is the test statistic uniformly most powerful for the null hypothesis and how is it distributed under the null?

2. Is β^* unbiased? Why?

I-B.

Theil, p. 603 of his text, Principles of Econometrics, recognizing the difficulties of selecting an estimator based on prior testing using the same data, said, "No special problems arise when these two successive steps [pre-testing, estimation] are based on independent sets of data."

Is Theil correct? Going back to Part I, Theil is suggesting using part of the data, say Y_1, X_1, sample size n_1 for testing the null, then using the remaining data, say Y_2, X_2, sample size n_2 for producing either b or $\tilde{\beta}$ depending on the outcome of the test. Would this yield an unbiased estimator for β? Why?

Can you give any intuitive argument about whether to pretest using only part of the data or all of the data? If so, make it.

II-A.
Briefly describe three of the following five concepts. (There is no need for extensive formulas. Just give the main ideas in a few sentences.)

1. Uniform law of large numbers

2. Dickey-Fuller distribution

3. Cointegration

4. Heteroskedasticity robust standard errors

5. ARCH model

II-B.
Suppose the model connecting the variable y_t to x_t is

$$y_t = f(x_t, \beta_0) + u_t$$

$$u_t = \rho_0 u_{t-1} + \epsilon_t, \quad |\rho_0| < 1$$

where $\{x_t\}$ is an $r \times 1$ iid process, $\{\epsilon_t\}$ is a scalar $(0,\sigma^2)$ iid process independent of $\{x_t\}$, and β_0 is $k \times 1$.

A. Sketch the main ideas of the proof of the consistency of the nonlinear least squares (NLS) estimator.

B. State the asymptotic distribution of the NLS estimator.

C. Show how to compute a feasible nonlinear GLS estimator of β_0 that is asymptotically more efficient than NLS.

Part III

You are analyzing the relationship between two (cointegrated) variables y and x, where x is a variable subject to government intervention (for the sake of simplicity you can assume that first order dynamics suffice to characterize the (x,y) process).

A sample is available for $t: 1 \rightarrow T$. The analysis of the (marginal) x process unambiguously suggests that its coefficients have changed at some known time T_1, (reflecting a change in government policy).

Provisionally assuming (weak) exogeneity of the x's you ran an OLS regression of the form

$$y_t = \beta_0 + \beta_1 x_t + \beta_2 x_{t-1} + \beta_3 y_{t-1} + \epsilon_t$$

Recursive application of Chow test indicates a shift in the OLS estimates of β_1 and β_2 around time T_1. In contrast the estimate of β_3 appears to be stable over the observation period.

Comment upon this situation. What are potential sources of the instability of the OLS estimates (relevant concepts are: the Lucas critique, (lack of) exogeneity, coefficient invariance, cointegration, Error-Correction-Mechanism representation,...)

Discuss additional testing and potential remedies that might be appropriate within this context.

University of Maryland

Comprehensive Examination in Econometrics

June 13, 1994

Answer 4 of the following 5 questions:

Question 1:

Consider the causal stationary AR(2) process

$$y_t = a_1 y_{t-1} + a_2 y_{t-2} + \varepsilon_t, \qquad (*)$$

where the ε_t are i.i.d. $WN(0, \sigma^2)$ random variables.

(a) Derive the Yule-Walker equations for the autocorrelations ρ_k, $k \geq 1$, for the model (*).

(b) Give the general solution for ρ_k, $k \geq 0$, in terms of a_1 and a_2. (Observe that the Yule-Walker equations form a homogeneous system of difference equations.)

(c) Use your answer from part (b) to compute ρ_2 given $a_1 = 0.5$, $a_2 = 0.14$.

Question 2:

Consider the simultaneous equation model (t=1,...T)

$$y_{t1} = \alpha y_{t2} + u_{t1},$$
$$y_{t2} = \beta z_t + u_{t2},$$

satisfying standard assumptions. The variable z_t is a scalar exogenous variable where $T^{-1}\sum_{t=1}^{T} z_t^2 \rightarrow Q_z$, $0<Q_z<\infty$. Assume that in the true structure $\beta \neq 0$.

(a) Derive the reduced form of the model.

(b) Show that α and β are identified.

(c) Define the 2SLS estimator for α and derive its asymptotic distribution.

Question 3:

Consider the nonlinear regression model

$$y_t = g(x_t, \theta_0) + u_t, \quad t=1,\dots,T,$$

where the random variables y_t, x_t and u_t take their values in $\mathbb{R}$, $\mathbb{R}^K$ and $\mathbb{R}$, respectively, $\theta_0 \in \mathbb{R}$, and $g: \mathbb{R}^{K+1} \to \mathbb{R}$ is twice continuously differentiable. Assume that the (u_t, x_t) are i.i.d., with $Eu_t = 0$, $Eu_t^2 = \sigma^2 > 0$ and finite, and that u_t and x_t are independent. Let $M = E[\partial g(x_t, \theta_0)/\partial\theta]^2$ and $Q = E[\partial^2 g(x_t, \theta_0)/\partial\theta\partial\theta]$ (abusing notation in an obvious way); assume further that $0 < M < \infty$ and $0 < Q < \infty$.

(a) Give the normal equations for the ordinary least squares estimator, say $\hat{\theta}_T$.

(b) Normalize the normal equations by $T^{-1/2}$ to obtain an expression of the form

$$T^{-1/2} \sum_{t=1}^T h(y_t, x_t, \hat{\theta}_T) = 0.$$

Calculate the expected value of $Eh(y_t, x_t, \theta_0)$ and $Eh(y_t, x_t, \theta_0)^2$ and express those expectations in terms of σ^2, M and Q.

(c) Derive the limiting distribution of the normalized normal equations evaluated at the true parameter value θ_0, i.e., $T^{-1/2} \sum_{t=1}^T h(y_t, x_t, \theta_0)$. (State the central limit theorem you may use.)

(d) Expand the normalized normal equations in a Taylor series around the true parameter value θ_0 to obtain an expression of the form

$$0 = T^{-1/2} \sum_{t=1}^T h(y_t, x_t, \theta_0) + [T^{-1} \sum_{t=1}^T \partial h(y_t, x_t, \tilde{\theta}_T)/\partial\theta] T^{1/2} (\hat{\theta}_T - \theta_0)$$

where $|\tilde{\theta}_T - \theta_0| \le |\hat{\theta}_T - \theta_0|$ (and where $\tilde{\theta}_T$ is assumed to be a proper random variable).

(e) Calculate the probability limit of $T^{-1} \sum_{t=1}^T \partial h(y_t, x_t, \theta_0)/\partial\theta$ and express that limit in terms of σ^2, M and Q. (State the law of large numbers you may use.)

(f) Assuming that

$$\operatorname{plim} T^{-1} \sum_{t=1}^T \partial h(y_t, x_t, \theta_0)/\partial\theta = \operatorname{plim} T^{-1} \sum_{t=1}^T \partial h(y_t, x_t, \tilde{\theta}_T)/\partial\theta$$

derive the asymptotic distribution of the ordinary least squares estimator $\hat{\theta}_T$.

Question 4:

Consider the linear regression model

$$y = X\beta + u, \qquad u \sim N(0,\sigma^2 I_T),$$

where y is Tx1, X is Tx3, β is 3x1, and u is Tx1. Suppose a researcher runs a least squares regression to estimate β based on a sample of size T=30 and obtains the following:

$$\hat{\beta} = \begin{bmatrix} \hat{\beta}_1 \\ \hat{\beta}_2 \\ \hat{\beta}_3 \end{bmatrix} = \begin{bmatrix} 5 \\ -4 \\ 2 \end{bmatrix} \text{ and } (X'X)^{-1} = \begin{bmatrix} 3 & 1 & 1 \\ 1 & 2 & 1 \\ 1 & 1 & 2 \end{bmatrix} \; ; \quad \hat{\sigma}^2 = 1.$$

(a) On the basis of this information estimate β (efficiently) given you believe the $\beta_1 + \beta_2 = \beta_3$. To do this, you need to derive the formula for the restricted least squares estimator.

(b) Test H_0: $\beta_1 + \beta_2 = \beta_3$ against H_1: $\beta_1 + \beta_2 \neq \beta_3$ at the 5 percent level of significance.

Question 5:

(a) Assume $y_1,\ldots,y_T$ are i.i.d. with common p.d.f. $f(y,\theta)$, where θ is a scalar parameter and $f(y,\theta)$ satisfies standard regularity conditions. Define the information matrix and give its dimension. State the asymptotic distribution of the maximum likelihood estimator for θ.

(b) Assume now that $f(y,\theta)=\exp(-\theta)\theta^y/y!$ for $y=0,1,2,3,\ldots$, and $f(y,\theta)=0$ else. The parameter θ is assumed to be positive. Derive the maximum likelihood estimator $\hat{\theta}$ for θ. Suppose further that you have obtained $\hat{\theta}=2$ from a sample of size 64. Based on the asymptotic theory, construct a 90%-confidence interval for the true parameter θ.

University of Maryland

Comprehensive Examination in Econometrics

January 11, 1994

Answer 4 of the following 5 questions:

Question 1:

Let x_t be i.i.d. with $(0,\sigma^2)$, t=1,...,T. Suppose x_t is regressed via OLS on x_{t-1} and x_{t-2}; let $\hat{\rho}_T$ be the resulting 2x1 estimator of the coefficients of x_{t-1} and x_{t-2}.

(a) Derive the large sample distribution of $T^{1/2}\,\hat{\rho}_T$ (give details).

(b) Determine the large sample distribution of $T\,\hat{\rho}_T'\hat{\rho}_T$.

Question 2:

(a) Give a brief discussion of what we mean by saying that the structural parameters of a (classical) linear simultaneous equation system are identified.

(b) Consider the two variable regression model

$$\underset{1\times1}{y_t} = \underset{1\times1}{\alpha} + \underset{1\times1}{x_t}\underset{1\times1}{\beta} + \underset{1\times1}{u_t}, \qquad t=1,\ldots,T,$$

where u_t is i.i.d. $N(0,\sigma^2)$ and $x_t \equiv 1$. Explain why the parameters α and β are not identified.

(c) Consider the following specific simultaneous equation system:

$$y_{t1} = y_{t2}b_{12} + x_{t1}c_{11} + u_{t1} \quad ,$$
$$y_{t2} = y_{t1}b_{21} + x_{t1}c_{21} + u_{t2} \quad , \qquad t=1,\ldots,T,$$

where y_{t1} and y_{t2} are the endogenous variables, x_{t1} is the (only) exogenous variable, u_{t1} and u_{t2} are the disturbances, and b_{12}, b_{21}, c_{11}, and c_{21} are parameters. The disturbance vectors $u'_{t.} = (u_{t1}, u_{t2})$ are i.i.d. with zero mean and positive definite variance covariance matrix. Suppose no additional information is available. Discuss whether the parameters of the model are identified.

(d) Consider the model in (c). Suppose it is known that $b_{12}+b_{21}=1$ and $c_{11}-c_{21}=0$. Discuss whether the parameters of the model are identified.

Question 3:

Consider the single equation model

$$y = X\beta + u$$

where y is the Tx1 vector of observations on the dependent variable, X is the TxK matrix of observations on the nonstochastic regressors with rank(X)=K, β is the Kx1 parameter vector, and u is the Tx1 disturbance vector with $u \sim N(0, \sigma^2 I_T)$.

(a) Derive the density of y. (If you use a result on the distribution of linear combinations of normally distributed random variables, please state the result.)

2

(b) Give the log-likelihood function.

(c) Give the objective function of the maximum likelihood estimator under the parameter constraint $R\beta = r$, where R is a GxK matrix of constants, rank(R) = G, and r is a Gx1 vector of constants. (Hint: Formulate the problem as a Lagrangian problem).

(d) Derive the maximum likelihood estimator for β and σ^2 under the parameter constraint $R\beta = r$.

(e) Derive the distribution of the constraint maximum likelihood estimator for β.

Remark: Let $v \sim N(\mu,\Omega)$ where v is a nx1 vector, then

$$f(v) = \frac{1}{(2\pi)^{n/2}|\Omega|^{1/2}} e^{-(v-\mu)'\Omega^{-1}(v-\mu)/2}$$

Question 4:

Consider the model (t=1,...,T)

$$\underset{1x1}{y_t} = \underset{1x1}{\alpha} + \underset{1x1}{x_t}\underset{1x1}{\beta} + \underset{1x1}{u_t} .$$

The disturbances u_t are distributed independently normal over time with $E(u_t)=0$ and $E(u_t^2) = 1/(a+bx_t^2)$, a>0, b>0. Furthermore x_t is nonstochastic and uniformly bounded (in absolute value) and $\lim_{T\to\infty} T^{-1}\sum_{t=1}^T x_t^k$ exists for k=1,2,... Suppose you have estimators $\hat{a}_T$ and $\hat{b}_T$ where $\hat{a}_T = a + \phi_T$ and $\hat{b}_T = b + \psi_T$ with $\text{plim}_{T\to\infty} \phi_T = \text{plim}_{T\to\infty} \psi_T = 0$.

(a) Define the true generalized least squares (GLS) estimator for α and β.

(b) Define the feasible GLS estimator for α and β that utilizes $\hat{a}_T$ and $\hat{b}_T$.

(c) Derive the probability limit of the feasible GLS estimator for α and β.

(d) Derive the limiting distribution of the feasible GLS estimator for α and β.

Question 5:

Consider the static simultaneous equations model $Y=YB+ZC+U$ where Y is the $T\times G$ matrix of observations on the endogenous variables, Z is the $T\times K$ matrix of observations on the exogenous variables, U is the $T\times G$ matrix of values of the disturbance terms, and B and C are parameter matrices of dimensions $G\times G$ and $K\times G$, respectively. The norming conditions $b_{ii}=0$ are assumed to hold. The typical elements of Y, Z and U are denoted with y_{ti}, z_{ti} and u_{ti}, respectively. The matrix Z is assumed to be nonstochastic and to have full column rank. The rows $u_{t.}$ of U are assumed to be i.i.d. $N(0,\Sigma)$ with Σ positive definite. All standard assumptions for the classical case are in force. The reduced form is written as $Y=Z\Pi+V$.

(a) State the relationship between the structural parameters (B,C,Σ) and the reduced form parameters (Π,Ω), where Ω is the covariance matrix of V. Is it true that the rows $v_{t.}$ of V are i.i.d. normal? State the rank condition for identifiability of the structural form parameters of the i-th equation.

(b) Give the OLS estimator $\hat{\Pi}_{OLS}$ of the reduced form parameters Π. Show that $\hat{\Pi}_{OLS}$ is consistent for Π. (You may assume that $Z'Z/T$ and $Z'U/T$ converge to appropriate limits.)

(c) Define the 2SLS-estimator for the structural parameters of the i-th equation as an instrumental variables estimator. Show that the 2SLS-estimator of the structural parameters in the i-th equation is consistent if the i-th equation is identified. Give (but do not derive) its asymptotic distribution. (You may assume that $Z'Y/T$, $Z'Z/T$ and $Z'U/T$ converge to appropriate limits.)

University of Maryland

Comprehensive Examination in Econometrics

June 16, 1993

USE A SEPARATE EXAMINATION BOOKLET FOR EACH QUESTION. WRITE YOUR SOCIAL SECURITY NUMBER AND THE QUESTION NUMBER ON THE OUTSIDE OF EACH BOOKLET.

Answer 4 of the following 5 questions:

Question 1:

Consider the classical simultaneous equation system

$$\underset{T\times G}{Y} = \underset{T\times G}{Y}\underset{G\times G}{B} + \underset{T\times K}{Z}\underset{K\times G}{C} + \underset{T\times G}{U}.$$

(a) Precisely state the classical assumptions on the model.

(b) Consider the first equation:

$$y_{.1} = Y_1\beta_1 + Z_1\gamma_1 + u_{.1} = X_1\delta_1 + u_{.1},$$
$$X_1 = [Y_1, Z_1],\ \delta_1 = [\beta_1', \gamma_1']',$$

where $y_{.1}$ denotes the vector of observations on the first endogenous variable, Y_1 and Z_1 denote the matrices of observations on the endogenous and predetermined explanatory variables that appear in the first equation, β_1 and γ_1 are the corresponding parameter vectors, and $u_{.1}$ denotes the disturbance vector in the first equation. Let $Z = [Z_1, Z_2^{*}, Z_2^{**}]$ and $\underline{Z} = [Z_1, Z_2^{*}]$. Consider the following "truncated" 2SLS estimator:

$$\tilde{\delta}_{1,T} = [\tilde{X}_1'X_1]^{-1}\tilde{X}_1'y_{.1}$$

where $\tilde{X}_1 = [\tilde{Y}_1, Z_1]$ with $\tilde{Y}_1 = \underline{Z}(\underline{Z}'\underline{Z})^{-1}\underline{Z}'Y_1$. (Note, in forming the instruments only a subset of the predetermined variables is used.) Derive the probability limit and the asymptotic distribution of $\tilde{\delta}_{1,T}$. Note: You may assume that the probability limit of any inverse matrix

1

you encounter exists.

Hint: It may be helpful to recognize that you can write $\tilde{X}_1 = \underline{Z}\underline{\tilde{R}}_1$, where $\underline{\tilde{R}}_1 = [\underline{\tilde{\Pi}}_{-1}, \underline{L}_{12}]$, $\underline{\tilde{\Pi}}_{-1} = (\underline{Z}'\underline{Z})^{-1}\underline{Z}'Y_1$, and $\underline{L}_{12}$ is a selector matrix selecting Z_1 from $\underline{Z}$.

Question 2:

Consider the following two equation model:

$$\underset{1\times1}{y_{t1}} = \underset{1\times1}{x_{t1}}\underset{1\times1}{\beta_1} + \underset{1\times1}{u_t} , \qquad \underset{1\times1}{y_{t2}} = \underset{1\times1}{x_{t2}}\underset{1\times1}{\beta_2} + \underset{1\times1}{v_t} , \qquad t=1,\ldots,T.$$

The regressors x_{ti} are assumed to be nonstochastic. The disturbances are defined as

$$u_t = \sum_{\tau=1}^{t}\varepsilon_\tau , \qquad v_t = \sum_{\tau=1}^{t}\eta_\tau , \qquad t=1,\ldots,T,$$

where the random variables (ε_t, η_t) are i.i.d. $N(0,\Phi)$ with Φ positive definite.

(a) Determine Euu', Euv', and Evv' where $u = (u_1,\ldots,u_T)'$ and $v = (v_1,\ldots,v_T)'$.

(b) Specify a consistent estimator for Φ. (Explain, but do not prove, why the estimator is consistent.

(c) Suppose Φ is known, give the BLUE for $(\beta_1,\beta_2)'$. (Explain, but do not prove, why the estimator is BLUE.)

Question 3:

Consider the model

$$y_t = x_t\beta + \varepsilon_t , \quad t=1,\ldots,T$$

where

(i) $E(\varepsilon_t) = 0$, $E(\varepsilon_t^2) = d_t^2$, and $0 < d_t^2 < m_2 < \infty$, where m_2 is a constant;

(ii) x_t is a nonstochastic scalar such that $0 < |x_t| < m_1 < \infty$, where m_1 is

University of Maryland

Comprehensive Examination in Econometrics

January, 1993

Answer 4 of the following 5 questions:

Question 1:

Consider the model

(1.1) $$y_{t1} = a_1 + a_2 e^{y_{t2}} + a_3 x_{t1} + \varepsilon_{t1} ,$$

(1.2) $$y_{t2} = b_1 + b_2 x_{t2} + b_3 y_{t1} + \varepsilon_{t2} , \quad t=1,\ldots, T,$$

where x_{t1} and x_{t2} are nonstochastic, $\varepsilon_t=(\varepsilon_{t1},\varepsilon_{t2})$ is i.i.d. $N(0,\Sigma_\varepsilon)$, where Σ_ε is a 2x2 matrix, and the remaining notation is obvious. Assume all of the conditions of the Amemiya model hold.

(a) Outline a nonlinear two stage least squares approach for estimating (1.1).

(b) Discuss problems which may be associated with the number of instruments used in relation to the sample size, which will (typically) be finite in practice.

(c) Determine the likelihood function for the model in (1.1) and (1.2).

Question 2:

Let y_{it}=1 if the i-th applicant for a loan at a given bank during a sampled year, t, receives a loan, and y_{it}=0, otherwise, i=1,...,N. Suppose the probability that y_{it}=1 depends upon the index I_{it} where

$$I_{it}=a_0 + a_1 z_i + b_0 D_{it} + b_1 D_{it-1} +\ldots +b_{10} D_{it-10}$$

where z_i is a relevant variable relating the i-th applicant, and D_{it} is the i-th applicant's net debt position during the sampled year, t, D_{it-1} is that debt position at time t-1, etc.

(a) Specify a model which might be useful for explaining y_{it}.

(b) Describe a likelihood ratio test for the hypothesis

$$H_0: b_i= \alpha_0 +\alpha_1 i + \alpha_2 i^2 , \quad i=1,\ldots,10$$

against the alternative that H_0 is not true.

(c) Suggest a Wald test for the hypotheses describe in (b). In doing this, show that the Almon specification, H_0 , can be expressed as restrictions of the form: RB=r, where $B'=(b_0,\ldots,b_{10})$.

Question 3:

Consider the nonlinear regression model

$$y_t = g(x_t, \theta_0) + u_t, \quad t=1,\ldots,T.$$

where the random variables y_t, x_t and u_t take their values in $\mathbb{R}$, $\mathbb{R}^K$ and $\mathbb{R}$, respectively, $\theta_0 \in \mathbb{R}$, and $g:\mathbb{R}^{K+1} \longrightarrow \mathbb{R}$ is twice continuously differentiable. Assume that (u_t, x_t) are i.i.d., with $Eu_t=0$, $Eu_t^2=\sigma^2>0$ and finite, and that u_t and x_t are independent. Let $M = E[\partial g(x_t,\theta_0)/\partial\theta]^2$ and $Q = E[\partial^2 g(x_t,\theta_0)/\partial\theta\partial\theta]$ (abusing notation in an obvious way); assume further that $0<M<\infty$ and $0<Q<\infty$.

(a) Give the normal equations for the ordinary least squares estimator, say $\hat{\theta}_T$.

(b) Normalize the normal equations by $T^{-1/2}$ to obtain an expression of the form

$$T^{-1/2}\sum_{t=1}^{T} h(y_t, x_t, \hat{\theta}_T) = 0.$$

Calculate the expected value of $Eh(y_t,x_t,\theta_0)$ and $Eh(y_t,x_t,\theta_0)^2$ and express those expectations in terms of σ^2, M and Q.

(c) Derive the limiting distribution of the normalized normal equations evaluated at the true parameter value θ_0, i.e., $T^{-1/2}\sum_{t=1}^{T} h(y_t,x_t,\theta_0)$. (State the central limit theorem you may use.)

(d) Expand the normalized normal equations in a Taylor series around the true parameter value θ_0 to obtain an expression of the form

$$0 = T^{-1/2}\sum_{t=1}^{T} h(y_t,x_t,\theta_0) + [T^{-1}\sum_{t=1}^{T} \partial h(y_t,x_t,\tilde{\theta}_T)/\partial\theta]T^{1/2}(\hat{\theta}_T-\theta_0)$$

where $|\tilde{\theta}_T-\theta_0| \le |\hat{\theta}_T-\theta_0|$ (and where $\tilde{\theta}_T$ is assumed to be a proper random variable).

(e) Calculate the probability limit of $T^{-1}\sum_{t=1}^{T} \partial h(y_t,x_t,\theta_0)/\partial\theta$ and express that limit in terms of σ^2, M and Q. (State the law of large numbers you may use.)

(f) Assuming that

$$\text{plim } T^{-1}\sum_{t=1}^{T} \partial h(y_t,x_t,\theta_0)/\partial\theta = \text{plim } T^{-1}\sum_{t=1}^{T} \partial h(y_t,x_t,\tilde{\theta}_T)/\partial\theta$$

derive the asymptotic distribution of the ordinary least squares estimator $\hat{\theta}_T$.

Question 4:

Consider the simple regression model:

$$y_t = x_t\beta + u_t, \quad t=1,\ldots,T,$$

with $x_t=t$. The disturbances u_t are assumed to be distributed i.i.d. over t with $E(u_t)=0$ and $E(u_t^2)=\sigma^2$ with $0<\sigma^2<\infty$. Let $\hat{\beta}_T$ denote the OLS estimator corresponding to a sample size T.

(a) Prove that $\hat{\beta}_T$ is a consistent estimator for β. (Hint: $\sum_{t=1}^{T} t^2 = T(T+1)(2T+1)/6$.)

(b) Assuming that the u_t's are normally distributed, derive the exact distribution of $\hat{\beta}_T$.

(c) Without assuming that the u_t's are normally distributed derive the probability limit of $T^{1/2}(\hat{\beta}_T-\beta)$.

(d) Without assuming that the u_t's are normally distributed derive the asymptotic distribution of $\hat{\beta}_T$. (To do this determine the limiting distribution of $T^{\alpha/2}(\hat{\beta}_T-\beta)$, where α should be chosen such that $T^{-\alpha}\sum_{t=1}^{T} t^2$ converges to a finite constant. Please check carefully the assumptions of any central limit theorem that you may want to apply in answering this question.)

Question 5:

Consider the classical linear regression model

$$\underset{1\times1}{y_t} = \underset{1\times1}{x_t}\,\underset{1\times1}{b} + \underset{1\times1}{z_t}\,\underset{1\times1}{c} + \underset{1\times1}{u_t} \tag{5.1}$$

and let the standard assumptions hold. Suppose you fit the misspecified model

$$y_t = x_t b + v_t \tag{5.2}$$

by ordinary least squares. Let $\hat{b}$ be the estimator of b so obtained.

(a) Calculate the bias of $\hat{b}$.

(b) Under which conditions is $\hat{b}$ unbiased?

(c) Suppose you want to test the null-hypothesis $H_0: b=0$ against the alternative $H_1: b\neq0$. Does the t-test based on (5.2) provide a valid procedure? What if the conditions you found in part (b) are met?

University of Maryland

Comprehensive Examination in Econometrics

August 25, 1992

Answer 4 of the following 5 questions:

Question 1:

(a) Consider the data process $\{y_t\}_{t=1,\ldots,T}$ with corresponding probability density function $f_T(y_1,\ldots,y_T,\theta)$ where the parameter vector θ is some element of the parameter space Θ. We may refer to the set of all densities $\{f_T(y_1,\ldots,y_T,\theta):\theta\in\Theta\}$ as the "model" for the probability law of the data process, and we may refer to a particular density corresponding to a particular parameter vector as a "structure". Explain the concept of observationally equivalent structures and the concept of identifiability in a brief and concise manner.

(b) Consider the following model

$$Q_t = A\,e^{\lambda t} L_t^{\alpha} K_t^{\beta} e^{u_t}, \quad t=1,2,\ldots,$$

where u_t is i.i.d. normal with mean zero and finite variance, and L_t and K_t are nonstochastic. Furthermore, let $L_t = e^{\rho t}$ (where ρ is known) and let K_t exhibit some general growth pattern (more specifically, assume K_t is not proportional to $e^{\kappa t}$ for some $\kappa\geq 0$). Discuss the identifiability of the parameters A, λ, α, β and/or linear combinations thereof with and without the assumption that $\alpha+\beta=1$.

(c) Consider the following simultaneous equation system:

$$y_{t1} = y_{t2}b_{12} + x_{t1}c_{11} + u_{t1},$$
$$y_{t2} = y_{t1}b_{21} + x_{t1}c_{21} + u_{t2}, \quad t=1,\ldots,T,$$

where y_{t1} and y_{t2} are the endogenous variables, x_{t1} is the (only) exogenous variable, u_{t1} and u_{t2} are the disturbances, and b_{12}, b_{21}, c_{11}, and c_{21} are parameters. The disturbances (u_{t1},u_{t2}) are i.i.d. with zero mean and positive definite variance covariance matrix. Suppose $b_{12}=1$ and $c_{11} = c_{21}$. Discuss whether the parameters of the model are identified.

Question 2:

Consider the model

$$\underset{1\times1}{y_t} = \underset{1\times K}{x_t}\underset{K\times1}{\beta} + \underset{1\times1}{u_t}, \quad t=1,\ldots,T$$

where the process (u_t, x_t) is i.i.d. Assume furthermore that u_t and x_t are contemporaneously independent, that u_t is distributed normal with zero mean and finite nonzero variance σ^2, and that the probability density function of x_t is given by $f_x(x_t)$, which does not depend on β or σ^2. Let $\hat{\beta}_T$ denote the ordinary least squares estimator.

(a) Derive the joint density of y_t and x_t.

(b) Show that $\hat{\beta}_T$ can be interpreted as a maximum likelihood estimator from the conditional and also from the joint density.

(c) Show that $\hat{\beta}_T$ can be interpreted as a moments estimator.

(d) Show that $\hat{\beta}_T$ can be interpreted as an instrumental variable estimator.

Question 3:

Let D_{t1} and D_{t2} be the demand at time t for goods 1 and 2, respectively. Suppose the units of D_{t1} and D_{t2} are comparable and let $D_t = D_{t1} + D_{t2}$. Suppose we do not observe D_{t1} and D_{t2}, but instead we observe D_t whenever $D_t < D^*$, where D^* is known. Let T^* be the number of periods in which $D_t < D^*$. Suppose the models determining D_{t1} and D_{t2} are

$$D_{t1} = X_t B + \varepsilon_t \;; \qquad D_{t2} = Z_t C + u_t,$$

where X_t and Z_t are nonstochastic row vectors of regressors which have no elements in common, and $\psi_t = (\varepsilon_t, u_t)$ is i.i.d. as $N(0,\Sigma)$, $\Sigma = (\sigma_{ij})$, $i,j=1,2$. Suppose we observe X_t and Z_t for all periods, i.e., when $D_t \geq D^*$ as well as when $D_t < D^*$. Suggest a two-step procedure for consistently estimating B and C; do not discuss issues relating to the VC matrix involved.

Question 4:

Let x_t be i.i.d. with $(0,\sigma^2)$, $t=1,\ldots,T$. Suppose x_t is regressed via OLS on x_{t-1} and x_{t-2}; let $\hat{\rho}_T$ be the resulting 2x1 estimator of the coefficients of x_{t-1} and x_{t-2}.

(a) Derive the large sample distribution of $T^{1/2}\hat{\rho}_T$ (give details).

(b) Determine the large sample distribution of $T\hat{\rho}_T'\hat{\rho}_T$.

Question 5:

Consider the model

$$y_t = a y_{t-1} + x_t b + \varepsilon_t, \quad t=1,\ldots T,$$

$$\varepsilon_t = \rho\varepsilon_{t-1} + u_t,$$

where x_t is a scalar nonstochastic regressor, u_t is i.i.d. as $N(0,\sigma^2)$ and a, b, and ρ are corresponding parameters. Suggest a Hausman-type test for $H_0: \rho=0$ against $H_1: \rho\neq0$.

Michigan State University

Econometrics Prelim

Fall, 1994

DO ALL FOUR QUESTIONS.

1. Suppose that the food consumption of the i-th household at time t is given by

$$(1) \qquad y_{it} = x_{it}'\beta_i + z_{it}'\gamma + u_{it}\,, \quad i = 1,\ldots,N\,,\ t = 1,\ldots,T\,.$$

Here β_i is a $k \times 1$ parameter vector (note that β_i depends on i); γ is an $m \times 1$ parameter vector; and the u_{it} are errors with $E(u_{it}) = 0$ and $E(u_{it}^2) = \sigma^2$ for all i and t, and with $E(u_{it}u_{js}) = 0$ for $i \neq j$ or $t \neq s$.

Now consider the macro (e.g., national) food consumption model

$$(2) \qquad \bar{y}_t = \bar{x}_t'\beta + \bar{z}_t'\gamma + v_t\,,$$

where $\bar{y}_t = N^{-1}\Sigma_{i=1}^{N} y_{it}$, $\bar{x}_t = N^{-1}\Sigma_{i=1}^{N} x_{it}$, and $\bar{z}_t = N^{-1}\Sigma_{i=1}^{N} z_{it}$. Note that the true data generating process is (1), while (2) is a model for the macro (aggregated) data that may or may not be correct.

A. Suppose that the following condition holds:

$$(3) \qquad \beta_1 = \beta_2 = \ldots = \beta_N\,.$$

What are the properties of the error v_t in the macro equation (2)? How would you estimate equation (2), using the aggregate data? What properties would your estimates have?

B. Suppose that condition (3) does not hold. Suppose that you estimate the macro model (2) by least squares. Give an expression for the expected value of the estimates of β and γ. Are they biased or unbiased? Explain.

C. If you have micro data on y_{it}, x_{it} and z_{it}, explain how you would test the restriction (3).

2. Consider the following panel data model, to be estimated using a sample with large cross sectional dimension (N) and small time series dimension (T):

$$(1) \qquad y_{it} = \alpha_i + \gamma_i t + x_{it}\beta + u_{it}\,,$$

where α_i and γ_i are unobserved individual effects, t is a linear time trend, and x_{it} contains observable explanatory variables. Note that each cross sectional unit (e.g., individual) is allowed to have its own intercept and time trend. In what follows, the cross section observations are i.i.d. draws from the population. Unless otherwise stated, we assume that, for each t,

$$(2) \qquad E(u_{it}|\alpha_i,\gamma_i,x_{i1},\ldots,x_{iT}) = 0.$$

A. Write the composite error as $v_{it} = \alpha_i + \gamma_i t + u_{it}$. Assume that α_i and γ_i have zero means, and that $E(u_{it}^2) = \sigma^2$ for all t, $cov(u_{it}, u_{is}) = 0$ for all $t \neq s$, and $cov(\alpha_i, \gamma_i) = 0$. Find $var(v_{it})$ and $cov(v_{it}, v_{is})$, $t \neq s$.

B. Under the same assumptions as in part A. above, and with the added assumptions that $E(x_{it}'\alpha_i) = E(x_{it}'\gamma_i) = 0$ for all t, what are the statistical properties of the pooled OLS estimator of β from the equation $y_{it} = x_{it}\beta + v_{it}$? Discuss unbiasedness, consistency and asymptotic distribution.

C. Under the assumptions in part A above, but now adding the assumption that $(u_{i1}, \ldots, u_{iT}, \alpha_i, \gamma_i)$ is independent of $x_i = (x_{i1}, \ldots, x_{iT})$, suggest a more (asymptotically) efficient estimator than the pooled OLS estimator.

D. Now drop all previous assumptions except (2), so that, in particular, α_i and γ_i are allowed to be correlated with x_{it}. Outline a method for consistently estimating β. What is the minimum number of time series observations (value of T) needed to estimate β?

3. Suppose that you are hired as a consultant by Ford. They wish to know why some car buyers buy U.S. cars and others buy foreign-made cars. They provide the following information, for each of 10,000 car buyers:

(i) Type of car -- foreign or U.S.
(ii) Age of buyer
(iii) Region of buyer's residence: west, midwest, south or east
(iv) Buyer's income.

A. <u>As explicitly as possible</u>, propose a model to use to estimate the effect of buyer's age, income and region of residence on type of car bought. Write the model down mathematically. Be clear about what assumptions you make.

B. How would you estimate the model? What properties would your estimates have?

C. How would you test the hypothesis that buyer's age does not affect the type of car bought?

D. Now consider each of the following possible complications. For each, indicate what problems (if any) it causes what what (if anything) can be done about them. (i) The sample is not a random sample of buyers; young buyers are overrepresented. (ii) The sample is not a random sample of buyers: buyers of foreign cars are overrepresented. (iii) Ford forbids you to make any distributional assumptions.

4. Suppose that you have observations on a pair of random variables (y_y, x_t), $t = 1,\ldots,T$. Suppose that economic theory indicates that

(1) $$E(y_{t+1} | \Omega_t) = x_t ,$$

where the "information set" Ω_t contains values of y and x dated "t" and earlier (that is, it contains y_t, x_t, y_{t-1}, x_{t-1}, y_{t-2}, x_{t-2}, ...) and also possibly other variables that economic agents may observe but you do not observe. You want to test this theory. You write the regression equation

(2) $$y_{t+1} = \alpha + \beta x_t + \epsilon_{t+1} , \quad t = 1,\ldots,T-1 .$$

You wish to test the hypothesis $\alpha = 0$, $\beta = 1$.

A. What properties does the economic model imply for the error series ϵ_t? Be clear about the relationships that do or do not exist among different ϵ_t, and between ϵ's and x's.

B. Suppose that (y_t, x_t) is a covariance stationary series. What are the properties of least squares applied to (1)? Explain briefly, in terms of your answer to A. above.

C. Explain how you would test H_0: $\alpha = 0$, $\beta = 1$, using only those properties of the ϵ_t that are implied by the economic theory (as identified in your answer to part A. above).

D. How would your answers to A., B. and C. change if (y_t, x_t) is a vector I(1) series [I(1) = "integrated of order one"]?

Michigan State University

Econometrics Prelim

January 20, 1994

<u>Instructions</u>: Do all four questions, each in a separate blue book.

1. Consider the following regression model for quarterly observations from 1950-I through 1989-IV:

$$y_t = \alpha + \beta x_t + \epsilon_t, \quad t=1,2,\ldots,160. \tag{1.1}$$

Assume that this model satisfies the ideal conditions under which ordinary least squares is unbiased and efficient.

Suppose that the data actually available are as follows: (1) We have the 120 quarterly observations from 1960-I through 1989-IV. (2) For each of the first ten years (1950-1959) we observe only the <u>annual totals</u> of y and x; that is, $\hat{y}_1 = y_1 + y_2 + y_3 + y_4$, $\hat{x}_1 = x_1 + x_2 + x_3 + x_4$ (1950); $\hat{y}_2 = y_5 + y_6 + y_7 + y_8$, $\hat{x}_2 = x_5 + x_6 + x_7 + x_8$ (1951); ...; $\hat{y}_{10} = y_{37} + y_{38} + y_{39} + y_{40}$, $\hat{x}_{10} = x_{37} + x_{38} + x_{39} + x_{40}$ (1959).

(i) Suppose you run an OLS regression of y on a constant and x using the available 130 observations (the first ten are the annual observations, the remaining 120 are the quarterly observations). Does this produce unbiased estimators of α and β? Justify your answer.

(ii) How should you estimate α and β? Be specific and explain.

(iii) Explain <u>in detail</u> how to test the hypothesis that β is constant over the whole period (that is, (1.1) holds) against the alternative that there are different slopes for the periods 1950-59 and 1960-1989.

2. In the two equation model

$$y_{i1} = \alpha X_{i1} + \epsilon_{i1}$$

$$y_{i2} = \beta X_{i1} + \gamma X_{i2} + \epsilon_{i2},$$

all quantities are scalars, the observations are independently distributed across i, and you have available n observations. Treat X_{i1} and X_{i2} as nonstochastic such that

$$\frac{1}{n}\sum_{i=1}^{n} X_{i1}^2 \to 2, \quad \frac{1}{n}\sum_{i=1}^{n} X_{i2}^2 \to 1, \quad \text{and } \frac{1}{n}\sum_{i=1}^{n} X_{i1}X_{i2} \to 1$$

as $n \to \infty$. Further, $\{(\epsilon_{i1},\epsilon_{i2})' : i=1,2,\ldots,n\}$ are identically distributed with

$$\begin{bmatrix} \epsilon_{i1} \\ \epsilon_{i2} \end{bmatrix} \sim \text{Normal}(0,\Sigma) \quad \text{where } \Sigma = \begin{bmatrix} \sigma_1^2 & \rho\sigma_1\sigma_2 \\ \rho\sigma_1\sigma_2 & \sigma_2^2 \end{bmatrix}$$

and $|\rho| < 1$.

(i) Explain how to obtain the asymptotically efficient estimators of α, β, and γ.

(ii) Let θ be the 3x1 vector containing α, β, and γ, and let $\hat{\theta}$ denote the estimator of θ from part (i). Derive the asymptotic variance of $\sqrt{n}(\hat{\theta} - \theta)$. (It should be a function of ρ, σ_1, and σ_2.)

(iii) Let $\tilde{\alpha}$, $\tilde{\beta}$, and $\tilde{\gamma}$ denote the estimators obtained by applying OLS to each equation in turn, and let $\tilde{\theta}$ denote the vector of these estimators. Derive the asymptotic variance of $\sqrt{n}(\tilde{\theta} - \theta)$.

(iv) Compare the asymptotic variances obtained in parts (ii) and (iii) and explain your findings.

3. Some studies have found a negative relationship between cigarette smoking and wages, conditional on various observed individual attributes. Suppose you have two years of panel data, say 1986 and 1990, on individual wages, cigarettes smoked per day, and various other individual attributes that affect both wages and cigarette smoking. Consider the following model:

$$wage_{it} = \theta_{10} + \theta_{11}d90_t + \gamma_{11}cigs_{it} + \mathbf{z}_{it1}\delta_1 + \alpha_i + u_{it1} \quad (3.1)$$

$$cigs_{it} = \theta_{20} + \theta_{21}d90_t + \gamma_{21}price_{it} \quad (3.2)$$
$$+ \gamma_{22}income_{it} + \mathbf{z}_{it2}\delta_2 + \rho_2\alpha_i + u_{it2}$$

$$income_{it} = wage_{it}hours_{it} + nonlabor_{it} \quad (3.3)$$

for $t=1,2$. Equation (3.1) is the equation of primary interest, (3.2) is a demand equation for cigarettes (per day), and (3.3) simply defines total income as labor income plus nonlabor income. Assume that $\mathbf{z}_{it}$ -- which consists of the elements in $\mathbf{z}_{it1}$ and $\mathbf{z}_{it2}$, all of which are time-varying -- $price_{it}$, and $nonlabor_{it}$ are strictly exogenous conditional on α_i. Here, $price_{it}$ is the average price of cigarettes (including taxes) in the state where person i resides. The unobserved factor α_i may be correlated with any of the observables.

(i) Why is it reasonable to take $price_{it}$ as strictly exogenous in (3.1) and (3.2)? Explain why $income_{it}$ is not exogenous to equation (3.1).

(ii) Does first differencing (3.1) and then applying OLS generally consistently estimate γ_{11} and δ_1? Explain.

(iii) Carefully outline a procedure for consistently estimating γ_{11} and δ_1, and for obtaining standard errors. State any assumptions you use in addition to the ones given above.

(iv) Is the linear model (3.2) for $cigs_{it}$ likely to be the best description of the demand for cigarettes? Explain.

4. A linear time series model relating a variable, y_t, to the rational expectation of the 1xK vector, $\mathbf{x}_t$, is given by

$$y_t = E(\mathbf{x}_t | I_{t-1})\beta + u_t,$$

where $E(\mathbf{x}_t | I_{t-1})$ is the expected value of $\mathbf{x}_t$ given all information known up to time t-1, I_{t-1}. Note that, at a minimum, $(y_{t-1}, \mathbf{x}_{t-1}, y_{t-2}, \mathbf{x}_{t-2}, \ldots)$ is contained in I_{t-1}. Throughout this problem assume that $\{u_t\}$ is I(0) such that $E(u_t | I_{t-1}) = 0$. For simplicity, there is no intercept in the model.

(i) Assume initially that $\{\mathbf{x}_t\}$ is an I(0) process. Let $\tilde{\beta}$ be the OLS estimator from the regression

$$y_t \text{ on } \mathbf{x}_t, \quad t=1,2,\ldots,T.$$

Show that $\tilde{\beta}$ is not generally a consistent estimator of β.

(ii) Still assuming that $\{\mathbf{x}_t\}$ is I(0), suggest a method for consistently estimating β. State any assumptions that you need in addition to those already made. Call this estimator $\hat{\beta}$.

(iii) How would you estimate the asymptotic variance of $\hat{\beta}$ under the assumptions given so far?

(iv) Now suppose that $\{\mathbf{x}_t\}$ is I(1), so that it can be written as $\mathbf{x}_t = \mathbf{x}_{t-1} + \mathbf{v}_t$ where $\{\mathbf{v}_t\}$ is a zero mean I(0) process. Evaluate the asymptotic properties of the OLS estimator, $\tilde{\beta}$, from part (i) of this question.

Michigan State University

Econometrics Prelim

January, 1994

DO ALL FOUR QUESTIONS.

1. Consider the two regressions

(a) $y = X\beta + \epsilon$ (T observations)

(b) $$\begin{bmatrix} y \\ y_0 \end{bmatrix} = \begin{bmatrix} X & 0 \\ X_0 & I_n \end{bmatrix} \begin{bmatrix} \beta \\ \gamma \end{bmatrix} + \begin{bmatrix} \epsilon \\ \epsilon_0 \end{bmatrix}$$ (T+n observations)

Let $\hat{\beta}$ = ordinary least squares of (a). Show that ordinary least squares of (b) equals

$$\begin{bmatrix} \hat{\beta} \\ y_0 - X_0\hat{\beta} \end{bmatrix} .$$

Describe, in words, what this result says about the effects of adding to a regression some extra observations and also dummy variables for those observations.

2. Let y, x_1 and x_2 be observable variables, and let z* be an unobserved (or latent) variable. Consider the model

(a) $y = \beta_0 + \beta_1 x_1 + \beta_2 x_2 + \gamma_1 z^* + \gamma_2 (x_2 z^*) + u$

(b) $E(u|x_1,x_2,z^*) = 0$.

Assume that z* is normalized so that $E(z^*) = 0$. As a specific example, y might be wage (or log wage) of an individual, x_1 is education, x_2 is education, and z* is unobserved ability.

(i) Find the partial effect of x_2 on $E(y|x_1,x_2,z^*)$. Show that β_2 can be interpreted as the partial effect of x_2 on $E(y|x_1,x_2,z^*)$, averaged over the population.

(ii) If $E(z^*|x_1,x_2) = 0$, explain why an OLS regression of y on $(1,x_1,x_2)$ produces consistent estimators of β_0, β_1 and β_2.

(iii) Now suppose that there is an observable variable z that is redundant in (a), so that $E(u|x_1,x_2,z^*,z) = 0$, and

(c) $E(z^*|x_1,x_2,z) = \delta_0 + \delta_1 z$.

Explain how to obtain consistent estimators of β_1 and β_2.

3. You are hired as a research assistant by Professor I.B. Rash. He has a univariate stationary time series y_1, y_2, ..., y_{100}. He wishes to forecast y_{101}, y_{102} and y_{103} and tells you to do so using an AR(1) model.

(i) Write down an AR(1) model for y. Be clear about what assumptions are made. DO NOT assume that the series y_t has zero mean.

(ii) How would you estimate the parameters of your AR(1) model? What properties would your estimates have?

(iii) Given your estimated model, explain specifically how you would use it to forecast y_{101}, y_{102} and y_{103}. That is, write the forecasts explicitly in terms of the data (y_1, ... , y_{100}) and estimated parameters. What properties would your forecasts have?

4. Suppose that we are interested in the pattern of numbers of worker injuries of small-sized firms (firms with less than 50 employees). We have three-year panel data on the injury rates of 1000 such firms. We postulate the following model:

(a) $$y_{it} = \alpha_i + \beta y_{i,t-1} + \epsilon_{it}$$

where the dependent variable y_{it} is the injury count of the i-th firm in year t, the single regressor is its lagged value, and the error term is assumed to be independently and identically distributed with mean zero and variance σ^2. The parameters of the model are β, σ^2, α_1, α_2, ... , α_N; thus we are treating the intercepts α_i as fixed.

(i) Assume that the errors are normally distributed and that the initial values y_{i0} are treated as fixed. Show that the MLE of β is the same as the OLS estimator with individual dummy variables included in the model; and show that this estimator is also the same as the OLS estimator with y_{it} converted to deviations from individual means (the "within estimator").

(ii) Is the MLE/OLS with dummies/within estimator consistent? Explain clearly. A rigorous proof is not necessary.

(iii) Suggest a consistent estimator of β that does not rely on any specific distributional assumption for ϵ.

(iv) The values of the data y_{it} are non-negative integers, since they are numbers of injuries. Explain why this conflicts with the assumption of a normal distribution for ϵ. Can you suggest an alternative to model (a), which may embody a specific distributional assumption, which takes into account the integer nature of the data? How would you estimate your model? In what sense is it true that a better distributional assumption leads to better estimates?

Michigan State University

Econometrics prelim

Fall, 1993

Do all four questions.

1. Let $M = I - X(X'X)^{-1}X'$. Show that the following least squares regressions imply the same estimates of γ.

A. $y = X\beta + Z\gamma + \epsilon_A$

B. $y = X\beta + (MZ)\gamma + \epsilon_B$

C. $(My) = X\beta + (MZ)\gamma + \epsilon_C$

D. $y = (MZ)\gamma + \epsilon_D$

E. $(My) = (MZ)\gamma + \epsilon_A$

Do B. and C. imply the same estimate of β as A.?

2. You have data for each member of a sample of economics graduate students on the following variables: X = number of statistics courses taken; Y = average grade in econometrics classes; D = dummy variable indicating whether or not the student ultimately takes the econometrics prelim. You wish to estimate the model

(*) $Y_i = \alpha + \beta X_i + \gamma D_i + \epsilon_i$.

Your main interest is in β, the effect of the number of statistics courses on grades in econometrics courses, but you include D_i because you think that students who plan to take the econometrics prelim will take more statistics course and also will have higher grades in econometrics courses. However, you are worried about the exogeneity of the variable D_i, because grades on econometrics courses may influence the decision to take the econometrics prelim.

There are (at least) two possible ways to modify the model (*) above. One is based on the assumption that the parameters α and β are different for students with D = 0 than for students with D = 1, and can be called a simultaneous equation (or endogenous switching) model. The other is based on the assumption that the parameters α and β are the same for all students, and can be called the self-selection model.

Explain these two approaches fully. Be sure to suggest, for each model:

A. The precise formulation of the model;

B. The assumptions made;

C. What is wrong with OLS applied to (*), given your model and assumptions;

D. The method of estimation for your model, and the properties of your estimates.

3. You wish to estimate a money demand function of the form

$$M_t = \alpha + \beta_1 Y_t + \beta_2 r_t + \epsilon_t \quad , \quad t = 1,2,\ldots,T \ ,$$

where M_t = log(real money balances), Y_t = log(real GNP), r_t = some specific interest rate. You also want to test the hypothesis that $\beta_1 = 1$. You have T = 120 quarterly observations for the U.S. on the variables (M,Y,r) over the period 1961-1990.

A. What is the relevance of the concepts of <u>integration</u> and <u>cointegration</u> to this empirical problem? Be sure to define these concepts.

B. Explain specifically what steps you would take to estimate (α,β_1,β_2) and to test the hypothesis $\beta_1 = 1$. These suggestions should reflect your answer to part A. about the relevance of the concepts of integration and cointegration.

4. You obtain a sample of 1000 individuals who are arrested for drunk driving in January, 1987. Five years later, in January, 1992, you are able to find out from police records how many (more) times they have been arrested for drunk driving during this five year period, and when these arrests occurred. You also observe a vector X_i of potentially relevant explanatory variables (such as race, sex, age in 1987) for person i, i = 1,...,1000. Assume that X_i does not change over time.

A. Suppose that the length of time between arrests for drunk driving is, for person i, distributed as exponential with mean $\lambda_i = \exp(X_i'\beta)$, where $\exp(x) \equiv e^x$. Suppose that the timing of subsequent arrests is independent of the number and timing of previous arrests. How would you estimate β? What properties does your estimate have? What properties would it have if the assumption of an exponential distribution is incorrect?

B. Suppose now that you observe the number of arrests during the five year period but you do not observe the timing of the arrests. That is, you know how often the individual was arrested, but not when he or she was arrested. Now how would you estimate β? What properties would your estimate have? What properties would it have if your distributional assumption is incorrect?

January 22, 1993

Michigan State University

Econometrics Prelim

Instructions: Answer all four questions, each in a separate exam book. Show your work, although you may rely on standard results from econometrics unless you are explicitly asked to prove or to show something.

1. A company employs workers for two jobs, job A and job B. Productivity in either job is determined by the worker's experience with the company, the worker's education, and an assortment of unobservable worker specific traits that do not change over time. These unobservable traits are orthogonal to education and experience; initially, they are also orthogonal to job type. The company attempts to set each worker's pay equal to his or her productivity, but it can only measure productivity with error. This error is orthogonal to education, experience, and job type.

You are hired by the company to determine how much a worker's productivity in the type A job increases with each year the worker spends with the company. Initially, you are provided data at one point in time on salary, education, experience, and job type.

You first use the data only on job A people to estimate the regression

$$\text{salary}_i = \hat{\beta}_0 + \hat{\beta}_1\text{educ}_i + \hat{\beta}_2\text{exper}_i + \hat{\beta}_3\text{exper}_i^2 + \hat{u}_i, \tag{1.1}$$

where $\hat{u}_i$ are the OLS residuals.

(i) Under the assumptions stated above, how does the fact that productivity is measured with error affect the usefulness of the OLS estimators to measure the impact of experience on productivity in the A job? It might be useful to write out the equations and assumptions corresponding to the verbal descriptions given above.

(ii) Suppose that, on average, the company moves people with more experience into job B. Does this cause a problem for the OLS estimators in (1.1) for estimating the effect of experience on productivity in the A job?

(iii) Suppose that, instead of grouping into jobs A and B based on experience, the company has a habit of moving permanantly into job B those workers who seem to be more productive in job A. What problem(s) does this create for the attempt to use the OLS estimates from (1.1) to measure the effect of experience on productivity in the job A?

(iv) Again consider the situation in part (iii). But now suppose you can collect data at another point in time on the same variables and for many of the same workers. Describe a strategy for combining information from the two samples to obtain an ubiased effect of experience on type A productivity. Make clear any additional assumptions that are needed to defend your chosen strategy. Again, writing down the theoretical equations will be helpful.

2. Consider a two equation system with i.i.d. observations:

$$y_{i1} = \alpha_1 y_{i2} + \beta_1 x_{i1} + u_{i1} \tag{2.1}$$

$$y_{i2} = \beta_2 x_{i2} + \beta_3 x_{i3} + u_{i2}, \tag{2.2}$$

where all quantities are scalars. Unless otherwise stated, u_{i1} and u_{i2} can be correlated. Throughout this question maintain the assumptions

$$E(\mathbf{x}_i' u_{i1}) = 0, \tag{2.3}$$

where $\mathbf{x}_i = (x_{i1}, x_{i2}, x_{i3})$, and

$$E(u_{i1}^2 | \mathbf{x}_i) = \sigma_1^2. \tag{2.4}$$

(i) Under (2.3) discuss identification of α_1 and β_1 in the first equation.

(ii) Explain the method of 2SLS for estimating α_1 and β_1. What are the statistical properties of the estimators? What role does assumption (2.4) play?

(iii) Suppose that $E(x_{i2}u_{i2}) = E(x_{i3}u_{i2}) = 0$ but $E(x_{i1}u_{i2}) \neq 0$ and $E(u_{i1}u_{i2}) \neq 0$, and you apply 3SLS to estimate both equations of the system. What are the properties of the 3SLS estimators of α_1 and β_1? Comparing this with part (ii), what lesson can be taken from this?

(iv) Make the same assumptions as in part (iii), except now $E(u_{i1}u_{i2}) = 0$. Find a simple method for improving over the 2SLS estimator from part (ii), assuming that $E(u_{i1}^2|\mathbf{x}_i,u_{i2})$ is constant.

3. Consider a linear model for time series data:

$$y_t = \mathbf{x}_t\beta + u_t, \quad t=1,2,\ldots,T, \tag{3.1}$$

where $\mathbf{x}_t$ is 1xK and β is Kx1; you can take the first element of $\mathbf{x}_t$ to be unity for concretensess, but this is no way affects the question. For parts (i), (ii), and (iii) you may assume that the time series is strictly stationary and ergodic, and that the law of large numbers and central limit theorem apply.

(i) Assuming that $\mathbf{A} = E(\mathbf{x}_t'\mathbf{x}_t)$ has rank K and $E(\mathbf{x}_t'u_t) = 0$, sketch a proof of consistency of the OLS estimator of β.

(ii) Suppose that $\{u_t\}$ follows an AR(1) process:

$$u_t = .5u_{t-1} + e_t, \tag{3.2}$$

where $\{e_t\}$ is a serially uncorrelated sequence with zero mean and constant variance. You estimate β by running OLS on the quasi-differenced data:

$$y_t - .5y_{t-1} \quad \text{on} \quad \mathbf{x}_t - .5\mathbf{x}_{t-1}. \tag{3.3}$$

Call this estimator $\tilde{\beta}$. Is this estimator consistent for β only under the assumptions in part (i) and (3.2)? Explain.

(iii) Suppose now that u_t satisfies

$$u_t = \rho u_{t-1} + e_t \tag{3.4}$$

where

$$E(e_t|\mathbf{x}_t, u_{t-1}, \mathbf{x}_{t-1}, \ldots) = 0$$

$$E(e_t^2|\mathbf{x}_t, u_{t-1}, \mathbf{x}_{t-1}, \ldots) = \sigma_e^2.$$

Carefully explain how to obtain the Lagrange multiplier test of the hypothesis of no serial correlation.

(iv) Now assume that y_t and all of the elements of $\mathbf{x}_t$ are I(1), and in equation (3.4), $|\rho| < 1$. What are the properties of the OLS estimator of β now? You do not have to give detailed descriptions; just discuss general features.

4. For a cross section of people older than (say) 25, let $y_i = \log(wage_i)$, let $\mathbf{x}_i$ and $\mathbf{z}_i$ be vectors of demographic characteristics, let $coll_i$ be a dummy variable equal to unity if person i graduated from a four year college, and let $abil_i$ denote the person's unobserved ability. We would like to know the return to attending college, accounting for the fact that this decision is probably correlated with ability. Thus, the expectation of interest (which controls for the level of ability) is

$$E(y_i|\mathbf{x}_i, \mathbf{z}_i, coll_i, abil_i).$$

Assume this takes the form

$$E(y_i|\mathbf{x}_i, \mathbf{z}_i, coll_i, abil_i) = \mathbf{x}_i\beta + \delta coll_i + abil_i,$$

so that the variables in $\mathbf{z}_i$ do not affect wage after the other variables are controlled for. Assume that $E(abil_i|\mathbf{x}_i, \mathbf{z}_i) = 0$, so that we can write this as a dummy endogenous variable model:

$$y_i = \mathbf{x}_i\beta + \delta coll_i + u_i \qquad (4.1)$$

$$E(u_i|\mathbf{x}_i,\mathbf{z}_i) = 0. \qquad (4.2)$$

Generally, u_i and $coll_i$ are correlated even after conditioning on $\mathbf{x}_i$ and $\mathbf{z}_i$. Suppose you believe that $coll_i$ follows a probit (this is a reduced form equation):

$$P(coll_i = 1|\mathbf{x}_i,\mathbf{z}_i) = E(coll_i|\mathbf{x}_i,\mathbf{z}_i) = \Phi(\mathbf{z}_i\gamma), \qquad (4.3)$$

where $\Phi(\cdot)$ denotes the standard normal cdf.

(i) Intepret a parameter value of $\delta = .21$.

(ii) Consider the following method for estimating β and δ in (4.1). First, estimate (4.3) by probit, and save the fitted values (estimated probabilities) $\hat{coll}_i = \Phi(\mathbf{z}_i\hat{\gamma})$. Then obtain $\hat{\beta}$ and $\hat{\delta}$ from the OLS regression

$$y_i \text{ on } \mathbf{x}_i, \hat{coll}_i.$$

Assuming that (4.1), (4.2), and (4.3) are all true, argue that this produces consistent estimators of $\hat{\beta}$ and $\hat{\delta}$. (Hint: An application of the law of iterated expectations suffices quite nicely for this. A detailed proof is not required.) Will the usual OLS standard errors be asymptotically valid? Why or why not?

(iii) Suppose that you use the procedure in part (ii) but $coll_i$ does not follow the probit in (4.3). Will $\hat{\beta}$ and $\hat{\delta}$ still be consistent?

(iv) Suppose we use an alternative procedure. As before, estimate a probit for $coll_i$, and obtain the fitted values $\hat{coll}_i$. Then, estimate the equation

$$y_i = \mathbf{x}_i\beta + \delta coll_i + u_i$$

by instrumental variables, using $\hat{coll}_i$ as the instrument for $coll_i$. For what reasons might you prefer this procedure over that from part (ii)?

Michigan State University

September 8, 1992

Econometrics Prelim

Answer all four questions, each in a separate exam book.

1. Consider the partitioned linear model

$$y = X_1\beta_1 + X_2\beta_2 + u,$$

where y is $T\times1$, X_1 is $T\times K_1$, X_2 is $T\times K_2$, and u is $T\times1$. Assume that the Gauss-Markov assumptions hold for this model. Let $\hat{\beta}_1$ be the OLS estimator of β_1 from the regression of y on X_1, X_2, and let $\hat{u}$ be the $T\times1$ vector of OLS residuals. Suppose you run the two regressions

$$y \text{ on } M_2X_1 \tag{1.1}$$

and

$$M_2y \text{ on } M_2X_1, \tag{1.2}$$

where $M_2 = I_T - X_2(X_2'X_2)^{-1}X_2'$.

(a) Which, if any, of these regressions produces the OLS estimator $\hat{\beta}_1$?

(b) Which, if any, of these regressions produces the OLS residuals $\hat{u}$?

(c) Now suppose you believe that $\beta_2 = \beta_1$. Let $\tilde{\beta}_1$ be the OLS estimator of β_1 with the restriction $\beta_2 = \beta_1$ imposed. Write down the expression for $\tilde{\beta}_1$ in terms of X_1, X_2, and y.

(d) Suppose that $\beta_2 \neq \beta_1$. If $X_1'X_2 = 0$ is $\tilde{\beta}_1$ unbiased for β_1? Justify your answer.

(e) If $\beta_2 = \beta_1$ do you prefer $\hat{\beta}_1$ or $\tilde{\beta}_1$ as an estimator of β_1? Justify your answer.

2. Consider the standard unobserved components panel data model for $T = 2$ time periods:

$$y_{it} = \alpha_i + \mathbf{x}_{it}\beta + u_{it}, \quad t=1,2.$$

Assume that the N cross section observations are independent and identically distributed. There are no *a priori* restrictions on the time dependence or heterogeneity across t. The following is a list of possible assumptions:

A.1: $E(u_{it}|\alpha_i,\mathbf{x}_{it}) = 0, \ t=1,2.$

A.2: $E(\alpha_i|\mathbf{x}_{it}) = 0, \ t=1,2.$

A.3: $E(u_{it}|\alpha_i,\mathbf{x}_{i1},\mathbf{x}_{i2}) = 0, \ t=1,2.$

A.4: $E(\alpha_i|\mathbf{x}_{i1},\mathbf{x}_{i2}) = 0.$

(a) Choosing only from assumptions A.1-A.4, what is the weakest set of conditions that ensures consistency of the pooled OLS estimator for β? Justify your answer.

(b) Repeat part (a) for the random effects estimator.

(c) Repeat part (a) for the fixed effects estimator.

(d) Rather than compute the fixed effects estimator, one can difference the equation over the two time periods and run OLS on the cross section of first differences. Show that (in the $T = 2$ case) the first difference estimator of β is identical to the fixed effects estimator.

(e) Note that the usual reported standard errors from the fixed effects and first difference procedures will <u>not</u> usually be the same. Which standard errors are more robust, and what are these standard errors robust to? Justify your answer.

3. The following model is a simple example of a *bilinear process*:

$$y_t = \alpha\epsilon_{t-1}y_{t-2} + \epsilon_t, \tag{3.1}$$

where $\{\epsilon_t\}$ is an i.i.d. process with zero mean and variance σ_ϵ^2. In particular, you may assume that $\{y_t\}$ is strictly stationary and, for all t,

$$E(\epsilon_t|\phi_{t-1}) = 0$$

$$Var(\epsilon_t|\phi_{t-1}) = E(\epsilon_t^2|\phi_{t-1}) = \sigma_\epsilon^2,$$

where $\phi_{t-1} \equiv (\epsilon_{t-1},\epsilon_{t-2},\ldots) = (y_{t-1},y_{t-2},\ldots)$ is information known at time t-1.

(a) Find the unconditional moments $E(y_t)$ and $Var(y_t)$, assuming that $\alpha^2\sigma_\epsilon^2 < 1$. Compare these with the conditional moments $E(y_t|\phi_{t-1})$ and $Var(y_t|\phi_{t-1})$.

(b) Show that $E(\epsilon_t y_t|\phi_{t-1}) = \sigma_\epsilon^2$.

(c) Let $\hat{\rho}$ be the OLS estimator of ρ in the AR(1) model

$$y_t = \rho y_{t-1} + \eta_t$$

based on T observations. If $\{y_t\}$ follows the model (3.1), show that plim $\hat{\rho} = 0$. (Hint: It suffices to show that $E(y_{t-1}y_t) = 0$. The result from part (b) might be useful here.)

(d) What do you conclude about the ability of linear models to forecast y_t when it follows the nonlinear model (3.1)?

(e) Explain how to construct the Lagrange multplier test of H_0: $\alpha = 0$. (Hint: Under H_0, $\epsilon_t = y_t$.)

4. Consider a latent variable model on i.i.d. observations:

$$y_i^* = \mathbf{x}_i\beta + u_i,$$

where $\mathbf{x}_i$ is a 1xK vector and β is the Kx1 vector to be estimated. The $\mathbf{x}_i$ are observed for everyone in the population, but the variable y_i^* is observed only when a selection indicator, s_i, is unity. Initially the selection indicator is defined by $s_i = 1[v_i > 0]$, where v_i is an observable random variable and $1[\cdot]$ is the indicator function equal to one if the event in brackets is true and zero otherwise. When $s_i = 1$ we write $y_i = y_i^*$.

(a) Under the assumption that the vector $(u_i, v_i)'$ is <u>independent</u> of $\mathbf{x}_i$ with zero mean, and $E(u_i|v_i)$ is linear, find $E(y_i^*|\mathbf{x}_i, v_i)$. (Hint: Recall that if (u_i, v_i) is independent of $\mathbf{x}_i$ then $E(u_i|\mathbf{x}_i, v_i) = E(u_i|v_i)$.)

(b) Argue that $E(y_i|\mathbf{x}_i, v_i, s_i = 1) = E(y_i^*|\mathbf{x}_i, v_i)$. Use this to suggest a feasible, consistent estimator of β. How would you test for sample selection bias?

(c) Now suppose that the selection mechanism is of the form

$$h_i^* = \mathbf{x}_i\delta + v_i$$
$$s_i = 1[h_i^* > 0].$$

We do not observe h_i^*, but we do observe $h_i = \max(0, h_i^*)$. Under the assumption that v_i is distributed as Normal$(0, \sigma_v^2)$ independently of $\mathbf{x}_i$, how would you estimate δ?

(d) Under the assumptions of part (a) and part (c), with the selection rule as in part (c), find $E(y_i|\mathbf{x}_i, v_i, s_i = 1)$.

(e) Use your answer from part (d) to suggest a feasible, consistent estimator of β. Note that v_i is no longer directly observable.

Michigan State University

Econometrics prelim

April, 1992

DO ALL FOUR QUESTIONS

1. Consider a two equation simultaneous equations model for cross section data, where all quantities are scalars. (The "i" subscripts have been omitted for simplicity.)

$$y_1 = \alpha_1 + \gamma_1 y_2 + \delta_{11} z_1 + \delta_{12} z_2 + \delta_{13} z_3 + u_1$$

$$y_2 = \alpha_2 + \gamma_2 y_1 + \delta_{21} z_1 + u_2$$

where $E(u_1|z_1,z_2,z_3) = 0$, $E(u_2|z_1,z_2,z_3) = 0$.

A. Using the order condition, discuss identification of each equation.

B. When does the rank condition hold for the second equation?

C. Assuming the rank condition holds, how would you estimate α_2, γ_2 and δ_{21}?

D. Explain how to test the overidentifying restrictions on the second equation, assuming that $var(u_2|z_1,z_2,z_3) = \sigma_2^2$.

E. Now suppose that you also know that the structural errors are uncorrelated. Show how this information identifies the first equation.

F. Under the assumptions in part E., outline a simple instrumental variables method for obtaining consistent, asymptotically normal estimates of the parameters of the first equation.

2. Consider the standard (censored) Tobit model:

$y_i^* = x_i'\beta + u_i$, u_i iid $N(0,\sigma^2)$, y_i^* not observed

$$y_i = \max(0, y_i^*) = \begin{cases} y_i^*, & \text{if } y_i^* > 0 \\ 0, & \text{otherwise} \end{cases}$$

We are generally interested in the expectation $E(y_i^* | x_i)$ and its partial derivatives with respect to the explanatory variables x_i. But, with the censoring problem, OLS does not give us a consistent estimate of β.

A. Present an intuitive explanation of this problem, based on the conditional and/or unconditional expectation of the observable y_i.

B. Show the possible direction of the bias of the OLS estimates.

C. How can you remedy the bias of OLS estimation without using maximum likelihood estimation? Associate your answer with the argument you presented in part A.

D. How would you conduct maximum likelihood estimation? Write down the likelihood function and briefly indicate the properties of the MLE.

E. How would you change your answers to parts A.-D. if, instead of a censored sample, you had a truncated sample?

3. A. What does it mean for a variable to be integrated of order one [I(1)]?

B. How would you test whether an observed series X_t, t = 1,...,T, is I(1)?

C. Suppose X_t and Y_t are each I(1). What does it mean for them to be cointegrated?

D. How would you test whether they are cointegrated?

E. If X_t and Y_t are cointegrated, what are the properties of an OLS regression of Y_t on X_t? Be explicit about any additional assumptions you have to make.

F. Under what circumstances (if any) would the t-statistic for the hypothesis that the coefficient of X_t equals zero be asymptotically valid [i.e., asymptotically distributed as N(0,1) under the null hypothesis]?

G. What is the "error correction model" for Y_t and X_t? How would you estimate it? What information does it contain that is not contained in a regression of Y_t on X_t?

4. Consider the model

$$y_{ij} = X_i\beta + \epsilon_{ij} \quad , \; i = 1,\ldots,m \; , \; j = 1,\ldots,n_i \; ,$$

where X_i (a 1×k vector of explanatory variables) depends on i but does not depend on j. As an example, let i index cities and j index individuals (so observation i,j means person j in city i); let y = expenditure on heating in a given month; and let X represent characteristics of the city such as average temperature or the price of fuel (assumed to be the same for every individual in the city). Assume that the ϵ_{ij} are mutually independent with zero mean and that

$$\mathrm{var}(\epsilon_{ij}) = \sigma_i^2$$

depends on i but not on j.

A. What are the properties of OLS applied to the model?

B. If you knew σ_i^2, i = 1,...,m, how would you estimate the model? What would be the properties of your estimates?

C. Suppose now that you don't know the σ_i^2 and want to estimate them. Consider the following suggestions, and evaluate each in terms of the estimates of σ_i^2 and β that they lead to. (All summations are over j, from 1 to n_i.)

(i) $\hat{\sigma}_i^2 = \Sigma\,(y_{ij} - \bar{y}_i)^2 \,/\, (n_i-1)$, where $\bar{y}_i = \Sigma\, y_{ij} \,/\, n_i$.

(ii) $\bar{\sigma}_i^2 = \Sigma\, e_{ij}^2 \,/\, n_i$, where the e_{ij} are OLS residuals from a regression of y on X using all observations.

(iii) $\check{\sigma}_i^2 = \Sigma\, \check{\epsilon}_{ij}^2 \,/\, n_i$, where the $\check{\epsilon}_{ij}$ are OLS residuals from a regression of y on X run separately for each city (i.e., from regressions of y on X using data only on city i).

University of Minnesota
Econometrics Preliminary Exam

Fall 1994 **G**

1. Suppose that

$$y_i = \mathbf{x}_i'\beta + \varepsilon_i \quad (i = 1,\ldots,n).$$

It is always the case that $\{y_i, \mathbf{x}_i\}_{i=1}^n$ are observed. The vector of coefficients β is unknown. The distribution of the disturbances is a *scale mixture of normals* and may be described as follows:

$$\{d_i\}_{i=1}^n \text{ is i.i.d Bernoulli, } P(d_i = 1) = P(d_i = 2) = .5;$$
$$\text{if } d_i = 1, \text{ then } \varepsilon_i \sim N(0, \sigma_1^2);$$
$$\text{if } d_i = 2, \text{ then } \varepsilon_i \sim N(0, \sigma_2^2).$$

The process $\{\mathbf{x}_i, d_i, \varepsilon_i\}_{i=1}^n$ is i.i.d.; $\mathbf{x}_i$ and d_i are independent; $\mathbf{x}_i$ and ε_i are independent; and $n^{-1}\sum_{i=1}^n \mathbf{x}_i\mathbf{x}_i' \xrightarrow{a.s.} \mathbf{Q}$, where $\mathbf{Q}$ is a positive definite matrix. The disturbances $\{\varepsilon_i\}_{i=1}^n$ are never observed.

(a) What is the asymptotic sampling distribution of the least squares estimator $\mathbf{b}$ of β? Carefully indicate whether this distribution is conditional or unconditional on $\{\mathbf{x}_i\}_{i=1}^n$.

(b) What is the exact sampling distribution of the least squares estimator $\mathbf{b}$ of β? Carefully indicate whether this distribution is conditional or unconditional on $\{\mathbf{x}_i\}_{i=1}^n$.

(c) Assume that $\{d_i\}_{i=1}^n$ are observed. State the best linear unbaised estimator $\hat{\beta}$ of β. What is the exact sampling distribution of $\hat{\beta}$? Carefully indicate whether this distribution is conditional or unconditional on $\{\mathbf{x}_i\}_{i=1}^n$.

(d) Suppose that $\{d_i\}_{i=1}^n$ is unobserved. Indicate a prior distribution for $(\beta, \sigma_1^2, \sigma_2^2)$ and then carefully describe how you would find the posterior distribution of β.

2. This question is about estimation in the classical linear simultaneous equation model,

$$\Gamma \mathbf{y}_t + \mathrm{B}\mathbf{x}_t = \mathbf{u}_t, \quad \mathbf{u}_t \overset{IID}{\sim} \mathrm{N}(\mathbf{0}, \Sigma) \quad (t = 1,\ldots,T),$$

where $\mathbf{y}_t : L \times 1$ is the vector of endogenous variables and $\mathbf{x}_t : K \times 1$ is the vector of predetermined variables. There are L equations. The coeffcients are normalized by the restrictions $\gamma_{\ell\ell} = 1 \quad (\ell = 1,\ldots,L)$.

(a) Derive the likelihood function for $(\Gamma, \mathrm{B}, \Sigma)$.

(b) Suppose that Γ is lower triangular and Σ is diagonal. Show that in this case the maximum likelihood estimates of the parameters in Γ and B may be found by least squares estimation.

(c) Suppose that Γ is lower triangular, but Σ is not necessarily diagonal. Provide the likelihood function for $(\Gamma, \mathrm{B}, \Sigma)$. Then *assuming that Σ is known,* provide closed-form expressions for the maximum likelihood estimators of Γ and B.

(d) Remove the assumption that Γ is lower triangular, and consider the problem of computing limited information maximum likelihood estimates for the coefficients of the first equation of the model,

$$y_{t1} + \sum_{j=2}^{L} \gamma_{1j} y_{tj} + \sum_{j=1}^{K} \beta_{1j} x_{tj} = u_{t1} \quad (t = 1,\ldots,T).$$

Continuing to assume that Σ is known, provide closed form expressions for the maximum likelihood estimators of the γ_{1j} and β_{1j}. [HINT: This is a special case of (c).]

(e) How would you estimate $(\Gamma, \mathrm{B}, \Sigma)$ in (c) if Σ were unknown? The method you suggest should take advantage of the fact that Γ is lower triangular.

3. Suppose that $\{x_t\}$ is a Gaussian, stationary first order autoregressive process with mean zero,

$$x_t = \beta x_{t-1} + \varepsilon_t, \quad \varepsilon_t \overset{IID}{\sim} N(0, \sigma^2), \quad t = 0, \pm 1, \pm 2, \ldots .$$

This time series is observed from time $t = 1$ to time $t = T$, but some of the observations are missing. Whether or not an observation is missing is independent of the process $\{x_t\}$ itself.

(a) Suppose the parameters β and σ^2 are known. If x_t is not observed at time $t = t_0$, what is the optimal linear interpolator of x_{t_0}? Explain.

(b) Suppose the parameters β and σ^2 are unknown. How would you construct asymptotically efficient estimators of these parameters? Your answer should indicate the objective function you would maximize or minimize. Feel free to make additional assumptions to obtain the results, but state them plainly.

(c) Suppose the parameters β and σ^2 are unknown, and as in part (a) suppose that x_t is not observed at time $t = t_0$. Describe an appropriate confidence interval for x_{t_0}, and how you would construct it.

4. Suppose

$$y_t = \beta x_t + u_t \quad (t = 1, \ldots T),$$

$$\begin{pmatrix} x_t \\ u_t \end{pmatrix} \overset{IID}{\sim} N(0, \Sigma), \quad \Sigma = \begin{bmatrix} \sigma_x^2 & \sigma_{xu} \\ \sigma_{xu} & \sigma_u^2 \end{bmatrix}.$$

The explanatory variable x_t is endogenous; *i.e.*, $\sigma_{xu} \neq 0$.

Despite the endogeneity a researcher tests $H_0: \beta = \beta_0$ using the usual, least-squares based, t statistic. Derive the exact distribution of this t statistic assuming the null hypothesis is true.

5. In this problem we consider two time series models.

Model I:

$$y_t = \beta t + u_t; \quad u_t = \sqrt{t}\varepsilon_t, \quad \varepsilon_t \overset{IID}{\sim} \left(0, \sigma^2\right) \quad (t = 1, \ldots, T);$$

Model II:

$$y_t = \alpha x_t + \beta t + u_t; \quad \begin{pmatrix} u_t \\ x_t \end{pmatrix} \overset{IID}{\sim} \left[\begin{pmatrix} 0 \\ 0 \end{pmatrix}, \begin{bmatrix} \sigma_u^2 & 0 \\ 0 & \sigma_x^2 \end{bmatrix} \right] \quad (t = 1, \ldots, T).$$

[In answering the following questions you may wish to take advantage of the facts $\sum_{t=1}^{T} t^2 = T(T+1)(2T+1)/6$ and $\sum_{t=1}^{T} t^3 = T^2(T+1)^2/4$.]

(a) In Model I, is the least squares estimator of β consistent? If so, calculate the rate of convergence of the estimator and find its limiting distribution.

(b) In Model I, derive the generalized least squares estimator of β and its asymptotic distribution. Does the generalized least squares estiator yield any asymptotic efficiency gain over the least squares estimator in this model?

(c) In Model II, consider the estimator $\left(\hat{\alpha}, \hat{\beta}\right)$ of (α, β) defined as follows: $\hat{\beta}$ is the least squares estimator in the regression of y_t on t, and $\hat{\alpha}$ is the least squares estimator in the regression of $y_t - \hat{\beta} t$ on x_t. Compare the asymptotic variance of $\left(\hat{\alpha}, \hat{\beta}\right)$ with that of the least squares estimator in Model II. Does least squares provide any asymptotic efficiency gain over $\left(\hat{\alpha}, \hat{\beta}\right)$?

6. A researcher is confronted with a simple, classical sample selection problem as follows:

$$y_i = \beta'\mathbf{x}_i + \varepsilon_{i,} \quad z_i^* = \gamma'\mathbf{w}_i + u_i \quad (i = 1,\ldots,n),$$

$$\begin{pmatrix} \varepsilon_i \\ u_i \end{pmatrix} \overset{IID}{\sim} \mathrm{N}(\mathbf{0}, \Sigma), \quad \Sigma = \begin{bmatrix} \sigma_\varepsilon^2 & \rho\sigma_\varepsilon\sigma_u \\ \rho\sigma_\varepsilon\sigma_u & \sigma_u^2 \end{bmatrix}.$$

The vectors $\mathbf{x}_i$ and $\mathbf{w}_i$ are always observed; whereas y_i is observed if and only if $z_i^* > 0$. The researcher's prior distribution is

$$\begin{pmatrix} \beta \\ \gamma \end{pmatrix} \sim \mathrm{N}\left(\begin{pmatrix} \underline{\beta} \\ \underline{\gamma} \end{pmatrix}, \underline{\mathbf{V}}_{(\beta,\gamma)} \right), \quad \Sigma^{-1} \sim \mathrm{W}(\underline{\mathbf{S}}^{-1}, \underline{\nu});$$

where (β, γ) and Σ are independent.

(a) Suppose -- contrary to fact -- that y_i and z_i^* were always observed, even if $z_i^* \le 0$. Describe the posterior distribution for (β, γ, Σ) in this case. If you cannot provide a closed-form expression for the posterior distribution, then indicate an algorithm for making draws from the posterior distribution.

(b) Now return to the original assumption that y_i is observed if and only if $z_i^* > 0$. Describe a Gibbs sampling - data augmentation algorithm for drawing from the posterior distribution for (β, γ, Σ). Provide a careful argument for convergence of the algorithm.

(c) The researcher has been asked the effect of a one-unit increase in x_{i2} on the observed y_i. Given the algorithm in (b), how might the reseracher answer this question?

University of Minnesota
Econometrics Preliminary Exam

Spring 1994

Part I

Answer both questions in this part.

1. Indicate whether each statement is true or false. For each statement sketch a proof, provide a couterexample, cite a pertinent theorem, or prove a correct version as appropriate.

   (a) *Statement:* If $\sqrt{n}(x_n - c) \xrightarrow{d} N(0, \sigma^2)$ then $x_n \xrightarrow{p} c$.

   (b) Suppose the random variables $y_1, \ldots, y_T$ are independent and identically distributed on the interval $[0, \theta]$. Three prior distributions for θ constitute three alternative hypotheses:

   (1) $P[\theta = 2] = 1$;
   (2) $p(\theta) = .5\exp(-.5\theta), \theta > 0$; $p(\theta) = 0, \theta \leq 0$;
   (3) $p(\theta) \propto \text{constant}, \theta > 0$; $p(\theta) = 0, \theta \leq 0$.
   (This prior distribution is improper.)

   Statement: Of the three posterior odds ratios possible between the three hypotheses, at least one must be positive and finite.

   (c) Suppose that

   $$y_i = \beta x_i^* + \varepsilon_i, \quad \text{var}(\varepsilon_i) = \sigma^2$$

   satisfies all the assumptions of the simple linear model except that x_i^* cannot be observed. However,

   $$x_i = x_i^* + \eta_i \quad \text{and} \quad z_i = x_i^* + \varsigma_i$$

   can be observed. The sequence $\{x_i^*, \varepsilon_i, \eta_i, \varsigma_i\}$ is independent and identically distributed, all four variables are mutually uncorrelated, the last three have mean zero, and all four have finite variance.

   Statement: In the equation

   $$y_i = \beta x_i + \omega_i,$$

   β can be consistently estimated by instrumental variables, using z_i as the instrument, and σ^2 can be consistently estimated from the resulting sum of squared residuals.

2. Suppose

$$y_i = \alpha + \beta x_i + \gamma z_i + \varepsilon_i,$$

$$\mathrm{E}\begin{pmatrix} x_i \\ z_i \\ \varepsilon_i \end{pmatrix} = \mathbf{0}, \quad \mathrm{var}\begin{pmatrix} x_i \\ z_i \\ \varepsilon_i \end{pmatrix} = \begin{bmatrix} \sigma_x^2 & \sigma_{xz} & 0 \\ \sigma_{xz} & \sigma_z^2 & \theta \\ 0 & \theta & \sigma_\varepsilon^2 \end{bmatrix} \equiv \mathbf{V},$$

where $\theta \neq 0$ and $\mathbf{V}$ is positive definite. The random vectors $(x_i, z_i, \varepsilon_i)'$ $(i = 1,2,\ldots)$ are independent and identically distributed.

(a) Show that the ordinary least squares estimator a_n of α is consistent.

(b) Show that the ordinary least squares estimator b_n of β is inconsistent, and that the sign of $\mathrm{plim}(b_n - \beta)$ is the same as that of $-\sigma_{xz}\theta$.

(c) Show that the ordinary least squares estimator g_n of γ is inconsistent, and that the sign of $\mathrm{plim}(g_n - \gamma)$ is the same as that of $\sigma_{xz}\theta$.

(d) If the model is generalized to

$$y_i = \alpha + \beta' \underset{k\times 1}{\mathbf{x}_i} + \gamma z_i + \varepsilon_i,$$

$$\mathrm{E}\begin{pmatrix} \mathbf{x}_i \\ z_i \\ \varepsilon_i \end{pmatrix} = \mathbf{0}, \quad \mathrm{var}\begin{pmatrix} \mathbf{x}_i \\ z_i \\ \varepsilon_i \end{pmatrix} = \begin{bmatrix} \Sigma_x & \Sigma_{xz} & 0 \\ \Sigma_{xz} & \sigma_z^2 & \theta \\ 0 & \theta & \sigma_\varepsilon^2 \end{bmatrix},$$

are there any results analogous to those in (a), (b), and (c)?

Part II

Answer two questions in this part.

3. Suppose that the normal linear regression model

$$\mathbf{y}_n = \mathbf{X}_n\beta + \varepsilon_n, \quad \varepsilon_n \sim \mathrm{N}(\mathbf{0}, \sigma^2\mathbf{I}_n)$$

is correctly specified for all $n = 1,2,\ldots$. Let i and j denote two particular observations on the variables; let ε_i and ε_j denote the corresponding disturbances; and let u_i^n and u_j^n denote the corresponding least squares residuals when there are n observations.

(a) Show that $(u_i^n - \varepsilon_i) \xrightarrow{a.s.} 0$. Explicitly make any additional assumptions needed for this result.

(b) Show that *ex ante*, $\mathrm{corr}(u_i^n, u_j^n) \xrightarrow{p} 0$. Explicitly make any additional assumptions needed for this result.

(c) Supposing that σ^2 is known and given the improper prior distribution $p(\beta) \propto$ constant $\forall \beta \in \Re^k$, show that *ex post*, $\mathrm{corr}(\varepsilon_i, \varepsilon_j) \xrightarrow{p}$ constant. Indicate the value of the constant and show that in general it is nonzero.

(d) In one page or less reconcile the findings in (b) and (c).

4. In each of m courses i $(i = 1, \ldots, m)$ students have rated their instructor's performance on a scale of 1 to 7, with 7 being the best rating. It is hypothesized that in each course i, student j $(j = 1, \ldots, n_i)$ forms a subjective assessment y_{ij}^* of the course instructor's performance,

$$y_{ij}^* = \mathbf{x}_i'\beta + \varepsilon_{ij}.$$

The vector $\mathbf{x}_i$ consists of a constant term and course- and instructor-specific variables; all ε_{ij} are independent of each other and of all $\mathbf{x}_i$, and $\varepsilon_{ij} \sim N(0, \sigma^2)$. The relation between the subjective assessment y_{ij}^* and the reported score of student j in course i is

$$y_{ij} = 1 \Leftrightarrow y_{ij}^* \le \gamma_1;$$

$$y_{ij} = k \Leftrightarrow \gamma_{k-1} < y_{ij}^* \le \gamma_k \;(k = 2, \ldots 6);$$

$$y_{ij} = 7 \Leftrightarrow y_{ij}^* > \gamma_6.$$

In (a) and (b) the full data set $\{(y_{ij}, j = 1, \ldots n_i), \mathbf{x}_i\}_{i=1}^m$ is available.

(a) Are the parameters β, σ^2, and $\gamma_1, \ldots, \gamma_6$ all identified? If not, indicate additional assumptions that will identify them without imposing further restrictions on the model.

(b) Propose a method for estimating the parameters. Demonstrate at least one attractive finite-sample or asymptotic property of your estimator.

(c) Now suppose only $n_i, \mathbf{x}_i$, and $\bar{y}_i = n_i^{-1}\sum_{j=1}^{n_i} y_{ij}$ are observed for each course. How would you proceed to estimate the parameters of the model? Demonstrate at least one attractive finite-sample or asymptotic property of your estimator.

5. Suppose we observe a stationary ergodic process $\left\{\begin{pmatrix} y_t \\ \mathbf{x}_t \end{pmatrix}\right\}$ with the nonlinear regression structure

$$y_t = g(\mathbf{x}_t, \theta_0) + \varepsilon_t$$

where ε_t is an unobserved error term, $g(\cdot,\cdot)$ is a known, differentiable function, and θ_0 is an unknown parameter to be estimated. It is also known that ε_t is symmetrically distributed about zero conditional on $\mathbf{x}_t$. Consider the estimator $\hat{\theta}$ of θ_0,

$$\hat{\theta} = \arg\min_\theta T^{-1} \sum_{t=1}^{T} \rho[y_t - g(\mathbf{x}_t, \theta)]$$

where $\rho(\cdot)$ is a convex, symmetric, differentiable function uniquely minimized at zero.

(a) Provide some additional assumptions about $\rho(\cdot)$, $g(\cdot,\cdot)$, and/or the data generating process that are sufficient for this estimator to be consistent. Argue (informally) why the estimator may fail to be consistent if your conditions are not satisfied in practice.

(b) As completely as possible, characterize the asymptotic distribution of $T^{1/2}(\hat{\theta} - \theta_0)$. Derive an expression for the asymptotic variance matrix.

(c) Propose a positive semi-definite, consistent estimator for the asymptotic variance matrix derived in (b).

6. Let a time-separable utility function have representation

$$V_t = \mathrm{E}\left[\sum_{s=0}^{S} \beta^s \mathrm{U}(c_{t+s}) \middle| \Phi_t\right] \quad (S > 0;\, S = \infty \text{ possible});$$

$$\Omega_t \equiv \{c_s, s = 0, \ldots, t-1\} \subseteq \Phi_t$$

where c_t is consumption at time t, Φ_t is the information set at time t, β is the discount factor $(|\beta| < 1)$, and $\mathrm{U}(c_t)$ is delivered utility at time t. Consumption follows the log first order autoregressive process

$$\log c_t = \alpha_0 + \alpha_1 \log c_{t-1} + \varepsilon_t$$

which may or may not be stationary.

Classify each of cases (a)-(e) into one of three categories:

(i) V_t does not exist; in this case, prove nonexistence;

(ii) V_t exists; in this case, provide an expression for V_t in terms of Φ_t;

(iii) V_t may exist or not.; in this case, indicate the conditions governing existence.

In your answers, keep in mind that the horizon S may be finite or infinite.

(a) $\mathrm{U}(c) = \log c$; $\varepsilon_t \overset{IID}{\sim} \mathrm{N}(0, \sigma^2)$; $\Phi_t = \Omega_t$ plus known values of α_0, α_1, and σ^2.

(b) $\mathrm{U}(c) = \log c$; $\varepsilon_t \overset{IID}{\sim} \mathrm{N}(0, \sigma^2)$; $\Phi_t = \Omega_t$ plus a known value for σ^2 and an improper prior density $\mathrm{p}(\alpha_0, \alpha_1) \propto$ constant, $(\alpha_0, \alpha_1) \in \Re^2$.

(c) $\mathrm{U}(c) = \log c$; $\varepsilon_t \overset{IID}{\sim} \mathrm{N}(0, \sigma^2)$; $\Phi_t = \Omega_t$ plus an improper prior $\mathrm{p}(\alpha_0, \alpha_1, \sigma^2) \propto \sigma^{-1}$, $(\alpha_0, \alpha_1, \sigma^2) \in \Re^2 \times \Re_{++}$.

(d) $\mathrm{U}(c) = c^{(1-\gamma)}/(1-\gamma)$; $\varepsilon_t \overset{IID}{\sim} \mathrm{N}(0, \sigma^2)$; $\Phi_t = \Omega_t$ plus a known value for σ^2 and an improper prior density $\mathrm{p}(\alpha_0, \alpha_1) \propto$ constant, $(\alpha_0, \alpha_1) \in \Re^2$.

(e) $\mathrm{U}(c) = \log c$; $\varepsilon_t \overset{IID}{\sim} \mathrm{t}(0, \sigma^2; \nu)$; $\Phi_t = \Omega_t$ plus known values of $\alpha_0, \alpha_1, \sigma^2$ and ν.

University of Minnesota
Econometrics Preliminary Exam

Spring 1993

Part I

Answer both questions in this part.

1. Indicate whether each statement is true or false. For each statement sketch a proof, provide a counterexample, cite a pertinent theorem, or prove a correct version as appropriate.

(a) The posterior odds ratio for two hypotheses is to be formed. Under both hypotheses, the model is $y = X\beta + \varepsilon$ and satisfies the specification of the normal linear regression model with fixed regressors X and $\varepsilon \sim N(0, \sigma^2 I)$. Under the first hypothesis, the prior distribution is improper with density function $p(\beta, \sigma) \propto \sigma^{-1}$. Under the second hypothesis the prior distribution fixes $\sigma^2 = 1$, and $\beta \sim N(\underline{\beta}, \underline{V})$, where $\underline{V}$ is a positive definite matrix. The prior probability of each hypothesis is 1/2.

Statement: In this circumstance, it is impossible for the posterior odds ratio in favor of the first model to exceed 1.

(b) In the linear regression model $y_t = \beta x_t + \varepsilon_t$, it is the case that $x_t = \alpha_0 \exp(\alpha_1 t)$ and the disturbances are mutually independently distributed with $E(\varepsilon_t) = 0$ and $\mathrm{var}(\varepsilon_t) = \gamma_0 \exp(\gamma_1 t)$. Let $\hat{\beta}$ denote the generalized least squares estimator of β.

(i) *Statement:* $\hat{\beta}$ is consistent for all values of α_1 and γ_1.

(ii) *Statement:* $T^{1/2}(\hat{\beta} - \beta) \Rightarrow N(0, \sigma^2)$, where σ^2 is a positive constant, if and only if $\gamma_1 = 2\alpha_1$.

2. Owners of private real estate pay taxes to local governments based on appraised property value. In many districts, the appraised value is set by experts and is supposed to reflect the the price the property would bring if it were sold. Property taxes owed are then a monotone function of the appraised value. You have been given 20 observations on private residential property sold in 1990. The data have been selected by searching deeds, to randomly choose five houses sold for $50,000, five sold for $100,000, five sold for $150,000, and five sold for $200,000. Denote these groups by 1, 2, 3, and 4, respectively. Let y_{ij} denote the assessed value of the i'th house in the j'th group, and $\bar{y}_j$ denote the mean assessed value of houses in the j'th group. Similarly x_{ij} is the assessed value of the i'th house in the j'th group, and $\bar{x}_j$ is the mean assessed value of houses in the j'th group. You are given the following information. (All data are in thousands of dollars.)

Mean sale price, $\bar{x}_j$	Mean assessed value, $\bar{y}_j$	s.d. $(y_j) = [(1/4)\sum_{i=1}^{5}(y_{ij} - \bar{y}_j)^2]^{1/2}$
$\bar{x}_1 = 50$	$\bar{y}_1 = 42.7$	s.d.$(y_1) = 1.04$
$\bar{x}_2 = 100$	$\bar{y}_2 = 117.4$	s.d.$(y_2) = 1.88$
$\bar{x}_3 = 150$	$\bar{y}_3 = 165.9$	s.d.$(y_3) = 3.16$
$\bar{x}_4 = 200$	$\bar{y}_4 = 188.2$	s.d.$(y_4) = 3.54$

(a) From this information, construct the least squares estimates and corresponding statistics (standard errors, sum of squared residuals, s^2, R^2) for the simple linear regression of y on x (i.e., a regression with intercept and slope coefficients).

(b) Assuming that the specification of the simple linear regression model is correct, and that the disturbances are normally distributed, test the null hypothesis that the intercept is zero and the slope coefficient is one. Be explicit about the distribution of your test statistic(s) including degree(s) of freedom, under the null hypothesis.

(c) Test the null hypothesis that the specification of linearity is correct, against the alternative that the regression need not be linear. Choose your alternative specification so that the test statistic can actually be computed using the information given. Be explicit about the distribution of your test statistic(s) including degree(s) of freedom, under the null hypothesis.

(d) Assuming that the specification of nonlinearity in part (c) is correct, test the restriction that the true regression is linear with an intercept of zero and a slope coefficient of one. Be explicit about the distribution of your test statistic(s) including degree(s) of freedom, under the null hypothesis.

Part II

Answer two questions in this part.

3. Suppose that $\{(x_t, y_t)'\}$ is a stationary bivariate time series in which

$$y_t = \beta x_t + \varepsilon_t, \qquad (1)$$

and for any T, $(\varepsilon_1, \ldots, \varepsilon_T) \mid (x_1, \ldots x_T) \sim N(0, \sigma^2 I_T)$. It is also the case that the autoregressive representation for x_t is

$$x_t = \rho x_{t-1} + \zeta_t$$

and that for ε_t is

$$\varepsilon_t = \rho \varepsilon_{t-1} + \eta_t.$$

Here are four procedures for reporting a point estimate and standard error for β.

(i) Report the ordinary least squares estimate and standard error for β in (1).

(ii) Report the ordinary least squares estimate and standard error for β in

$$(y_t - \hat{\rho} y_{t-1}) = \beta(x_t - \hat{\rho} x_{t-1}) + \varepsilon_t \qquad (t = 1, \ldots, T). \qquad (2)$$

In (2), $\hat{\rho} = \sum_{t=2}^{T} e_t e_{t-1} / \sum_{t=2}^{T} e_{t-1}^2$, where e_t denotes the least squares residual for observation t in (1).

(iii) Estimate

$$y_t = \sum_{s=-m}^{m} \beta_s x_{t-s} + \varepsilon_t \qquad (t = m+1, \ldots, T-m) \qquad (3)$$

by least squares, where $m \propto T^{1/3}$. Report the least squares estimate and standard error for β_0.

(iv) Estimate

$$(y_t - \hat{\rho} y_{t-1}) = \sum_{s=-m}^{m} \beta_s (x_{t-s} - \hat{\rho} x_{t-s-1}) + \varepsilon_t \qquad (t = m+2, \ldots, T-m) \qquad (4)$$

by least squares. In (4), $m \propto T^{1/3}$ and $\hat{\rho} = \sum_{t=2}^{T} e_t e_{t-1} / \sum_{t=2}^{T} e_{t-1}^2$, where e_t denotes the least squares residual for observation t in (3).

(a) Compare the asymptotic efficiency of all four estimators of β. Carefully distinguish situations in which the asymptotic efficiency of one estimator is strictly greater than, weakly greater than, or equal to the asymptotic efficiency of another estimator.

(b) Indicate which reported standard errors are asymptotically valid. If a particular standard error is asymptotically invalid in general, but valid if particular conditions hold, indicate these conditions.

4. An investigator working with the linear regression model

$$y = X\beta + \varepsilon, \quad E(\varepsilon) = 0, \quad E(\varepsilon\varepsilon') = \sigma^2 I,$$

where X is $n \times k$ of rank k and β is $k \times 1$, decides to estimate β by the so-called "ridge estimator"

$$\tilde{\beta} = (X'X + \rho^2 I)^{-1} X'y,$$

and to evaluate it by means of the matrix mean-square error

$$MSE(\tilde{\beta}) = E[(\tilde{\beta} - \beta)(\tilde{\beta} - \beta)'].$$

(a) Show that for any $\rho^2 > 0$, a sufficient condition for the mean-square error of $\tilde{\beta}$ to be less than or equal to that of the ordinary least-squares estimator $b = (X'X)^{-1}X'y$ is that

$$\beta'X'X\beta/\sigma^2 \leq 1.$$

Is there a way to test this hypothesis?

(b) Show that if

$$\beta'\beta/\sigma^2 \leq M$$

for sufficiently large M, then $\tilde{\beta}$ will have lower mean-square error than b for all ρ^2 in the interval $0 < \rho^2 < 2/M$.

5. An investigator is working with the linear regression model

$$y = X\beta + \varepsilon, \quad E(\varepsilon) = 0, \quad E(\varepsilon\varepsilon') = \sigma^2\Omega,$$

where X is $n \times k$ of rank k, β is $k \times 1$, and

$$\Omega^{-1} = \begin{bmatrix} 1+\rho^2-\rho & -\rho & 0 & \cdots & 0 & 0 & 0 \\ -\rho & 1+\rho^2 & -\rho & \cdots & 0 & 0 & 0 \\ 0 & -\rho & 1+\rho^2 & \cdots & 0 & 0 & 0 \\ & & & \cdots & & & \\ 0 & 0 & 0 & \cdots & 1+\rho^2 & -\rho & 0 \\ 0 & 0 & 0 & \cdots & -\rho & 1+\rho^2 & -\rho \\ 0 & 0 & 0 & \cdots & 0 & -\rho & 1+\rho^2-\rho \end{bmatrix}.$$

She decides to estimate β by $b = (X'X)^{-1}X'y$ and var(b) by $s^2(X'X)^{-1}$ where $e = y - Xb$, $s^2 = e'e/(n-k)$.

(a) Show that b is a minimum-variance unbiased linear estimator of β.

(b) If it is assumed that $0 < \rho < 1$, compare the expected value of the investigator's estimator of var(b) with its true value.

6. Suppose $\{X_i\}_{i=1}^{n}$ is a random sample from a distribution that is uniform on $[0, \alpha]$. Let $\gamma = \log(\alpha)$.

(a) Derive Jeffreys' prior for α, and for γ. Are these priors proper or improper?

(b) Indicate the posterior densities corresponding to the prior densities in (a). Show that for any constants a_1 and a_2 $(a_2 > a_1 > 0)$, $P[(a_1 < \alpha \le a_2) \mid \{x_i\}_{i=1}^{n}] = P[\log(a_1) < \gamma \le \log(a_2)]$.

(c) Suppose that instead of Jeffreys' prior, the prior distribution for α is the improper distribution $p(\alpha) \propto$ constant for $\alpha \in (0, \infty)$. Derive the posterior distribution and express $P[(a_1 < \alpha \le a_2) \mid \{x_i\}_{i=1}^{n}]$ in terms of $\{x_i\}_{i=1}^{n}$.

(d) Suppose that instead of Jeffreys' prior, the prior distribution for γ is the improper distribution $p(\gamma) \propto$ constant for $\gamma \in (0, \infty)$. Derive the posterior distribution and express $P[(g_1 < \gamma \le g_2) \mid \{x_i\}_{i=1}^{n}]$ in terms of $\{x_i\}_{i=1}^{n}$.

Fall, 1992

University of Minnesota
Econometrics Preliminary Exam
Part I

Answer both questions in this part.

1. Indicate whether each statement is true or false. For each statement sketch a proof, provide a counterexample, cite a pertinent theorem, or prove a correct version as appropriate.

(a) In the linear regression model,

$$\underset{n\times 1}{y_n} = \underset{n\times k}{X_n}\ \underset{k\times 1}{\beta} + \underset{n\times 1}{\varepsilon_n}, \quad E(\varepsilon_n \mid X_n) = 0,$$

suppose that $\text{plim}(X_n'X_n)^{-1} = A$; the rank of A is r, $0 \le r \le k$; and the distribution of ε_n conditional on X_n, $\varepsilon_n \mid X_n$, is $N(0, \sigma^2 I_n)$. Let b denote the least squares estimator of β. Then $\text{plim}\, c'b = c'\beta$ if and only if $Ac = 0$.

(b) In the normal linear regression model

$$\underset{n\times 1}{y_n} = \underset{n\times k}{X_n}\ \underset{k\times 1}{\beta} + \underset{n\times 1}{\varepsilon_n}, \quad \varepsilon_n \mid X_n \sim N(0, \sigma^2 I_n)$$

suppose we know $\beta_j \ge 0$ $(j = 1, \dots, k)$. A $100(1-\alpha)\%$ confidence region for β is given by

$$R^{k+} \cap \{\beta: (\beta - b)'[s^2(X'X)^{-1}]^{-1}(\beta - b)/k \le F_\alpha(k, n-k)\},$$

where R^{k+} is the positive orthant of k-dimensional Euclidean space, b is the ordinary least squares estimator of β, and $F_\alpha(k, n-k)$ is the conventional critical point for the $F(k, n-k)$ distribution:

$$f \sim F(k, n-k) \Rightarrow P[f > F_\alpha(k, n-k)] = \alpha.$$

Part I, continued

2. Consider a classical linear regression model,

$$y_i = \beta_1 + \beta_2 x_{i2} + \beta_3 x_{i3} + \varepsilon_i,$$
$$E(\varepsilon_i) = 0, \quad var(\varepsilon_i) = \sigma^2, \quad E(\varepsilon_i \varepsilon_j) = 0 \text{ if } j \neq i$$
$$(i = 1, \dots, n).$$

(a) An investigator estimates the model by least squares and reports

$$\underset{(.200)}{y_i = -.073} + \underset{(.219)}{.858x_{i2}} + \underset{(.335)}{.500x_{i3}}, \quad s^2 = .112$$

(Conventional least squares standard errors are given in parentheses.) Describe an unbiased estimator of $\beta_1^2 + \beta_2^2 + \beta_3^2$, prove that it is unbiased, and then compute the estimate from the results given above.

(b) Now suppose the investigator also reports $\hat{cov}(b_2, b_3) = -.032$, computed from the conventional least squares formulas for the estimated variance of the least squares estimator. Describe an unbiased estimator of $\beta_2\beta_3$, and compute the corresponding estimate from this new result plus those originally reported in (a).

Part II

3. An investigator trying to apply the model

$$y = X\beta + \varepsilon; \quad E(\varepsilon) = 0; \quad E(\varepsilon\varepsilon') = \sigma^2 I$$

(where y is an $n \times 1$ vector and X is an $n \times k$ matrix) finds that the data come only in grouped form. Specifically, partitioning the matrices of observations on the dependent and independent variables as

$$\begin{bmatrix} y^1 \\ y^2 \\ \vdots \\ y^{n^*} \end{bmatrix} \quad \text{and} \quad \begin{bmatrix} X^1 \\ X^2 \\ \vdots \\ X^{n^*} \end{bmatrix}$$

(where y^ν and X^ν are of orders $n_\nu \times 1$ and $n_\nu \times k$ respectively, and $\sum_{\nu=1}^{n^*} n_\nu = n$) only the column sums of each y^ν and X^ν are available. Denote the $n^* \times 1$ and $n^* \times k$ vectors of these columns sums by y^* and X^* respectively.

(a) Find the minimum variance unbiased linear estimator of β conditional on the data available to the investigator, i.e., y^* and X^*.

(b) Show that the estimator obtained in (a) is equivalent to the best linear unbiased estimator of β that could be obtained if all the data were available, if and only if in each block X^ν of X, the rows are identical.

Part II, continued

4. The placement officer for a large MBA program at a well known business school has available detailed data on job offers received by students in their final year of study. The data include x_i, a vector of personal characteristics of the i'th student $(i = 1, \ldots, n)$; z_j, a vector of characteristics of the j'th job offered $(j = 1, \ldots, m)$; $d_{ij} = 1$ if student i received an offer of job j and 0 otherwise; and $e_{ij} = 1$ if student i selected job j, 0 otherwise.

   Assume that if student i selects job j, he or she will realize utility
$$u_{ij} = \alpha_j' x_i + \beta' z_j + \varepsilon_{ij}.$$
The vectors $\varepsilon_i \equiv (\varepsilon_{i1}, \ldots, \varepsilon_{im})'$ are independent across students and have identical distribution $N(0, \Sigma)$. From among the jobs offered to him/her, each student selects the one from which he/she realizes the greatest utility.

   Students receive different numbers of job offers; each student receives at least one job offer; the same job may be offered to several students; and typically, a student is offered only a small subset of the available jobs.

(a) Write the likelihood function of the parameters $\alpha_1, \ldots, \alpha_m$, β, and Σ.

(b) State a set of restrictions on the parameters, and/or a set of further assumptions, that will identify all of the parameters.

(c) Given the conditions in (b), how would you compute maximum likelihood estimates of the parameters? Discuss any important computational problems, and indicate the asymptotic properties of the estimator.

(d) Indicate a practical prior distribution for a Bayesian approach to the problem. Outline the computation of posterior moments given this prior and the data.

(e) Now suppose the students are interviewed, and each student ranks his/her preference over all job offers received. Carefully write the likelihood function for this situation, and provide a *brief* indication of how your answers to (b), (c), and (d) might be changed.

Part II, continued

5. An agricultural economist has been asked to assist with the analysis of yield data for a new variety of wheat. For each of n plots, fertilizer applied per acre (x_i) and yield expressed in bushels per acre (y_i) are known. The data come from a well-controlled experiment, and it is assumed that no factors other than fertilizer per acre systematically affected yield. The agricultural economist and those involved with the experiment assume

$$y_i = f(x_i)\exp(\varepsilon_i),$$

where f is a monotone increasing, concave function over the range of the data, and ε_i is an independent, identically distributed disturbance with mean 0 and variance σ^2. Assume without loss of generality that $x_1 \leq x_2 \leq ... \leq x_n$.

The objectives of the analysis are

(i) Infer reasonable ranges for yeilds for a set of prespecified values of fertilizer per acre x_j^* $(j = 1, ..., m)$;

(ii) Infer reasonable ranges for the marginal physical product of fertilizer at these same values.

Each prespecified value lies within the range of the data [i.e., $x_1 \leq x_j^* \leq x_n$ $(j = 1, ..., m)$] but there is not necessarily a data point corresponding to each prespecified value [i.e., it may not be the case that for a given j, $x_i = x_j^*$ for some i].

(a) A traditional approach to this problem is to posit a functional form for $f(\cdot)$. Choose such a form and justify your choice. Indicate how you would then meet the objectives of the anlysis. Carefully and explicitly state any additional assumptions you require. How would you check or test your specification of the functional form?

This problem is continued on the next page.

Part II, Problem 5, continued

(b) If the agricultural economist were unwilling to assume a specific functional form for $f(\cdot)$, he might proceed in one of the following ways.

(i) For each application of fertilizer per acre for which one or more observations are available, estimate $\log[f(x_i)]$ as the arithmetic mean of the corresponding yields. That is, if $x_{ij} = \tilde{x}$ $(j = 1, \ldots, p)$ then the estimator of $\log[f(\tilde{x})]$ is $p^{-1}\sum_{j=1}^{p} y_{ij}$.

(ii) Denote $\mu_i \equiv \log[f(x_i)]$. The estimator of $(\mu_1, \ldots, \mu_n)$ is

$$\text{argmin}_{(\mu_1, \ldots, \mu_n)} \sum_{i=1}^{n} [\log(y_i) - \mu_i]^2$$

subject to the constraints

$$\mu_{i+1} - \mu_i = 0 \text{ if } x_{i+1} = x_i \quad (i = 1, \ldots, n-1)$$
$$\mu_{i+1} - \mu_i \geq 0 \text{ if } x_{i+1} \geq x_i \quad (i = 1, \ldots, n-1)$$
$$\mu_{i+1} - 2\mu_i + \mu_{i-1} \leq 0 \quad (i = 2, \ldots, n-1).$$

Indicate a set of assumptions that makes the resultant estimators maximum likelihood estimators. Provide a careful econometric argument why (ii) is a better procedure than (i). What are the limitations of procedure (ii) with respect to the objectives of the study?

(c) Can you suggest a method that might be preferred to either (a) or (b)? If so, describe it briefly and indicate its advantages.

6. Suppose that $\{x_t\}$ is a Gaussian, stationary first order autoregressive process with mean zero,

$$x_t = \beta x_{t-1} + \varepsilon_t, \quad \varepsilon_t \sim \text{IIDN}(0, \sigma^2), \ t \text{ integer.}$$

This time series is observed from time $t = 1$ to time $t = T$, but some of the observations are missing. Whether or not an observation is missing is independent of the process $\{x_t\}$ itself.

(a) Suppose the parameters β and σ^2 are known. If x_t is not observed at time $t = t_0$, what is the optimal linear interpolator of x_{t_0},? Explain.

(b) Suppose the parameters β and σ^2 are unknown. How would you construct asymptotically efficient estimators of these parameters? Your answer should indicate the objective function you would maximize or minimize. Feel free to make additional assumptions to obtain the results, but state them plainly.

(c) Suppose the parameters β and σ^2 are unknown, and as in part (a) suppose that x_t is not observed at time $t = t_0$. Describe an appropriate confidence interval for x_{t_0}, and how you would construct it.

7. Suppose that $\{z_i\}$ is an i.i.d. sequence of random variables with

$$E(z_i) = \mu_i, \quad 0 < \mathrm{var}(z_i) = \sigma^2 < \infty.$$

Furthermore, let $\{v_i\}$ be an i.i.d. sequence of random variables independent of $\{z_i\}$, with the discrete distribution

$$\Pr(v_i = c_i) = \Pr(v_i = -c_i) = p_i, \quad \Pr(v_i = 0) = 1 - 2p_i.$$

Here, $\{c_i\}$ and $\{p_i\}$ are sequences of constants with $c_i > 0$ and $0 \le p_i \le .5$ for each i. Let

$$X_n = v_n + n^{-1}\sum_{i=1}^{n} z_i, \quad n = 1, 2, 3, \dots .$$

(a) Characterize the necessary and sufficient conditions on the sequences $\{\mu_i\}$, $\{p_i\}$, and $\{c_i\}$ in order for X_n to converge in probability to a constant.

(b) Characterize the necessary and sufficient conditions on the sequences $\{\mu_i\}$, $\{p_i\}$, and $\{c_i\}$ in order for X_n to converge almost surely to a constant.

(c) Characterize the necessary and sufficient conditions on the sequences $\{\mu_i\}$, $\{p_i\}$, and $\{c_i\}$ in order for X_n to converge in mean square to a constant.

(d) Using your results from (a) - (c), construct examples in which

(i) X_n converges in mean square but not almost surely;

(ii) X_n converges almost surely but not in mean square;

(iii) X_n converges in probability but not in mean square or almost surely.

(e) Let θ denote the limiting constant in your answer to part (a). Characterize the necessary and sufficient conditions on the sequences $\{\mu_i\}$, $\{p_i\}$, and $\{c_i\}$ in order for $n^{1/2}(X_n - \theta)$ to converge in distribution to a limiting nondegenerate normal distribution. Show by an example that the limiting distribution need not have zero mean.

8. Suppose that $Q_T(\theta)$ is a random, convex function on $\Re^K$ for each T, and that $Q_T(\theta) \xrightarrow{p} Q(\theta)$ for each $\theta \in \Re^K$. Here $Q(\theta)$ is a nonstochastic function minimized at a point θ_0. Suppose also that $Q(\theta)$ is continuously twice differentiable, that its Hessian matrix $H(\theta)$ is continuously twice differentiable and $H(\theta)$ is nonsingular at θ_0.

Let $\Theta \subset \Re^K$ be a convex, compact set that includes θ_0 in its interior. Consider the two extremum estimators $\hat{\theta}_T$ and $\tilde{\theta}_T$ defined by minimizing Q_T over $\Re^K$ and Θ, respectively.

(a) Show that if $Q_T(\theta) \xrightarrow{p} Q(\theta)$ uniformly on Θ then $\tilde{\theta}_T$ is consistent for θ_0.

(b) Show that if $Q_T(\theta) \xrightarrow{p} Q(\theta)$ uniformly on Θ then $\Pr(\hat{\theta}_T = \tilde{\theta}_T) \rightarrow 1$.

(c) The preceding results show that compactness assumptions can be relaxed when the objective function is convex. Show by an example that $\hat{\theta}_T$ may be inconsistent when Q_T is not convex.

University of Minnesota

Econometrics Preliminary Examination
Fall, 1991

Part I

Answer both questions in this part.

1. Indicate whether each statement is true or false. For each statement sketch a proof, provide a counterexample, cite a pertinent theorem, or prove a correct version as appropriate.

   (a) Let $\{X_n\}$ be a sequence of random variables, and suppose $X_n \geq 0$ for all n. If $\lim_{n\to\infty} E(X_n) = 0$, then $\text{plim}(X_n) = 0$.

   (b) In the general linear regression model,
   $$\underset{n\times 1}{y_n} = \underset{n\times k}{X_n}\ \underset{k\times 1}{\beta} + \underset{n\times 1}{\varepsilon_n}, \quad E(\varepsilon_n \mid X_n) = 0, \quad \text{var}(\varepsilon_n \mid X_n) = V_n,$$
   the ordinary least squares estimator of β is consistent if $\text{plim}(X_n'X_n)^{-1} = 0$.

   (c) In the linear model
   $$y_i = \beta x_i + \varepsilon_i, \quad \varepsilon_i \sim \text{IIDN}(0, \sigma^2) \qquad (i = 1, \ldots, n) \qquad (1)$$
   the explanatory variables can take on exactly two values, x_A or x_B $(x_A \neq x_B)$. The total number of observations, n, in the sample is fixed, but we are free to allocate these n observations among n_A observations for which $x_i = x_A$, and n_B observations for which $x_i = x_B$. The test of (1) against the general alternative
   $$y_i = f(x_i) + \varepsilon_i, \quad \varepsilon_i \sim \text{IIDN}(0, \sigma^2) \qquad (i = 1, \ldots, n) \qquad (2)$$
   will be most powerful if we choose $n_1 = n_2 = n/2$.

2. Let $\{x_i^*, y_i^*\}_{i=1}^n$ be a set of i. i. d. random variables. This set of variables cannot be observed. However, we maintain that

$$x_i^* \sim N(0, \phi^2); \qquad y_i^* \sim N(0, \psi^2);$$
$$\varepsilon_i \equiv x_i - x_i^* \sim N(0, \tau^2); \qquad \zeta_i \equiv y_i - y_i^* \sim N(0, \sigma^2);$$

for all $i = 1, \ldots, n$. The random vector $(x_i^*, y_i^*, \varepsilon_i^*, \zeta_i^*)'$ is i.i.d. and normally distributed; all covariances in this distribution are zero, except for that between x_i^* and y_i^*. Only the set $\{x_i, y_i\}_{i=1}^n$ is observed. The model
$$y_i^* = \beta x_i^*$$
has been hypothesized to account for the relationship between x_i^* and y_i^*.

   (a) Is the parameter β identified? Be as explicit as possible in your answer.

(b) Simple least squares adjustment of x_i by y_i, and vice versa, yields the results

$$\hat{y}_i = \underset{(.013)}{.561}\, x_i, \qquad \hat{x}_i = \underset{(.012)}{1.602}\, y_i$$

(Standard errors are shown parenthetically.) What would you conclude about the hypothesized model, and about β?

(c) Would simple least squares adjustment results of this kind ever lead you to reject the idea that the hypothesized model accounts for the relationship between x_i^* and y_i^*?

Part II

Answer one question in this part.

3. Consider a censored regression model,

$$y_i^* = \alpha + \beta x_i + \gamma z_i + \varepsilon_i; \tag{1}$$

$$\varepsilon_i \sim \text{IIDN}(0, \sigma^2), \quad \varepsilon_i \text{ independent of } x_i \text{ and } z_i; \tag{2}$$

$$y_i = y_i^* \text{ if } y_i^* \geq 0, \ y_i = 0 \text{ otherwise.} \tag{3}$$

The i.i.d. sample $(x_i, z_i, y_i;\ i = 1, \ldots, n)$ is observed; the y_i^* are unobserved.; x_i and z_i possess moments of all orders; and x_i and z_i are mutually independent.

An econometrician faced with these data incorrectly assumes

$$y_i^* = \alpha + \beta x_i + \varepsilon_i \tag{1'}$$

instead of equation (1) and computes maximum likelihood estimates of α and β based upon these assumptions.

(a) Suppose that z_i is an i.i.d. sequence of Bernoulli random variables. That is, $z_i = 1$ with probability θ and $z_i = 0$ with probability $1 - \theta$, $0 < \theta < 1$. Are the estimates computed by the econometrician consistent in this case? Explain.

(b) Suppose now that $z_i \sim \text{IIDN}(\mu_z, \sigma_z^2)$. Are the estimates computed by the econometrician consistent in this case? Explain.

Note: Formal proofs are not need to answer this question adequately.

Part II, continued

4. Consider a model in which there are two wage equations:

$$y_{1i}^* = x_{1i}\theta_1 + \varepsilon_{1i},$$
$$y_{2i}^* = x_{2i}\theta_2 + \varepsilon_{2i}.$$

The first equation gives the wage that individual i will receive if he goes to college; the second equation gives the individual's wage otherwise. Thus the observed wage y_i satisfies

$$y_i = d_i y_{i1}^* + (1 - d_i) y_{i2}^*$$

where d_i is a dummy variable with $d_i = 1$ if person i goes to college and $d_i = 0$ otherwise. The variable d_i is in turn determined by the selection equation

$$d_i = 1, \text{ if } z_i\beta + u_i \geq 0; \quad d_i = 0, \text{ otherwise.}$$

Suppose further that the vector of unobserved error terms $(\varepsilon_{1i}, \varepsilon_{2i}, u_i)'$ is independent of the regressors $(x_{1i}, x_{2i}, z_i)'$, and that $(\varepsilon_{1i}, \varepsilon_{2i}, u_i)'$ has a trivariate normal distribution with mean zero and covariance matrix Σ. You are given an i.i.d. sample on the variables $(x_{1i}, x_{2i}, z_i;, d_i, y_i)$ $i = 1, \ldots, n$.

(a) Explain what restrictions, if any, are needed on the parameter vectors θ_1, θ_2 and β and on the matrix Σ in order to identify all of the remaining parameters.

(b) Propose a method for estimating θ_1, θ_2 and β. Be as explicit as possible. If your method involves an optimization problem, be sure to write out the objective function as completely as possible.

(c) Now suppose that you observe $(x_{1i}, x_{2i}, z_i, d_i)$ for an individual i (not in the original sample) and that $d_i = 0$ (i.e., this person has chosen not to attend college). How would you predict the wage y_{1i}^* that this person would have received if they had chosen to attend college instead?

Part III

Answer one question in this part.

5. An investigator is trying to assess the economic situation in a country that has annual but no quarterly data on GNP, but does have a quarterly index of industrial production. This investigator posits the model

$$y = x\beta + \varepsilon; \quad E[\varepsilon] = 0; \quad E[\varepsilon\varepsilon'] = \sigma^2 I;$$

where y is a $T \times 1$ vector of $T = 4S$ consecutive unobserved quarterly values of GNP and x is a $T \times 1$ vector of consecutive quarterly observations on the index of industrial production; S is the number of years in the sample. The investigator has observations on the $S \times 1$ vector z whose components are annual GNP, as well as on the $T \times 1$ vector x.

(a) Find a method for obtaining interpolated values $\tilde{y}$ of quarterly GNP such that

(i) $\tilde{y}$ is a linear (affine) function of z;

(ii) $E(\tilde{y} - y) = 0$ for all β;

(iii) For each $s = 1, 2, \ldots, S$, $\sum_{i=1}^{4} \tilde{y}_{4(s-1)+i} = z_s$;

(iv) Subject to the above, $E[(\tilde{y} - y)'(\tilde{y} - y)]$ is minimized.

(b) Assuming that β is a random variable with prior mean $\overline{\beta}$ and prior variance τ^2, and that β is uncorrelated with ε, find a method for obtaining interpolated values $\hat{y}$ of quarterly GNP such that

(i) $\hat{y}$ is a linear (affine) function of z;

(ii) For each $s = 1, 2, \ldots, S$, $\sum_{i=1}^{4} \hat{y}_{4(s-1)+i} = z_s$;

(iii) Subject to the above, $E[(\hat{y} - y)'(\hat{y} - y)]$ is minimized.

(c) Show that as τ^2 gets larger, the results of the second procedure will approach those of the first. Can you argue that this will also be true if τ^2 is fixed and the sample size S gets larger?

Part III, continued

6. Suppose that the wide sense stationary process $\{x_t\}$ has the representation

$$x_t = \varepsilon_t + \varepsilon_{t-1},$$

where $\{\varepsilon_t\}$ is a white noise process with mean 0 and variance σ^2.

(a) Derive the best linear predictor of x_t conditional on $x_1, \ldots, x_{t-1}$.

(b) Derive the variance σ_t^2 of the associated forecast error. Show that σ_t^2 is a monotonically decreasing sequence with limit σ^2.

Part IV

7. Suppose that $\{z_i\}$ is an i.i.d. sequence of random variables with

$$E(z_i) = \mu_i, \ 0 < \mathrm{var}(z_i) = \sigma^2 < \infty.$$

Furthermore, let $\{v_i\}$ be an i.i.d. sequence of random variables independent of $\{z_i\}$, with the discrete distribution

$$\Pr(v_i = c_i) = \Pr(v_i = -c_i) = p_i, \quad \Pr(v_i = 0) = 1 - 2p_i.$$

Here, $\{c_i\}$ and $\{p_i\}$ are sequences of constants with $c_i > 0$ and $0 \leq p_i \leq .5$ for each i. Let

$$X_n = v_n + n^{-1}\sum_{i=1}^{n} z_i, \quad n = 1, 2, 3, \ldots \ .$$

(a) Characterize the necessary and sufficient conditions on the sequences $\{\mu_i\}$, $\{p_i\}$, and $\{c_i\}$ in order for X_n to converge in probability to a constant.

(b) Characterize the necessary and sufficient conditions on the sequences $\{\mu_i\}$, $\{p_i\}$, and $\{c_i\}$ in order for X_n to converge almost surely to a constant.

(c) Characterize the necessary and sufficient conditions on the sequences $\{\mu_i\}$, $\{p_i\}$, and $\{c_i\}$ in order for X_n to converge in mean square to a constant.

(d) Using your results from (a) - (c), construct examples in which
(i) X_n converges in mean square but not almost surely;
(ii) X_n converges almost surely but not in mean square;
(iii) X_n converges in probability but not in mean square or almost surely.

(e) Let θ denote the limiting constant in your answer to part (a). Characterize the necessary and sufficient conditions on the sequences $\{\mu_i\}$, $\{p_i\}$, and $\{c_i\}$ in order for $n^{1/2}(X_n - \theta)$ to converge in distribution to a limiting nondegenerate normal distribution. Show by an example that the limiting distribution need not have zero mean.

Part IV, continued

8. Suppose that $Q_T(\theta)$ is a random, convex function on $\Re^K$ for each T, and that $Q_T(\theta) \xrightarrow{p} Q(\theta)$ for each $\theta \in \Re^K$. Here $Q(\theta)$ is a nonstochastic function minimized at a point θ_0. Suppose also that $Q(\theta)$ is continuously twice differentiable, that its Hessian matrix $H(\theta)$ is continuously twice differentiable and $H(\theta)$ is nonsingular at θ_0.

   Let $\Theta \subset \Re^K$ be a convex, compact set that includes θ_0 in its interior. Consider the two extremum estimators $\hat{\theta}_T$ and $\tilde{\theta}_T$ defined by minimizing Q_T over $\Re^K$ and Θ, respectively.

   (a) Show that if $Q_T(\theta) \xrightarrow{p} Q(\theta)$ uniformly on Θ then $\tilde{\theta}_T$ is consistent for θ_0.

   (b) Show that if $Q_T(\theta) \xrightarrow{p} Q(\theta)$ uniformly on Θ then $\Pr(\hat{\theta}_T = \tilde{\theta}_T) \to 1$.

   (c) The preceding results show that compactness assumptions can be relaxed when the objective function is convex. Show by an example that $\hat{\theta}_T$ may be inconsistent when Q_T is not convex.

University of North Carolina at Chapel Hill

G

Econometrics Field Exam August 1994

Question 1

Consider the model

(1) $$y_t = \alpha + \beta x_t + \gamma z_t + \epsilon_t,$$

where x_t and z_t are exogenous and ϵ_t is an i.i.d. error term.

a) Suppose you are estimating this model by OLS with a very basic regression package that does not print out anything but coefficient estimates and t ratios. Show how to test the hypothesis that $\beta = \gamma$.

Suppose you mistakenly leave out z_t and estimate the model

(2) $$y_t = \alpha + \beta x_t + \epsilon_t.$$

b) Prove or disprove the conjecture that the OLS residuals from this regression are orthogonal to the variable x_t.

c) Give conditions under which the OLS estimate of β from (2) is consistent.

Suppose now that the coefficient of x_t is not a constant, but that it depends on z_t. That is, b_t is now a time-varying coefficient, and the model is now

$$y_t = \alpha + b_t x_t + \gamma z_t + \epsilon_t,$$

$$b_t = \beta + \delta z_t.$$

d) Explain how you might obtain consistent estimates of the parameters in this model, and describe a specific method for testing the null hypothesis that $\delta = 0$. Is this possible with your basic regression package? If not, describe the additional features that your computer program must include.

Suppose now that the model is

$$y_t = \alpha + \exp\{\beta x_t\} + \gamma z_t + \epsilon_t,$$

where $\exp\{\cdot\}$ is the exponential function.

e) Describe how one might obtain consistent estimates of the parameters in this model, and derive a computationlly feasible expression for the asymptotic variance-covariance matrix of those estimates. Is this possible with your basic regression package? If not, describe the additional features that your computer program must include.

Question 2

You are interested in the model

(1) $$y_t = \beta x_t + \gamma E_{t-1}z_t + \epsilon_t,$$

where $E_{t-1}z_t$ denotes the expectation of z_t formed using period t-1 information. Because you do not have data on the unobservable expectation, you instead run the regression

(2) $$y_t = \beta x_t + \gamma z_t + \epsilon_t,$$

substituting the realized value z_t for the expectation $E_{t-1}z_t$.

a) Discuss the general conditions that determine whether or not the OLS estimate of β is consistent.

b) Discuss the general conditions that determine whether or not the OLS estimate of γ is consistent.

Suppose now ϵ_t, u_t, and v_t are independent error terms and that x_t and z_t are generated by

(3) $$x_t = \rho x_{t-1} + \theta z_{t-1} + u_t$$

(4) $$z_t = \phi_1 z_{t-1} + \phi z_{t-2} + v_t$$

c) Is the OLS estimate of β from (2) consistent? Why or why not?

d) Is the OLS estimate of γ from (2) consistent? Why or why not?

Finally, suppose that (3) and (4) are replaced by

(5) $$x_t = \rho x_{t-1} + u_t$$

(6) $$z_t = \alpha_1 x_t + \alpha_2 x_{t-1} + v_t.$$

e) Is the OLS estimate of β from (2) consistent? Why or why not?

f) Is the OLS estimate of γ from (2) consistent? Why or why not?

g) For those cases that lead to inconsistent estimates, please give a specific estimation procedure that does lead to consistent estimates.

University of Pennsylvania

G

PRELIMS - ECONOMETRICS I (705)
SEPTEMBER 1994

INSTRUCTIONS: Answer all questions. Explain your answers as clearly and fully as possible. The percentage points indicate the relative importance of each question and may therefore be useful to your allocation of time to the different problems.

I. Suppose x_1 and x_2 are independent N(0,1).

20% 1. What is the moment generating function of x_1? Show analytically that $(x_1 + x_2)/2$ is also N(0,1). Describe in detail how you would verify this result through Monte Carlo simulations.

15% 2. Suppose x_1 and x_2 form a random sample of size 2 from the distribution having probability density function (pdf).

$$f(x) = e^{-x}, \quad 0 < x < \infty$$
$$= 0, \quad \text{elsewhere,}$$

and

$$y_1 = x_1 + x_2$$
$$y_2 = x_1/(x_1 + x_2).$$

Derive the joint pdf of y_1 and y_2 and show that y_1 and y_2 are stochastically independent.

II. Suppose $x_1, x_2, \ldots, x_n$ are independent and identically distributed with probability density function $f(x;\theta)$ and finite mean μ, finite variance σ^2. Consider the two statistics:

$$\bar{x} = \Sigma x_i/n$$

$$s^2 = \Sigma(x_i - \bar{x})^2/(n-1)$$

15% 3. Under the given assumptions, for any arbitrary pdf $f(x;\theta)$, show that $\bar{x}$ is an unbiased and consistent estimator of μ. Show also that s^2 is unbiased for σ^2. Do you need any additional assumptions for s^2 to be a consistent estimator of σ^2? Explain your answer.

20% 4. If the population pdf is <u>normal</u>, show that $\bar{x}$ and s^2 are jointly sufficient and complete for μ and σ^2. Explain the technical meaning of sufficiency and completeness and discuss why these properties are useful in statistical inference.

III. Let x_1, x_2, and x_3 be a random sample of size 3 from the exponential distribution

$$f(x;\theta) = (1/\theta)\exp(-x/\theta), \quad 0 < x < \infty$$
$$= 0 \quad , \quad \text{elsewhere}$$

Suppose we are interested in testing the null hypothesis

H_0: $\theta \leq 2$

against the alternative hypothesis

H_1: $\theta > 2$.

15% 5. For the significance test which rejects H_0 in favor of H_1 if

$x_1 + x_2 + x_3 > 12$,

indicate how you would calculate

a. the significance level of the test
b. the power function of the test.

(No need to perform the integration to calculate numerical values.)

15% 6. Show that the test given above (in #5) is uniformly most powerful among tests with size equal to the size of this test.

Jinyong Hahn University of Pennsylvania September 1994

Preliminary Examination
Economics 706

1. (20 pt.) Assume that

$$y_i^* = x_i'\beta + \epsilon_i \qquad i = 1, \ldots, n,$$

where (x_i, ϵ_i) are *i.i.d.*, x_i and ϵ_i are independent of each other, and $\epsilon_i \sim N(0, \sigma^2)$. The latent dependent variable is subject to censoring at c_i. We observe y_i^* only when $y_i^* \geq c_i$. Assume that the censoring point c_i is observed. To summarize, we observe (y_i, x_i, c_i), where $y_i = y_i^*$ when $y_i^* \geq c_i$ and $y_i = c_i$ otherwise. Assume that c_i is independent of x_i and has a normal distribution. For simplicity, you may assume that the expectation of c_i is equal to 0. We do not have any knowledge about the covariance between c_i and ϵ_i.
(a) (10 pt.) How would you apply Heckman's two stage method to estimate β?
(b) (10 pt.) Assume that c_i is independent of (x_i, ϵ_i). Thus, the covariance between c_i and ϵ_i is now assumed to be zero. Show that OLS of y_i with $y_i > c_i$ on x_i yields a consistent estimator of β. (*Hint*: What is the conditional expectation of y_i^* given that $y_i^* > c_i$?)

2. (20 pt.) Consider the linear regression model

$$y_i = \beta x_i + \epsilon_i.$$

Suppose that ϵ_i satisfies

$$E[\epsilon_i x_i] = E[\epsilon_i z_i] = 0. \qquad (M)$$

(x_i, z_i, ϵ_i) are *i.i.d.* (For simplicity, assume that x_i and z_i are scalars.) A friend of yours argues that the OLS estimator of β is asymptotically inefficient because it does not use all the moment restrictions implied by (M).
(a) (10 pt.) Suggest an optimal GMM estimator which uses all the moment restrictions in (M).
(b) (10 pt.) Show that the OLS estimator of y_i on x_i has the same asymptotic distribution as this particular estimator if $Var(\epsilon_i | x_i, z_i) = \sigma^2$.

3. (20 pt.) Consider the following regression model:

$$y_i = \beta x_i + \epsilon_i \quad i = 1, \ldots, n,$$

where (x_i, ϵ_i) are *i.i.d.*, $E[\epsilon_i x_i] = 0$, and x_i is a scalar random variable. Assume that $E[|\epsilon_i x_i^3|] < \infty$ and $E[x_i^4] < \infty$.
(a) (5 pt.) Show that the OLS estimator b of β is consistent.
(b) (10 pt.) Show that $n^{1/2}(b - \beta)$ is asymptotically normal with variance

$$\frac{E[\epsilon_i^2 x_i^2]}{E[x_i^2]^2}.$$

(c) (5 pt.) Let e_i denote the ith residual from the OLS estimation:

$$e_i \equiv y_i - b x_i = \epsilon_i - (b - \beta) x_i.$$

Show that

$$n^{-1} \sum_i e_i^2 x_i^2$$

converges in probability to $E[\epsilon_i^2 x_i^2]$. Conclude that

$$\hat{\sigma}^2 \equiv \frac{n^{-1} \sum e_i^2 x_i^2}{(n^{-1} \sum x_i^2)^2}$$

is a consistent estimator of the asymptotic variance.

Hint $$n^{-1} \sum_i e_i^2 x_i^2 = n^{-1} \sum_i \epsilon_i^2 x_i^2 - 2(b - \beta) \cdot \left[n^{-1} \sum_i \epsilon_i x_i^3 \right] + (b - \beta)^2 \cdot \left[n^{-1} \sum_i x_i^4 \right]$$

University of Pennsylvania

PRELIMS - ECONOMETRICS I (705)
May 1994

INSTRUCTIONS: Answer all questions. Explain your answers as clearly and fully as possible. The numbers next to the questions indicate their comparative importance and may therefore be useful to you in gauging your time.

I. In deriving the probability distribution of $Y = g(X)$, given the distribution of the random variable X, one can use the following approaches:

a. use of moment-generating functions
b. change-of-variable technique
c. Monte Carlo simulations

15% 1. Briefly describe the essential steps involved in these approaches and state (without proof) any important theorems or propositions upon which each of these procedures are based. (Assume that g is continuously differentiable up to the second order.)

15% 2. If X_1, X_2, and X_3 are independent N(0,1), derive the moment generating function of $Y = X_1^2 + X_2^2 + X_3^2$ and show that Y has a central Chi-squared distribution with three degrees of freedom. Note: Take the following propositions as given -- you are not required to prove them.

Proposition 1. For $t < 1/2$,

$$E(e^{tX_1^2}) = (1-2t)^{-1/2}$$

Proposition 2. The moment generating function of a Chi-squared random variable with r degrees of freedom is

$$(1-2t)^{-r/2}, \text{ for } t < 1/2.$$

II. **Suppose $X_1,\ldots,X_n$ are independent and identically distributed with probability density function $f(x;\theta)$, where θ is a finite dimensional vector of unknown parameters.**

15% 3. Define the notion of efficiency of a point estimator of θ. Distinguish between finite-sample efficiency and large-sample asymptotic efficiency. Provide a brief definition of the following and discuss their relationships to efficiency

a. Cramer-Rao inequality

b. sufficiency
c. completeness

15% 4. In sampling from a normal population with mean μ and variance 1, show that the sample mean is the maximum likelihood estimator of μ and that it is sufficient, complete, and is minimum variance unbiased.

III. Suppose $X_1, X_2, \ldots, X_n \sim$ i.i.d. $N(\mu, 1)$, as in II, but now, we are interested in testing the null hypothesis

$$H_0: \mu = 0 \qquad \text{versus} \qquad H_1: \mu \neq 0.$$

15% 5. Show that the likelihood ratio test in this case (with a 5% significance level) is:

$$\text{reject } H_0 \text{ if } |\bar{x}| > (1.96/\sqrt{n}).$$

Discuss the Wald and Lagrange Multiplier tests for this problem.

15% 6. Is this LR test in #5 uniformly most powerful among 5%-size tests for the given problem? Why or why not? How would you calculate the power of this test for alternative values of μ under the alternative hypothesis?

IV. Consider the investment function

$$I_t = \beta_1 + \beta_2 Y_t + \beta_3 R_t + e_t$$

where

I_t = investment in year t
Y_t = real GNP in year t
R_t = interest rate in year t

Based on thirty observations on I, Y, and R, the following regression results were obtained (standard errors in parentheses):

a. Least Squares

$$I_t = \underset{(2.51)}{6.22} + \underset{(0.072)}{0.770}\, Y_t - \underset{(0.126)}{0.184}\, R_t$$

$R^2 = 0.816$, $DW = 0.852$, $SSE = 299.3$

b. Generalized Least Squares (correcting for AR(1) Autocorrelation)

$$I_t = \underset{(2.86)}{8.434} + \underset{(0.114)}{.742}\, Y_t - \underset{(0.079)}{0.285}\, R_t$$

$R^2 = 0.636$, $DW = 1.548$, $SSE = 186.6$, $\hat{\rho} = 0.568$

10% 7. Compare the results in the least squares (a) and GLS regressions (b). Note any important differences between these two regressions and explain how the least squares regression results in (a) could be misleading. Why not just use the least squares regression reported in (a), since the coefficient estimates are supposed to be Best Linear Unbiased Estimates?

September 1993 *University of Pennsylvania*

Economics 706 Prelim

1. Consider the generalized regression model: $y = X\beta + \varepsilon$, $E(\varepsilon) = 0$, $E(\varepsilon\varepsilon') = \sigma^2\Omega$, where Ω is a $n \times n$ positive definite matrix, y is $n \times 1$, X is $n \times K$ and nonstochastic, β is a $K \times 1$ vector of unknown parameters and ε is a $n \times 1$ vector of disturbances.

(a) Is the OLS estimator b unbiased? Why or why not?

(b) Let s^2 be the OLS estimator of σ^2, which is the sum of squared residuals divided by n-K. Is it an unbiased estimator of σ^2? Why or why not?

(c) Suppose X is a column of ones and suppose Ω is given by

$$\begin{bmatrix} 1 & \rho & \cdot & \cdot & \cdot & \cdot & \rho \\ \rho & 1 & \rho & \cdot & \cdot & \cdot & \rho \\ \rho & \rho & 1 & \rho & \cdot & \cdot & \rho \\ \cdot & \cdot & \cdot & \cdot & \cdot & \cdot & \cdot \\ \rho & \cdot & \cdot & \rho & 1 & \rho & \rho \\ \rho & \cdot & \cdot & \cdot & \rho & 1 & \rho \\ \rho & \cdot & \cdot & \cdot & \cdot & \rho & 1 \end{bmatrix}.$$

Here, ρ is positive and less than 1. Is b consistent for β? Why or why not?

2. Consider the simultaneous equations model:

$$\begin{array}{llllll} y_1 & + \gamma_{21}y_2 & & + \beta_{11}x_1 & & + \beta_{31}x_3 & = \varepsilon_1 \\ \gamma_{12}y_1 & + y_2 & + \gamma_{32}y_3 & + \beta_{12}x_1 & + \beta_{22}x_2 & & = \varepsilon_2 \\ & \gamma_{23}y_2 & + y_3 & + \beta_{13}x_1 & & & = \varepsilon_3. \end{array}$$

Here, y's are endogenous variables and x's are exogenous. The coefficients of included variables are non-zero. Determine the identifiabililty of each equation. Which equation is under-identified? Which equation is over-identified?

3. Suppose y^* has a normal distribution with mean μ and variance σ^2. There is a sample of size n, $(y_1^*,\cdots,y_n^*)$, but only those values of y^* that are *less than* a constant c are recorded. Thus if y_i is the i-th observation, $y_i = y_i^*$ if $y_i^* < c$, $= c$ otherwise.

(a) Write down the log likelihood function of the cencored sample $(y_1,\cdots,y_n)$ for estimation of the parameters (μ, σ^2).

(b) Re-parameterize the log likelihood function by $\alpha = \mu/\sigma$ and $h = 1/\sigma$. Derive the first-order condition with respect to α and h.

END

University of Pennsylvania

Econometrics Field Exam, Spring 1993. Answer ***BOTH*** questions. Good luck!

I. Consider the multivariate dynamic stochastic process:

$$\begin{bmatrix} X_{1t} \\ X_{2t} \end{bmatrix} = \begin{bmatrix} \phi_{11} & \phi_{12} \\ 0 & \phi_{22} \end{bmatrix} \begin{bmatrix} X_{1t-1} \\ X_{2t-1} \end{bmatrix} + \begin{bmatrix} \varepsilon_{1t} \\ \varepsilon_{2t} \end{bmatrix} + \begin{bmatrix} \theta_{11} & 0 \\ 0 & \theta_{22} \end{bmatrix} \begin{bmatrix} \varepsilon_{1t-1} \\ \varepsilon_{2t-1} \end{bmatrix}.$$

$$\begin{bmatrix} \varepsilon_{1t} \\ \varepsilon_{2t} \end{bmatrix} \sim (\underline{0}, \Sigma)$$

1. Under what conditions is the process covariance stationary? Strictly stationary? Invertible? Discuss.

2. Derive and discuss the (matrix) autocorrelation function.

3. Derive and discuss the (matrix) spectral density in terms of
   (a) Cospectrum and quadrature spectrum
   (b) Gain and phase
   (c) Coherence and phase.

4. Derive and interpret the impulse-response function. Discuss and defend the implicit normalization that you adopt.

5. Find a state-space representation for the process and, assuming covariance stationarity and known parameter, show how to use the Kalman filter to produce an "optimal" k-step-ahead point forecast. In what sense is your point forecast optimal? How, and under what additional assumptions, would you construct an interval forecast?

6. Assuming covariance stationarity, show how to use the Kalman filter to obtain exact maximum-likelihood estimates of the parameters. How does your answer change if one or both of X_{1t} and X_{2t} are I(1)?

7. How would you use Dickey-Fuller procedures to examine the integration status of X_{1t} and X_{2t} individually? Jointly? Is it possible that $X_1 \sim I(1)$ and $X_2 \sim I(1)$ and yet the system has only one unit root? Relate your answer to models of cointegration and error-correction.

8. How would you assess the adequacy of this model as fitted to real data under a normality assumption? You may want to consider, among other things:
   (a) Neglected conditional mean dynamics (short memory or long memory)
   (b) Neglected conditional variance dynamics (short memory or long memory)
   (c) Adequacy of the normality assumption
   (d) Structural Change.

ECONOMETRICS FIELD EXAM

II. Consider the following model of real wages, employment and inflation (Lucas-Rapping):

$$\text{Log}(N/M)_t = \alpha_1 + \alpha_2 \text{ Log } \hat{W}_t + \alpha_3 \text{ Log } W_{t-1} + \alpha_4 \text{ Log } (P_t/P_{t-1}) + \alpha_5 \text{ Log } (N/M)_{t-1} + \epsilon_{1t}$$

$$\text{Log } (NQ/Y)_t = \beta_1 + \beta_2 \text{ Log } (\hat{W}/Q)_t + \beta_3 \text{ Log } (NQ/Y)_{t-1} + \beta_4 \text{ Log } (Y_t/Y_{t-1}) + \epsilon_{2t}$$

$$U_t = \gamma_1 + \gamma_2 \text{ Log } (P_t/P_{t-1}) + \gamma_3 \text{ Log } (\hat{W}_t/W_{t-1}) + \gamma_4 U_{t-1} + \epsilon_{3t}$$

where

N = total hours supplied annually
M = number of households
P = GNP deflator
W = real wage rate (money wages divided by the GNP deflator)
Y = level of output in constant dollars
Q = index of labor quality (years-of-schooling-completed index)
U = unemployment rate
$\hat{W}$ = expected real wage rate.

The variables Q_t, Y_t, M_t and P_t are taken to be exogenous. The current values of N_t, W_t, and U_t are taken to be endogenous.

1. What econometric complications in the estimation of the model arise from the presence of $\hat{W}_t$ in the model? Lucas-Rapping use as proxy for $\hat{W}$ the value of W calculated from an OLS regression of Log W_t on Log W_{t-1}, Log P_t/P_{t-1}, Log Y_t/M_t, Log Q_t, Log $(NQ/Y)_{t-1}$, Log Y_t/Y_{t-1}, Log $(N/M)_{t-1}$, based on aggregate annual time series data. They then proceed to estimate each equation in the model by ordinary least squares. Does This procedure yield consistent estimates of the standard coefficients? Explain your answer.

2. Devise a statistical test for the hypothesis that the GNP deflator (P_t) is exogenous.

3. Suppose you find that P_t is not exogenous. Develop a generalized method of moments estimator for the above three structural equations taking into account the endogeneity of P_t.

University of Pennsylvania

Econometrics I
Preliminary Examination, Fall 1991

Part I: Do either I.1 or I.2.

Question I.1

Suppose that the vector $X = (X_1, X_2, \ldots, X_N)'$ has a multivariate Gaussian distribution with mean vector 0 and covariance matrix I. Let i be any element of (1, 2, ..., N), and let a subscript of "ii" denote the (i, i) element of a matrix.

a. Determine the distribution of each of the following (and discuss your reasoning).

1. X_i

2. $$\frac{X_i - EX_i}{[E[(X - EX)(X - EX)']]_{ii}}$$

3. $$\left[\frac{X_i - EX_i}{[E[(X - EX)(X - EX)']]_{ii}}\right]^2$$

4. $$\sum_{i=1}^{N}\left[\frac{X_i - EX_i}{[E[(X - EX)(X - EX)']]_{ii}}\right]^2$$

5. $$\lim_{N\to\infty}\left(\frac{\sum_{i=1}^{N}\left[\frac{X_i - EX_i}{[E[(X - EX)(X - EX)']]_{ii}}\right]^2 - N}{\sqrt{2N}}\right)$$

b. Write down and discuss in detail the density function of the vector X, the joint marginal density of any subset of the elements of X, and the joint conditional density of any subset of the elements of X (where the conditioning is upon the remaining elements of X). Use your results to motivate and discuss the relationship between multivariate normality and the linear regression model.

Question I.2

Let X be a real-valued continuous random variable with probability density function f(x) and cumulative density function F(x). Prove each of the following assertions if true; otherwise, correct the assertion and prove the correct version.

1. $f(x) > 0, \ \forall x \in \mathbf{R}$

2.

$$0 \leq F(x) < 1, \ \forall x \in \mathbf{R}$$

$$\lim_{x \to -\infty} F(x) = 0$$

$$\lim_{x \to \infty} F(x) = 1 - \delta, \ \delta > 0$$

3.

$$F(a) \leq F(b), \ \forall a < b$$

4.

$$\int_{x_1}^{x_2} f(x)\, dx = F(x_2) + F(x_1), \ \forall x_2 > x_1$$

5.

$$\lim_{h \to 0} F(x + h) = F(x), \ \forall x \in \mathbf{R}, \ h > 0$$

6.

$$cov(X, c) = var(X), \ \forall \text{ constants } c > 0.$$

7.

$$var(X) = [E(X)]^2 - E(X^2)$$

Part II: Do <u>either</u> II.1 or II.2.

Question II.1

a. Write down and discuss the "full ideal conditions" associated with regression analysis. When and why are they likely to be violated in econometric analyses?

b. Consider the regression model, $Y = X\beta + \epsilon$, under the full ideal conditions, with one exception: Assume that the disturbances are iid Cauchy. (The Cauchy is symmetric and leptokurtic, with infinite moments of all orders.) Derive the least-squares estimator of β, and discuss its efficiency properties relative to the maximum-likelihood estimator.

c. In what sense is the least-squares estimator "good" when the disturbances are Cauchy, as above? In what sense is it less attractive than if the disturbances were Gaussian? Can you think of any alternative estimators that might be preferable to least squares, in light of the fact that we are often unsure as to the correct distributional assumption, but wish to insure ourselves against fat-tailed disturbances?

Question II.2

a. In random sampling from the exponential distribution, with probability density function

$$f(X) = (1/\theta)\exp(-X/\theta), \qquad X \geq 0, \qquad \theta > 0,$$

find the maximum likelihood estimator of θ and obtain the asymptotic distribution of this estimator.

b. Based on a random sample of 16 observations from the exponential distribution above, we wish to test the hypothesis that $\theta = 1$. We will reject the hypothesis if the sample mean is greater than 1.2 or less than 0.8. Use your answer in (a) to get an asymptotic approximation to the power of this test at $\theta = 1.5$.

University of Pennsylvania

Econometrics II
Preliminary Examination, Fall 1991

Part I: Do <u>either</u> I.1 or I.2.

<u>Question I.1</u>

Consider the linear regression model:

$$Y_t = \beta_0 + \beta_1 X_{1t} + \beta_2 X_{2t} + \beta_3 X_{3t} + u_t$$

$$u_t \sim N(0, \sigma^2)$$

$$t = 1, \ldots, T.$$

(a) Discuss in general the concept of a likelihood ratio test, and in particular the likelihood ratio test for the general linear hypothesis $R\beta = r$. (R is a matrix and r is a vector.)

(b) Show how each of the following hypotheses falls under the rubric of the general linear hypothesis, and be sure to note any context-specific simplifications that arise in the form of the likelihood ratio statistic:

b1. H_0: $\beta_1 = 0$

b2. H_0: $\beta_1 + \beta_2 = 1$

b3. H_0: $\beta_1 = \beta_2 = 0$

b4. H_0: $\beta_1 = \beta_2 = \beta_3 = 0$

(c) Suppose you suspect, on a priori grounds, that a structural change occured at time t^*. That is, you suspect that one probability structure (assumed to conform to the linear regression model) governs observations $1, \ldots, (t^*-1)$, and a different structure governs observations $t^*, \ldots, T$. How would you construct a test for such structural change within the framework of the general linear hypothesis?

Question I.2

Cagan's model of hyper-inflation relates the demand for real cash balances to the expected rate of inflation. Let:

m_t = log money supply

p_t = log price level

p^*_{t+1} = expectation of p_{t+1} as of t

u_t = stochastic term representing the effects of all left out variables.

The expected rate of inflation between t and t+1 is

$$\pi^*_{t+1} = p^*_{t+1} - p_t \tag{1}$$

whereas the realized rate is

$$\pi_{t+1} = p_{t+1} - p_t. \tag{2}$$

Cagan assumes adaptive expectations:

$$\pi^*_{t+1} - \pi^*_t = (1-\lambda)[\pi_t - \pi^*_t]. \tag{3}$$

Write the demand for money as

$$y_t = a + b\,\pi^*_{t+1} + u_t, \tag{4}$$

where

$$y_t = m_t - p_t.$$

1. Show that

$$y_t = a(1-\lambda) + \lambda\, y_{t-1} + b(1-\lambda)\pi_t + v_t, \tag{5}$$

where

$$v_t = u_t - \lambda u_{t-1}.$$

2. Cagan estimated (5) by OLS. Is OLS in this situation unbiased? Consistent? Efficient? Why or why not?

3. Discuss the estimation of Cagan's model by instrumental variables. What instruments would you choose?

3. Discuss the estimation of Cagan's model by maximum likelihood. Does a closed-form expression for the likelihood exist? If not, how would you proceed?

Part II: Do *either* II.1 or II.2.

Question II.1

The CES production function may be written as

$$(1) \quad \text{Log } Q = \text{Log } \gamma - \frac{v}{\rho} \log [\delta K^{-\rho} + (1-\delta) L^{-\rho}] + u,$$

and a Taylor series approximation to this function around the point $\rho = 0$ is

$$(2) \quad \text{Log } Q = \beta_1 + \beta_2 X_2 + \beta_3 X_3 + \beta_4 X_4 + \epsilon,$$

where $X_2 = \text{Log } K$, $X_3 = \text{Log } L$, $X_4 = \text{Log}^2 (K/L)$, and

$$\beta_1 = \text{Log } \gamma$$
$$\beta_2 = v\delta$$
$$\beta_3 = v\ (1-\delta)$$
$$\beta_4 = -\rho v \delta\ (1-\delta)/2.$$

a. Discuss how you would estimate the parameters $(\gamma, v, \delta, \rho)$ by nonlinear least squares applied directly to equation (1).

b. How would you estimate $(\gamma, v, \delta, \rho)$ from the Taylor series approximation given in (2)?

c. Are the estimates of $(\gamma, v, \delta, \rho)$ in (a) and (b) the same? Why or why not?

Question II.2

Consider the following simultaneous equations model:

$$Y_1 = \beta_1 Y_2 + \gamma_{11} X_1 + \gamma_{21} X_2 + \gamma_{31} X_3 + u_1$$
$$Y_2 = \beta_2 Y_1 + \gamma_{12} X_1 + \gamma_{22} X_2 + \gamma_{32} X_2 + u_2$$

a. Verify that, as stated, neither equation is identified.

b. Establish whether or not the following restrictions are sufficient to identify (or partially identify) the model:

(1) $\gamma_{12} = \gamma_{22} = 0$

(2) $\beta_1 = \beta_2$ and $\gamma_{32} = 0$

(3) $\gamma_{21} + \gamma_{22} = 1$

(4) $\sigma_{12} = 0$, $\gamma_{21} = \gamma_{22} = \gamma_{31} = \gamma_{32} = 0$
(σ_{12} = covariance between u_1 and u_2.)

University of Pennsylvania

705 Prelim, May 1991

I. Answer I.1 or I.2

I.1. Let X_1, X_2 and X_3 have the joint p.d.f.

$$f(x_1,x_2,x_3) = 1/4, \quad (x_1,x_2,x_3) \in \{(1,0,0), (0,1,0), (0,0,1), (1,1,1)\}$$
$$= 0, \quad \text{otherwise.}$$

(a) Compute the joint p.d.f.'s of X_i and X_j, $i = 1, 2, 3$, $j = 1, 2, 3$, $i \neq j$, and discuss their form. Also compute the marginal p.d.f.'s of X_1, X_2 and X_3, and discuss their form.

(b) Define (in terms of relationships between joint and marginal distributions) stochastic independence and pairwise stochastic independence of the set of random variables X_1, X_2 and X_3.

(c) Using your definitions from (b), determine whether X_1, X_2 and X_3 are pairwise stochastically independent, and whether they are stochastically independent.

(d) Let $M(t_1,t_2,t_3)$ be the moment-generating function of the random variables X_1, X_2 and X_3. Write out an explicit expression for $M(t_1,t_2,t_3)$. Recast your definitions in (b) and findings in (c) in terms of $M(t_1,t_2,t_3)$, $M(0,t_2,t_3)$, $M(t_1,0,t_3)$, $M(t_1,t_2,0)$, $M(0,0,t_3)$, $M(t_1,0,0)$ and $M(0,t_2,0)$.

I.2. Consider the regression model, $Y = X\beta + \epsilon$, under the full ideal conditions. Assume that σ^2, the disturbance variance, is known.

(a) Define and derive the LS estimator of β and its covariance matrix.

(b) Write down the likelihood function and compute Fisher's information matrix.

(c) In light of the Cramer-Rao theorem and your results above, comment on the efficiency of the LS estimator. How would your answer change if normality were not assumed?

(d) Derive and discuss the ML estimator of β.

II. ANSWER II.1 OR II.2

II.1. Let X_1, X_2, and X_3 be independently and identically distributed as normal with mean μ and variance σ^2 and define the following statistics:

$$W = (X_1 + X_2 + X_3)/3$$

$$V = [(X_1 - W)^2 + (X_2 - W)^2 + (X_3 - W)^2] / 2.$$

a. What are the probability distributions of W and V? (Just specify the type of distributions and appropriate parameters. There is no need to write the explicit expressions for the probability density functions.)

b. Outline a proof for the statistical independence between V and W.

c. Prove that W and V are the minimum variance unbiased estimators of μ and σ^2, respectively. [Note: First, prove unbiasedness; then show the minimum variance property.]

II.2 A random sample of size 64 is to be used to test the null hypothesis that the mean μ of a normal population (with known variance $\sigma^2 = 256$) is less than or equal to 40 against the alternative hypothesis that it is greater than 40. If the null hypothesis is to be rejected if and only if the mean of the random sample exceeds 43, find:

a. the probability of a Type I error when $\mu = 38$

b. the probability of a Type II error when $\mu = 45$

c. What would your rejection region be if you want a 10% probability of a Type I error when $\mu = 40$?

d. What is the uniformly most powerful test, with a 5 % significance level, in this problem?

University of Pennsylvania

706 Prelim, May 1991

I. Answer I.1 or I.2

I.1. Suppose that the linear regression model,

$$Y_t = x_t' \beta + \epsilon_t \qquad \epsilon_t \sim N(0, \sigma^2_\epsilon),$$

is estimated by OLS. The full ideal conditions are satisfied, with one possible exception: It is not known whether the disturbances are serially correlated.

(a) Are you concerned by the possibility of serial correlation, if interest centers on obtaining a point (interval) estimate of β and sample size is large (small)? How (if at all) would your answers change if one regressor were a lagged dependent variable?

(b) Suppose that you determine that the disturbances <u>are</u> serially correlated, and are best characterized as AR(1). That is,

$$Y_t = x_t' \beta + \epsilon_t \qquad \epsilon_t = \rho\, \epsilon_{t-1} + v_t \qquad v_t \overset{iid}{\sim} N(0, \sigma^2).$$

Discuss and contrast estimation of this model by exact ML, by Schweppe/Newbold approximate maximum likelihood based on a prediction-error decomposition ("nonlinear least squares"), and by various feasible GLS estimators. How (if at all) would your answers change if a lagged dependent variable were included among the regressors?

I.2. Consider the "geometric" distributed lag model,

$$y_t = \alpha + \beta \sum_{i=0}^{\infty} w^i x_{t-i} + \epsilon_t$$

where $0 < w < 1$.

(a) Write the model in lag-operator notation, and find a transformation that converts the infinite-ordered distributed lag into an estimable form. Is the OLS estimator of the estimable form consistent? Is the IV estimator of the estimable form consistent? Efficient? Is the ML estimator of the estimable form consistent? Efficient? If IV estimation were adopted, what would you use as an instrument?

(b) In the context of a <u>general</u> distributed-lag model, define and discuss the concepts of T-period response, long-run response, mean lag and median lag. Compute, for the <u>geometric</u> lag model, the T-period response, long-run response, mean lag and median lag.

II. ANSWER II.1 OR II.2

II.1. Suppose

$$Q_{1t} = \beta_0 + \beta_1 P_{1t} + \beta_2 P_{2t} + \ldots + \beta_k P_{kt} + \gamma \bar{P}_t + \delta Y_t + u_{1t}$$

where Q_{1t} is the demand for commodity 1, P_{1t} is the price of commodity 1, $P_{2t}, \ldots, P_{kt}$ are the prices of (k-1) other goods, $\bar{P}_t = \frac{1}{k} \sum_{i=1}^{k} P_{it}$ is the general price level, and Y_t is income.

a. Why would it not be possible to use direct least squares to estimate the above model?

b. Show that β and δ are identifiable while the other coefficients are not.

c. Characterize the linear combinations of β_0, β_1, β_2, ..., β_k, γ, and δ which are identifiable based on the above model.

d. Further assuming that the u_{1t} are uncorrelated, with mean zero and variance σ^2, how would you estimate the above equation? Would it be reasonable to assume that the explanatory variables are all uncorrelated with the error term u_{1t}? Why or why not?

e. How would you estimate the equation if u_{1t} is correlated with some of the explanatory variables?

II.2. The labor-force participation (LF) of wives in the population -- their being in the labor force or not -- is to be explained in terms of the age (A) and education level (E) of the woman and the income (Y) of her husband. Discuss the alternative ways of modeling and empirically estimating the structural relationship between LF (which is a zero-one variable) and A, E, and Y:

a. If you have data for n wives: (LF_i, A_i, E_i, Y_i), i=1,2,...,n.

b. If you have data for m sets of wives: (P_j, A_j, E_j, Y_j), j=1,2,...,m

where, within each set, each wife is of the same age, has attained the same education level, and whose husband has the same income. P_j is the proportion of wives in the jth set who are in the labor force. (Assume that there is a large number of wives in each set.)

G

PRINCETON UNIVERSITY

Department of Economics

General Examination for the Degree of Doctor of Philosophy

Econometrics General Examination

Time: 3 hours May 20, 1994

Do not write your name on any of your examination papers, but identify them with a Code Number which you have obtained from Ms. Alito.

Start a new paper or book for each question so that the examination can be assembled by question rather than by candidate. Be sure that your Code Number appears on each sheet or book.

Part I

Question 1

Define and briefly discuss SIX of the following eight concepts (30 minutes).

- The Lagrange Multiplier test
- Influence functions
- Stochastic volatility
- Nonparametric estimation
- Long memory process
- Probabilistic modes of convergence
- Coherence and phase
- Error correction and cointegration

Part II

Answer TWO of the following three questions (30 minutes each).

Question 2

Consider the following quadratic regression model:

$$y_i = \alpha + \beta z_i + \gamma z_i^2 + \varepsilon_i,$$

where it is assumed that ε_i is independent of z_i with finite moments and zero mean. Suppose that the variable z_i is unobserved; instead, you observe

$$x_i = z_i + u_i,$$

where the measurement error u_i is independent of both z_i and ε_i, again with finite moments and zero mean. You are interested in the parameters β and γ, which characterize the derivative of $E[y_i | z_i]$ with respect to the variable z_i; a random sample of observations on y_i and x_i is available.

A. Demonstrate that a least-squares regression of y_i on 1, x_i, and x_i^2 will yield inconsistent estimates of β and γ.

B. Suppose you knew that the unobservable regressor z_i satisfied

$$z_i = w_i + v_i,$$

for some observable variable w_i that was independent of the measurement errors ε_i, u_i, and v_i, and that you knew that v_i was independent of ε_i and u_i with bounded moments and zero mean. Will a least-squares regression of y_i on 1, w_i, and w_i^2 give consistent estimators of β and γ?

C. Suppose instead that the variable w_i is an independent measurement of z_i:

$$w_i = z_i + v_i,$$

where now it is assumed that z_i (not w_i) that is independent of v_i; as before, you know that v_i, ε_i, and u_i are mutually independent with zero means and bounded moments. If you use instrumental variables to fit y_i as a quadratic function of x_i using 1, w_i, and w_i^2 as instruments, will the resulting estimators of β and γ be consistent?

Question 3

Answer the following two questions.

A. State and prove the Gauss-Markov theorem.

B. For the partitioned linear model

$$y = X_1\beta_1 + X_2\beta_2 + \varepsilon,$$

where X_1 and X_2 are $(N\times K_1)$ and $(N\times K_2)$ matrices, respectively, with full column rank, prove the Frisch-Waugh theorem: namely, if y^* is the vector of residuals of a regression of y on X_2 and X_1^* is the matrix of residuals of a regression of X_1 on X_2, then the coefficients of a least-squares regression of y^* on X_1^* will be identical to the coefficients on X_1 in a least-squares regression of y on X_1 and X_2.

Question 4

Consider the regression model

$$y_t = x_t'\beta + \varepsilon_t,$$

where the x_t are nonrandom K-vectors with $x_{t1} = 1$ and all other components strictly positive, and where the error terms ε_t have $E(\varepsilon_t) = 0$ but are autocorrelated and heteroskedastic. In fact,

$$E(\varepsilon_t\varepsilon_s) = \rho^{t-s}[(x_t'\gamma)\cdot(x_s'\gamma)]^{1/2},$$

where $|\rho| < 1$ and the coefficients of γ are all positive, but the true values of β, ρ, and γ are unknown.

If you have access to a statistical package which can only do linear regression and simple algebraic transformations of data series, discuss how you could use this package to obtain an (asymptotically) efficient FGLS estimator. [HINT: deal with one problem at a time.]

Part III

Answer TWO of the following four questions (45 minutes each).

Question 5

Suppose you have monthly data on yields of one- and three-month bonds (with zero default risk) and wished to test the hypothesis that

$$(1) \qquad E_t \left[\frac{D_t}{d_t d_{t+1} d_{t+2}} \right] = 1 ,$$

where D_t is the three-month yield (one plus the interest rate) and d_t the corresponding yield on one-month bonds in month t. A particular theoretical model of term structure behavior gives you the alternative relation

$$(2) \qquad E_t \left[\frac{D_t}{d_t (d_{t+1})^{1-\theta} (d_{t+2})^{1+\theta}} \right] = 1 ,$$

where you expect $\theta \neq 0$ if the alternative theory is correct.

Given T realizations from the observed (D_t, d_t) process, which is assumed to be stationary, ergodic, *et cetera*, discuss how you would estimate the parameter θ and test the null hypothesis that $\theta = 0$. You need not worry about the regularity conditions for any limit theorems you use; however, you should be very clear about the steps you use in construction of your estimator and test statistic, giving algebraic details where appropriate.

Also, you should discuss the efficiency of your proposed estimator and test. There are two aspects to the efficiency question to be considered. For a given set of unconditional moment restrictions derived from the conditional moment restriction (2), one question is the efficiency of the particular estimator (and corresponding test procedure) you propose. Additionally, there is the question of the efficient choice of unconditional moment restrictions derived from the conditional restriction (2). Discuss the efficiency of your method with regard to these two aspects, pointing out any implementation problems if your approach is not fully efficient.

Question 6

For the censored Tobit model with a single regressor,

$$y_i = \max\{0, \beta_0 \cdot x_i + u_i\}, \qquad i = 1, \ldots, N,$$

suppose that the error terms u_i are symmetrically distributed about zero conditionally, not on the regressor x_i, but instead on some set of "instrumental variables" z_i. The regressor x_i is assumed to be related to the instruments z_i by a linear reduced form,

$$x_i = z_i'\pi_0 + v_i,$$

where (u_i, v_i) are continuously and spherically symmetrically distributed given z_i; that is, for any scalars α and γ, $\alpha u_i + \gamma v_i$ is continuously distributed and symmetric about zero given z_i.

A. Consider the following "two-stage" procedure: first, estimate π_0 by least squares, then estimate β_0 by symmetrically-censored least squares (SCLS) estimation, after replacing the "endogenous" regressors x_i with their fitted values $\hat{x}_i = z_i'\hat{\pi}$; that is, $\hat{\beta}$ solves

$$0 = \sum_{i=1}^{n} 1(\hat{x}_i'\hat{\beta} > 0) \cdot \min(y_i - \hat{\beta} \cdot \hat{x}, \hat{\beta} \cdot \hat{x}) \cdot \hat{x}_i \equiv \sum_{i=1}^{n} \psi(y_i, z_i, \hat{\pi}, \hat{\beta}).$$

Assuming that this estimator is consistent, and assuming random sampling and that all necessary moments exist, derive the asymptotic distribution of the second stage estimator $\hat{\beta}$.

B. Suppose instead that the reduced form for x_i was substituted into the model for the dependent variable y_i, and the parameters $\delta_0 = \beta_0 \pi_0$ of the resulting relationship between y_i and z_i were estimated using SCLS. Given this SCLS estimator $\hat{\delta}$ and the least squares estimator $\hat{\pi}$ of the reduced form coefficients π_0, propose an efficient way to estimate the coefficients β_0 of the original model, and derive its asymptotic covariance matrix (as usual, don't bother to check regularity conditions).

C. Now suppose that the second stage estimator was censored least absolute deviations (CLAD) rather than SCLS, so that $\hat{\beta}$ solves

$$0 = \sum_{i=1}^{n} 1(\hat{x}_i'\hat{\beta} > 0) \cdot \mathrm{sgn}(y_i - \hat{\beta} \cdot \hat{x}) \cdot \hat{x}_i \equiv \sum_{i=1}^{n} \psi^{*}(y_i, z_i, \hat{\pi}, \hat{\beta}).$$

How does your answer to part A. change?

Question 7

In order to study the effects of government expenditures on real output, one does not wish to assume that government expenditures are exogenous.

A. Explain how a VAR can be used to estimate the effects of past exogenous changes in government expenditures on real output. What assumptions are required in obtaining your estimates?

B. Incorporate stochastic trends in your model and rewrite the model in state-space form. Assuming normal residuals, set up the likelihood function for estimating the parameters of the model.

Question 8

Consider a time series process $\{y(t): -\infty < t < +\infty\}$ with a moving average representation:

$$y(t) = v(t) + 2v(t-1)$$

where $\{v(t): -\infty < t < +\infty\}$ is a process that has mean zero, is serially uncorrelated, and has variance one for all t. Let H(t) be the space of all linear combinations of current and past values of y(t) and the (mean-square) limit points of such sequences. Let $H^{*}(t)$ be the corresponding space that is constructed with "v(t)" replacing "y(t)".

A. Calculate the autocovariznces $E[y(t)y(t-\tau)]$ for all integer values of τ.

B. Calculate the Wold decomposition of $\{y(t): -\infty < t < +\infty\}$. In other words, find a representation of the form:

$$y(t) = \sum_{j=0}^{\infty} \alpha_j w(t-j)$$

where $y(t)-P[y(t)|\ (t-1)] = \alpha_0 w(t)$ and $E[w(t)^2] = 1$. [Hint: First show that $P[y(t)|\ (t-2)] = 0$. Second show that $\alpha_j = 0$ for $j \geq 2$. Third express $E[y(t)^2]$ and $E[y(t)y(t-1)]$ in terms of α_0 and α_1. Fourth equate these expressions to the corresponding numbers calculated in part A. Finally, solve these two equations for α_0 and α_1. In this last step there will be multiple solutions. Find a solution such that w(t) is in H(t).]

C. Does $H^{*}(t)$ contain H(t)? Does H(t) contain $H^{*}(t)$?

PRINCETON UNIVERSITY
Department of Economics

General Examination for the Degree of Doctor of Philosophy

Econometrics General Examination

Time: 3 hours May 19, 1993

Do not write your name on any of your examination papers, but identify them with a Code Number which you have obtained from Mrs. Alito.

Start a new paper or book for each question so that the examination can be assembled by question rather than by candidate. Be sure that your Code Number appears on each sheet or book.

Part I

Question 1

Define and briefly discuss SIX of the following eight concepts (30 minutes).

- Stochastic equicontinuity
- Vector error correction models
- Quantile restrictions
- Mixing conditions
- Regular estimator
- Roots local to unity
- Latent variable models
- Chain rule of forecasting

Part II

Answer TWO of the following three questions (30 minutes each).

Question 2

For the simple linear model

$$y_t = \beta_0 x_t + u_t , \qquad t = 1, \ldots, T,$$

suppose you wish to test the null hypothesis H_0: $E(x_t u_t) = 0$, under the maintained hypothesis $E(z_t u_t) = 0$, where y_t, x_t, and z_t are scalar observable random variables and β_0 is an unobservable coefficient. To simplify calculations, assume that all variables have mean zero ($E(x_t) = E(z_t) = E(u_t) = 0$), and that, under the null hypothesis, the errors are homoskedastic ($E(u_t^2 | x_t, z_t) = \sigma_u^2$).

Consider the following two approaches for testing this hypothesis:

(i) Estimate β_0 by the IV estimator $\tilde{\beta} = (z'y)/(z'x)$, where x, y, and z are T-dimensional vectors of observed variables. Then, using the residual vector $\tilde{u} = y - \tilde{\beta}x$, check whether the sample covariance of x and $\tilde{u}$ is significantly different from zero using $S_1 = (x'\tilde{u})/\sqrt{T}$.

(ii) Check whether the IV estimator $\tilde{\beta}$ is significantly different from the least squares estimator $\hat{\beta} = (x'y)/(x'x)$, using $S_2 = \sqrt{T}\,(\hat{\beta} - \tilde{\beta})$.

For either of these two approaches, a consistent estimator of the unknown variance σ_u^2 is given by $s_u^2 = (\tilde{u}'\tilde{u})/T$.

A. Show that the ratio of S_1 to S_2 does not depend upon the dependent variable y_t, and that (suitably normalized) test statistics for each of these approaches are algebraically identical.

B. Derive the limiting distribution of this (suitably normalized) test statistic under the sequence of local alternative hypotheses $H_{A,T}$: $u_t = x_t(\delta_0/\sqrt{T}) + v_t$, where δ_0 is an arbitrary scalar and v_t is independent of x_t.

Question 3

Consider the nonparametric regression model

$$y_t = g(x_t) + u_t, \quad t = 1, \ldots, T,$$

where y_t and x_t are jointly continuously distributed with finite variances, joint density function $f_{y,x}(y, x)$, marginals $f_y(y)$ and $f_x(x)$, and with $E[u_t|x_t] = 0$ (i.e., $g(x_t) = E[y_t|x_t]$) and $E[u_t^2|x_t] = \sigma^2$. Furthermore, f_x and g_x are Lipschitz continuous, i.e., $|f_x(a)-f_x(b)| \le f_0|a-b|$ and $|g(a)-g(b)| \le g_0|a-b|$ for some f_0 and g_0. An estimator for the value of $g(x)$ at a fixed point $x = x_0$ is the uniform kernel estimator

$$\hat{g}(x_0) = \left[\frac{1}{T}\sum_{t=1}^{T} w_{tn}y_t\right] \cdot \left[\frac{1}{T}\sum_{t=1}^{T} w_{tn}\right]^{-1}, \text{ where}$$

$$w_{tn} = (h_T)^{-1} \cdot 1(|x_t - x_0| \le h_T/2),$$

and h_T is a nonrandom bandwidth sequence.

Suppose u_t and x_s are independent for all t and s, x_t is i.i.d., $f_x(x_0) > 0$, and u_t is weakly stationary with autocovariance sequence $\gamma_u(s) = Cov(y_t, y_{t-s})$ that is absolutely summable, i.e.,

$$\sum_{s=0}^{\infty} |\gamma(s)| < \infty.$$

Find conditions on the bandwidth sequence h_T under which $\hat{g}(x_0)$ is (weakly) consistent. Try to make your assumptions as weak (general) as possible.

Question 4

It has sometimes been argued by time series analysts that the nature of the relationship between two series is best evaluated by differencing to achieve stationarity, and then examining the sample cross-correlation function. Discuss the usefulness of this approach by considering the following common trend model:

$$\begin{bmatrix} y_{1t} \\ y_{2t} \end{bmatrix} = \begin{bmatrix} 1 \\ \theta \end{bmatrix}\mu_t + \begin{bmatrix} 0 \\ \bar{\mu} \end{bmatrix} + \begin{bmatrix} \varepsilon_{1t} \\ \varepsilon_{2t} \end{bmatrix}, \qquad Var(\varepsilon_t) = \Sigma_\varepsilon$$

$$\mu_t = \mu_{t-1} + \beta + \eta_t, \qquad Var(\eta_t) = \sigma_\eta^2$$

where the irregular components $\varepsilon_t = (\varepsilon_{1t}, \varepsilon_{2t})$ are mutually uncorrelated and their variances are much greater than the variance of the disturbance driving the common trend (η_t).

Part III

Answer TWO of the following three questions (45 minutes each).

Question 5

Consider the model $y_t = \begin{cases} \alpha + \beta y_{t-1} + \varepsilon_t, & 1(z_t = 1) \\ \gamma + \beta y_{t-1} + \varepsilon_t, & 1(z_t = 0) \end{cases}$,

where z_t is a Bernoulli random variable [takes on the value 1 with probability p and 0 with probability (1-p)] and $1(\cdot)$ is the indicator function (takes on the value 1 when its argument is true). In addition, ε_t is i.i.d. $N(0,\sigma^2)$. Assume z_t is unobserved.

a) (5 minutes) Under what conditions is y_t stationary?

b) (8 minutes) Calculate the mean and variance of y_t under the assumptions you defined in a).

c) (11 minutes) Under the assumptions you made above, suggest a method of estimating the parameters in the model and derive the joint asymptotic distribution of $(\hat{\alpha}, \hat{\beta}, \hat{\gamma})$.

d) (8 minutes) For what true values of p are the parameters σ^2, α, β, γ identified? If p were unknown but equal to one of these values, could you also identify it? [HINT: can you use the moments of the residuals to identify the parameters?].

e) (8 minutes) Suppose you wanted to test the persistence of shocks in this model (that is, $\beta=1$). Propose such a test. What is its asymptotic distribution under the null of no permanent effects? Under the alternative?

f) (5 minutes) Suppose the model above were true but we were to estimate

$$y_t = \delta + \theta t + \beta y_{t-1} + v_t$$

instead (t is the usual time trend). What would be the properties of the estimated residuals?

Question 6

For each of the following three questions, give a derivation of the desired result, implicitly assuming existence of any derivatives or bounded moments needed. You need not rigorously check regularity conditions for the limit theorems you use, but you should keep track of any remainder terms and explicitly state why they are negligible.

A. Prove the "one-step" theorem. That is, suppose a (consistent) estimator $\hat{\theta}$ of a parameter θ_0 uniquely solves a set of estimating equations $T_n(\hat{\theta}, \omega) = 0$, where the Hessian matrix $\partial T_n(\theta, \omega)/\partial\theta'$ converges continuously to some square matrix $H(\theta)$ which is nonsingular at $\theta = \theta_0$ and $\sqrt{n}\ T_n(\theta_0, \omega) \xrightarrow{d} \mathcal{N}(0, V_0)$ for some V_0. Let $\tilde{\theta}$ be some other root-n-consistent estimator of θ_0, and define a one-step estimator of θ_0 as

$$\hat{\theta}_{os} = \tilde{\theta} - \left[\partial T_n(\tilde{\theta}, \omega)/\partial\theta'\right]^{-1} \cdot T_n(\tilde{\theta}, \omega).$$

Show that $\sqrt{n}(\hat{\theta} - \hat{\theta}_{os}) = o_p(1)$.

B. Suppose $\hat{\theta}$ is an efficient estimator of a (scalar) parameter θ_0 in a linear class $\mathfrak{C}$ of root-n-consistent, asymptotically normal estimators. (Linearity here means that if $\tilde{\theta}_1$ and $\tilde{\theta}_2$ are in $\mathfrak{C}$, then $a \cdot \tilde{\theta}_1 + (1 - a) \cdot \tilde{\theta}_2$ is in $\mathfrak{C}$ for any real number a). Show that, for any $\tilde{\theta}$ in $\mathfrak{C}$, $AV(\tilde{\theta} - \hat{\theta}) = AV(\tilde{\theta}) - AV(\hat{\theta})$, where "AV" denotes asymptotic variance.

C. Let $\mathcal{L}_n(\theta) = n^{-1} \sum_i \ln f(z_i | \theta)$ be the log-likelihood for an i.i.d. sample of observations on z_i with density $f(z | \theta_0)$, and the (unrestricted) maximum likelihood estimator be $\hat{\theta}_U$. Under the null hypothesis that $g(\theta_0) = 0$ (where $g: R^p \to R^q$, for $q \leq p = \dim(\theta)$), denote the restricted MLE by $\hat{\theta}_R$. The likelihood ratio test statistic is of the form

$$LR = 2n \cdot [\mathcal{L}_n(\hat{\theta}_U) - \mathcal{L}_n(\hat{\theta}_R)].$$

Derive the asymptotic distribution of LR under the null hypothesis $g(\theta_0) = 0$. You may use the fact that the unrestricted and restricted MLEs satisfy the relation

$$\hat{\theta}_R = \hat{\theta}_U + \mathcal{I}_0^{-1} G_0' \cdot \hat{\lambda} + o_p(1/\sqrt{n}),$$

where $\mathcal{I}_0$ is Fisher's information matrix, $G_0 = \partial g(\theta_0)/\partial\theta'$, and the q-vector $\hat{\lambda}$ of Lagrange multipliers for the restricted MLE has

$$\sqrt{n}\ \hat{\lambda} \xrightarrow{d} \mathcal{N}(0, [G_0 \mathcal{I}_0^{-1} G_0']^{-1}).$$

Question 7

You wish to decompose quarterly data on log real GNP (y_t) into three components, trendcycle x_t, seasonal s_t, and irregular r_t, as follows:

(1) $$y_t = x_t + s_t + r_t \qquad (r_t \text{ i.i.d.}).$$

You assume that x_t follows a second-order autoregressive process

(2) $$x_t = a_1 x_{t-1} + a_2 x_{t-2} + a_0 + \varepsilon_{1t} \qquad (\varepsilon_{1t} \text{ i.i.d.}),$$

and that the seasonal component s_t follows

(3) $$s_t = s_{t-4} + \varepsilon_{2t} \qquad (\varepsilon_{2t} \text{ i.i.d.}).$$

a. (8 minutes) Write the above model in state-space form with a dynamic equation

(4) $$\alpha_t = T\alpha_{t-1} + \eta_t$$

and an observation equation

(5) $$y_t = Z\alpha_t + \xi_t$$

by specifying the vector α_t, the matrices T and Z, and the random errors η_t and ξ_t in the present context.

b. (18 minutes) Defining $a_{t|s} = E_s\alpha_t$, $a_{t|t} = a_t$ and $P_{t|s} = E_s[(\alpha_s - a_t)(\alpha_s - a_t)']$, where E_s denotes conditional expectation given information available at time s,

(i) express $a_{t|t-1}$ as a function of a_{t-1} and $P_{t|t-1}$ as a function of P_{t-1};

(ii) express a_t as a function of $a_{t|t-1}$ and P_t as a function of $P_{t|t-1}$.

Relax. You might not be able to derive the equations in part (ii) completely. Spend up to 14 minutes to explain a derivation using the regression of α_t on y_t given information at t-1. Start with the coefficient matrix of this regression.

c. (8 minutes) Assuming that you are given the formulas in part b., how can you use them to solve the decomposition problem given by equation (1)? How are these formulas different from the "smoothing" formulas? Define the "smoothing" formulas and explain how they can be used for the above decomposition.

d. (10 minutes) If you did not know the coefficients a_0, a_1, and a_2 and the other parameters of the model in part a., explain how you can estimate these parameters. State your method of estimation and the main computational steps.

PRINCETON UNIVERSITY
Department of Economics

General Examination for the Degree of Doctor of Philosophy

Econometrics General Examination

Time: 3 hours October 13, 1992

Do not write your name on any of your examination papers, but identify them with a Code Number which you have obtained from Mrs. Alito.

Start a new paper or book for each question so that the examination can be assembled by question rather than by candidate. Be sure that your Code Number appears on each sheet or book.

Part I

Question 1

Define and briefly discuss SIX of the following eight concepts (30 minutes).

- Specification tests
- ARCH models and their relatives
- Covariance matrix for two-step estimators
- Brownian bridge
- The Wold decomposition
- Asymptotic distribution of U-statistics
- E-M algorithm
- Hazard function

Part II

Answer TWO of the following three questions (30 minutes each).

Question 2

Data collected on individuals in J groups are assumed to follow a linear model,

$$y_{ij} = x'_{ij}\beta_0 + u_{ij}, \qquad \text{for } i = 1, \ldots, n_j \quad \text{and} \quad j = 1, \ldots, J.$$

For each group j, a random sample of y_{ij} and x_{ij} are drawn; it is assumed that $E(u_{ij}) = 0$, $E(u_{ij})^2 = \sigma^2$, $E(x_{ij}) = \mu_j$, $E(x_{ij} \cdot x'_{ij}) = D_j$, and that x_{ij} is independent of u_{ij} for all i and j. Also, it is assumed that third moments of all variables exist and are bounded above.

Suppose now that only average values of the dependent variable and regressors are available for each group, i.e., only

$$\bar{y}_j = \frac{1}{n_j}\sum_{i=1}^{n_j} y_{ij} \quad \text{and} \quad \bar{x}_j = \frac{1}{n_j}\sum_{i=1}^{n_j} x_{ij}$$

are observed for $j = 1, \ldots, J$. The number of groups J is fixed, and $J \geq K$, i.e., there are at least as many groups as unknown regression coefficients.

(a) Let $n \equiv \min(n_1, \ldots, n_J)$. Under what conditions will the classical least squares estimator $\hat{\beta}$ obtained using the grouped data $\{(\bar{y}_j, \bar{x}_j), j = 1, \ldots, J\}$ be consistent for β_0 as $n \to \infty$?

(b) For the same LS estimator calculate the limiting distribution of $\sqrt{n}(\hat{\beta} - \beta_0)$ as $n \to \infty$ in terms of the unknown parameters and $w_j \equiv \lim n_j/n$, assuming $w_j < \infty$ for all j.

(c) Is it possible to consistently estimate the asymptotic covariance matrix of the LS estimator $\hat{\beta}$ using the $\{\bar{x}_j\}$ and the residuals $\{\hat{u}_j \equiv \bar{y}_j - \bar{x}_j\beta_0\}$ if $n \to \infty$ for J fixed? If so, how? If not, why not?

Question 3

Let $X_1, X_2, \ldots, X_N$ be a random sample from a population with density function

$$F(x) = \frac{2}{\Gamma(1/4)} \exp\{-(x - \mu)^4\},$$

where μ is an unknown parameter and $\Gamma(\cdot)$ denotes the gamma function. It can be shown that, for this distribution,

$$E[(X - \mu)^k] = 1\{k \text{ is even}\} \cdot \Gamma((k+1)/4)/\Gamma(1/4)$$

Let

$$\hat{\mu}_1 = \hat{\mu}_{MLE},$$

$$\hat{\mu}_2 = \bar{X},$$

$$\hat{\mu}_3 = \left[\frac{1}{N} \sum_{i=1}^{N} (X_i^2 - 1/4) \right]^{1/2}. \qquad \text{[NOTE: } \Gamma(3/4)/\Gamma(1/4) = 1/4.]$$

(a) Find the asymptotic distribution of $\hat{\mu}_1$, the maximum likelihood estimator of μ.

(b) Determine the asymptotic distribution of $\hat{\mu}_2$.

(c) Show that if $\mu \neq 0$,

$$\Pr\left\{ \frac{1}{N} \sum_{i=1}^{N} (X_i^2 - 1/4) < 0 \right\} \to 0 \quad \text{as} \quad N \to \infty.$$

(d) Assume that $\mu \neq 0$. Find the asymptotic distribution of $\hat{\mu}_3$. [Note that (c) guarantees that this estimator is well-defined with probability approaching one as the sample size increases.]

Question 4

A. Suppose that $X_t = .9X_{t-1} - .2X_{t-2} + \varepsilon_t$, where ε_t is a white noise process and $V(\varepsilon_t) = 1$.

(a) What is the best forecast of X_{t+3} at time t?

(b) What is the moving average representation of X_t?

(c) What are the autocovariances of X_t?

B. A random variable x_t is said to be bounded in probability if there exists some $M < \infty$ such that $\Pr(|X_t| < M) = 1$ for all t. A filter a(L) is said to be stable if, for x_t bounded in probability, $y_t = a(L)x_t$ is bounded in probability. Show that an absolutely summable (i.e. 0-summable) filter is stable.

Part III

Answer TWO of the following three questions (45 minutes each).

Question 5

Suppose $\begin{pmatrix} y_t \\ x_t \end{pmatrix} = C(L)w_t$, where $\{w_t: -\infty < t < +\infty\}$ is a second moment stationary bivariate process, satisfying:

$$E(w_t) = 0 \qquad E(w_t w_t') = I$$

and $$E(w_t w_{t-\tau}') = 0, \text{ for } \tau \neq 0.$$

In addition

$$(*)\ C(z) = \sum_{j=0}^{\infty} c_j z^j \qquad \text{where } \sum_{j=0}^{\infty} |c_j|^2 < +\infty.$$

Suppose that the power series in (*) converges for $|z| < \rho$, where $\rho > 1$, and

$$\det[C(z)] \neq 0 \qquad \text{for } |z| < \rho.$$

Finally, suppose that

$$C(z) = \begin{bmatrix} C_{11}(z) & C_{12}(z) \\ 0 & C_{22}(z) \end{bmatrix}.$$

(a) Find an expression for $B(z)$, where $P[y_t | x_t, x_{t-1}, \ldots] = B(L)x_t$.

(b) Is it true that $P[y_t | x_t, x_{t-1}, x_{t+1}, \ldots] = P[y_t | x_t, x_{t-1}, \ldots]$?
Why or why not?

(c) Is it true that

$$P[x_t |\ x_t, x_{t-1}, y_{t-1}, x_{t-2}, y_{t-2}\ \ldots] = P[x_t |\ x_{t-1}, x_{t-2}, \ldots]?$$

Why or why not?

(d) Let

$$S(\theta) = \begin{bmatrix} S_{11}(\theta) & S_{12}(\theta) \\ S_{21}(\theta) & S_{22}(\theta) \end{bmatrix}$$

denote the spectral density matrix for the composite process $\{(x_t, y_t): -\infty < t < +\infty\}$ at frequency θ. Show that

$$B[\exp(-i\theta)] = S_{12}(\theta)/S_{22}(\theta).$$

[Hint: Recall that $S(\theta) = C[\exp(-i\theta)]C[\exp(-i\theta)]'$.]

Question 6

An economist estimates a production function of the form

$$y_i = \alpha_0 \cdot (x_i)^{\lambda_0} + \beta_0 \cdot (z_i)^{\lambda_0} + u_i$$

where it is assumed that u_i is i.i.d. with $E[u_i | x_i, z_i] = 0$ and $E[u_i^2 | x_i, z_i] = \sigma^2$ (the "input" random variables x_i and z_i are positive random variables that are also i.i.d. and have bounded support). Knowing *a priori* that the true $\lambda_0 \in (\varepsilon_0, 1/\varepsilon_0)$ for a known $\varepsilon_0 \in (0, 1)$, the economist fits the model as follows:

(i) Given a fixed value of λ in the parameter space, $\hat{\alpha} \equiv \hat{\alpha}(\lambda)$ and $\hat{\beta} \equiv \hat{\beta}(\lambda)$ are obtained by regressing y_i on $(x_i)^\lambda$ and $(z_i)^\lambda$ using a least squares program, with $\hat{\sigma}^2 \equiv \hat{\sigma}^2(\lambda)$ obtained from the sum of squared residuals (divided by n);

(ii) The parameter λ_0 is then estimated by that value $\hat{\lambda}$ that minimizes $\hat{\sigma}^2(\lambda)$ over the parameter space (though this was done by a grid search, you may assume the true minimizer of $\hat{\sigma}^2$ was obtained), and the corresponding estimators $\hat{\alpha}(\hat{\lambda})$ and $\hat{\beta}(\hat{\lambda})$ were reported.

The economist makes three claims about this procedure:

(a) The resulting estimators of α_0, β_0, and λ_0 are consistent and asymptotically normal;

(b) The estimators are asymptotically efficient if $\{u_i\}$ are normally distributed; and

(c) The estimated covariance matrix for $\hat{\alpha}$ and $\hat{\beta}$ taken from the program which computes the least squares regression of y_i on $(x_i)^\lambda$ and $(z_i)^\lambda$ for $\lambda = \hat{\lambda}$ is appropriate for large-sample inference on α_0 and β_0.

Determine whether each of these claims is correct or incorrect, giving a brief argument when the claim is true and, for any claim that is untrue, an appropriate modification of the approach which is correct.

Question 7

Suppose an economic model yields a conditional moment condition of the form

$$E_{t-2}[r(z_t, \theta_o)] = 0,$$

where θ_o is a p-dimensional vector of unknown parameters, z_t is a strictly stationary random vector, and $r(z_t, \theta)$ is a continuous function of θ. From this conditional moment restriction you obtain the unconditional moment restrictions

$$E[m_t(\theta_o)] \equiv E[w_{t-2} \cdot r(z_t, \theta_o)] = 0,$$

where w_{t-2} is an r-dimensional vector of random variables dated t-2 or earlier ($r > p$). Assuming $m_t(\theta)$ is twice continuously differentiable in θ and that it has uniformly bounded third moments (as do its derivatives), you estimate θ_o by minimizing the GMM criterion function

$$S_T(\theta) \equiv [\bar{m}_T(\theta)]' \hat{A}_T [\bar{m}_T(\theta)],$$

where $\bar{m}_T(\theta)$ is the sample average of the moment functions

$$\bar{m}_T(\theta) = \frac{1}{T} \sum_{t=1}^{T} m_t(\theta) ,$$

and $\hat{A}_T$ is an $r \times r$ positive definite matrix which converges in probability to some positive definite matrix A_o.

Derive the asymptotic distribution of the GMM estimator which minimizes $S_T(\theta)$ over the (compact) parameter space Θ, and find the matrix A_o which will yield the most efficient GMM estimator based on the given (unconditional) moment restrictions. Also, give a consistent estimator of the optimal weighting matrix A_o. You need not rigorously verify the regularity conditions for the limit theorems you use, but you should derive the results algebraically rather than citing results in the literature. Be sure to account for the fact that the moment functions $m_t(\theta)$ will generally not be serially independent, but simplify your results as much as possible.

PRINCETON UNIVERSITY
Department of Economics

General Examination for the Degree of Doctor of Philosophy

Econometrics General Examination

Time: 3 hours May 20, 1992

Do not write your name on any of your examination papers, but identify them with a Code Number which you have obtained from Mrs. Alito.

Start a new paper or book for each question so that the examination can be assembled by question rather than by candidate. Be sure that your Code Number appears on each sheet or book.

Part I

Question 1

Define and briefly discuss six of the following eight concepts (30 minutes).

- Hilbert space
- Continuous convergence
- Ordered vs. multinomial response
- Autocovariance generating function
- Heteroskedasticity and autocorrelation consistent covariance matrix estimation
- Ergodicity
- Selectivity bias
- Generalized information equality

Part II

Answer TWO of the following three questions (30 minutes each).

Question 2

Suppose $X_i = \theta + U_i$, where $E(U_i) = 0$ and

$$E(U_iU_j) = \begin{cases} 1 & \text{for} \quad i=j \\ \gamma & \text{for} \quad i \neq j \end{cases},$$

with $i,j = 1, \ldots, n$. Let $\bar{X} = (X_1 + \ldots X_n)/n$. Is $\bar{X}$ the minimum variance linear unbiased estimator of θ? Explain your answer.

Question 3

For the simple linear model (with no intercept)

$$y_i = \beta \cdot x_i + \varepsilon_i,$$

suppose you know that two moment conditions hold, namely, $E[x_i \cdot \varepsilon_i] = 0$ and $E[z_i \cdot \varepsilon_i] = 0$, for some observable instrumental variable z_i.

(a) If z_i and x_i have $E[z_i \cdot x_i] = 0$, but the conditional variance of ε_i depends on both z_i and x_i, will a GMM estimator of β using both z_i and x_i will be more efficient (in large samples) than the least squares estimator $b = x'y/x'x$? Show why or why not.

(b) Repeat the same exercise, now assuming in addition that the error terms are conditionally homoskedastic, i.e., $E[\varepsilon_i^2 | z_i, x_i] = E[\varepsilon_i^2] = \sigma^2$.

Question 4

Suppose a bivariate VAR(1) model is written as

$$\begin{pmatrix} y_t \\ x_t \end{pmatrix} = \begin{pmatrix} \phi_{11} & \phi_{12} \\ \phi_{21} & \phi_{22} \end{pmatrix} \begin{pmatrix} y_{t-1} \\ x_{t-1} \end{pmatrix} + \begin{pmatrix} \varepsilon_t \\ \eta_t \end{pmatrix},$$

where (ε_t, η_t) is a bivariate white noise process.

A. Assuming $E[\varepsilon_t \eta_t] = 0$ and $\phi_{21} = 0$, determine the order and derive the algebraic form of the univariate ARMA representation for y_t ("solving out" for x_t). Also, give a necessary and sufficient condition of the parameters of this process for y_t and x_t to be weakly stationary.

B. Given the usual (sample average) estimators $\hat{\Gamma}(s)$ of the autocovariance matrices

$$\Gamma(s) \equiv \begin{pmatrix} \gamma_{yy}(s) & \gamma_{yx}(s) \\ \gamma_{xy}(s) & \gamma_{xx}(s) \end{pmatrix} \equiv E \begin{pmatrix} y_t y_{t-s} & y_t x_{t-s} \\ x_t y_{t-s} & x_t x_{t-s} \end{pmatrix}$$

for s = 1 and 2, derive an expression for initial estimates of the ARMA coefficients for y_t (expressed in terms of the $\hat{\gamma}$'s) under the assumptions in part A. above. If the error terms are i.i.d. and normal, will these initial estimates be asymptotically efficient? Why or why not?

Part III

Answer TWO of the following four questions (45 minutes each).

Question 5

Consider a random sample $\{z_i, i = 1,\ldots,n\}$ from a population with known density function $f(z, \theta_o)$, where θ_o is an unknown k-dimensional vector assumed interior to some compact parameter space Θ. However, suppose that for each sample size n the true value of θ_o was treated as a random variable $\tilde{\theta}$ drawn from a prior distribution with density function $\pi_n(\theta)$. The posterior density of $\tilde{\theta}$ given the data $\{z_i\}$ is then proportional to the product of the prior density and the individual density functions, i.e., the posterior density takes the form

$$p_n(\theta|z_1,\ldots,z_n) \propto \pi_n(\theta)\cdot f(z_1, \theta)\cdot f(z_2, \theta)\cdots f(z_n, \theta).$$

One Bayesian approach to point estimation would pick the "estimator" $\hat{\theta}$ as the value that maximizes the posterior density function (or its logarithm) over the parameter space (this estimator is called the Bayesian posterior mode).

Now suppose the prior density for $\tilde{\theta}$ is normal with mean θ_n and covariance matrix $\sigma_n^2\cdot I$, i.e., the prior density is proportional to $(\sigma_n)^k\cdot\exp(-(\theta - \theta_n)'(\theta - \theta_n)/2\sigma_n^2)$; though the true value of $\tilde{\theta}$ is fixed at θ_o in the population, the prior distributions have a mean value θ_n which may or may not vary with the sample size n, as well as a (possibly) shifting scaling factor σ_n.

Under each of the following two sequences of prior densities, demonstrate the consistency of the Bayesian posterior mode $\hat{\theta}$ for the true value θ_o, and determine the asymptotic distribution of the estimator:

(i) $\theta_n = \theta_o + \delta_o$ and $\sigma_n = \sigma_o$, with δ_o and σ_o fixed;

(i) $\theta_n = \theta_o + \delta_o/\sqrt{n}$ and $\sigma_n = \sigma_o/\sqrt{n}$, again with δ_o and σ_o fixed.

You may presume (without proof) that the density function $f(z, \theta)$ satisfies sufficient smoothness and moment-dominance conditions for uniform convergence of the appropriate sample averages. [Please don't give a long list of regularity conditions; just do the calculations to show the limiting objective functions are uniquely maximized at the true value and to derive the form of the asymptotic distributions.]

Question 6

Define the average propensity to consume (APC) as the ratio of average consumption ($\bar{C}$) to average income ($\bar{Y}$), and the marginal propensity to consume as the OLS slope coefficient obtained by regressing C_t against a constant and Y_t:

(1) MPC: $$\hat{\beta} = \sum_{t=1}^{T} (C_t-\bar{C})(Y_t-\bar{Y}) \Big/ \sum_{t=1}^{T} (Y_t-\bar{Y})^2.$$

A puzzle which has often attracted economist's attention is the empirical finding that the estimated MPC appears smaller than the estimated APC. Friedman's explanation was that current income measures permanent income (Y_t^P) with error, and that "true" consumption is a linear function of Y_t^P, i.e. (assuming a zero intercept for simplicity):

(2) $$Y_t = Y_t^P + \eta_{yt},$$

(3) $$C_t = \beta Y_t^P + \eta_{ct},$$

where η_{yt} and η_{ct} are transitory income and consumption, respectively. Suppose also that η_{yt} and η_{ct} are uncorrelated with Y_t^P and with each other; neither η_{yt} nor η_{ct} are assumed to be serially uncorrelated, but they are both assumed to be stationary.

a) Assuming that Y_t^P is a covariance-stationary process, show that APC is consistent for β, but that $\hat{\beta}$ (MPC) is inconsistent and has a limit less than β.

b) Suppose now that Y_t has a time series representation with a unit root (as has often been claimed) and that η_{yt} and η_{ct} are stationary processes. Show that $\hat{\beta}$ (MPC) is then consistent for β.

c) In light of the framework described in (b), what time series interpretation can you give to the parameter β? Can this help you give an alternative explanation for the empirical puzzle? (Hint: think in terms of the properties of the asymptotic distribution of $\hat{\beta}$ in (b)).

d) Discuss several estimators of the parameter β in (3) that would have better asymptotic properties, in general, than $\hat{\beta}$ as defined in (1). In what special case would $\hat{\beta}$ in (1) be optimal for β in (3)?

Question 7

Suppose you are interested in the effects of individual-specific explanatory variables on the duration of individual unemployment. You are given a random sample of observations on the duration of unemployment spells, y_i, which you will use as the dependent variable in your analysis. Also, for each observation, you are given a vector of explanatory variables, x_i, which do not vary during the duration of the unemployment spell (x_i includes sociodemographic indicator variables, education level and work experience at the beginning of the unemployment spell, etc.).

Two additional features of the sample must be taken into consideration. First, there are two ways unemployment spells can end: either the individual finds a new job (which includes being rehired by her former employer), or the individual leaves the labor market. The data include an indicator variable d_i, which takes the value 1 if the individual finds a job and 0 if she leaves the labor market.

Second, the dependent variable is only measured in monthly intervals, i.e., $y_i = 1$ if unemployment lasted less than (or equal to) one month, $y_i = 2$ if unemployment lasted between one and two months, etc. Hence, there is a difference between the "true" unemployment duration (which is a continuous random variable) and the observed "grouped" dependent variable.

Propose a model for the analysis of these data, and discuss how you would estimate the parameters of interest. Be as specific as possible about the algebraic form of the model and the assumptions you make on any error terms. Be sure your analysis accounts for the discreteness of the dependent variable and the two distinct sources of exit from unemployment.

Question 8

Consider the time series model

(1) $$y_t = \alpha y_{t-1} + u_t,$$

(2) $$u_t = \beta u_{t-1} + e_t + \theta e_{t-1},$$

where $|\beta| < 1$, $|\theta| < 1$, and $e_t \sim$ i.i.d. $(0, \sigma^2)$.

(i) Derive the autocovariance function of the sequence $\{u_t\}$.

(ii) What is the spectral density function of $\{u_t\}$?

(iii) Suppose $\{y_t\}$ is generated by (1) and (2) with $\alpha = 1$. What is the limiting distribution of the least-squares estimator of δ in the following regression:

(3) $$y_t = \mu + \delta y_{t-1} + v_t \text{ ?}$$

(Note: you may use limiting results about weak convergence of partial sums of the data, e.g., $\sum y_{t-1}^2$, properly normalized. You need not derive these results from first principles. However, makes sure to make explicit the dependence of the limiting distribution on the nuisance parameters β, θ, and σ^2.)

(iv) How is the result in (iii) changed if additional deterministic components are included in the regression (3)?

(v) Discuss several possible ways to construct consistent (against $|\alpha| \neq 1$) tests of the hypothesis $\alpha = 1$ that are asymptotically valid (i.e., invariant to the nuisance parameters under the null hypothesis).

PRINCETON UNIVERSITY
Department of Economics

General Examination for the Degree of Doctor of Philosophy

Econometrics General Examination

Time: 3 hours

October 14, 1991

Do not write your name on any of your examination papers, but identify them with a Code Number which you have obtained from Mrs. Alito.

Start a new paper or book for each question so that the examination can be assembled by question rather than by candidate. Be sure that your Code Number appears on each sheet or book.

Part I

Question 1

Define and briefly discuss FIVE of the following seven concepts (30 minutes).

- The Wald test statistic
- Generalized method of moments
- Identification of structural VAR models
- Local power (Pitman drift)
- Beveridge-Nelson decomposition
- Convergence in distribution
- Near-integrated process.

Part II

Answer TWO of the following three questions (30 minutes each).

Question 2

In a certain population, $y = \alpha + \beta z + u$ and $x = z + v$, where z, u, and v are (unobserved) independent random variables, with $E(z) = \mu$, $E(u) = 0 = E(v)$.

In random sampling from that population, only x and y are observed. Let $\hat{y} = a + bx$ and $\hat{x} = c + dy$ denote the sample least-squares linear regression of y on x, and of x on y, respectively. Show that $\text{plim } b \le \beta \le \text{plim } (1/d)$. Also, develop the extension of that result to a multiple regression case, where $y = \alpha + \beta_1 z + \beta_2 x_2 + \dots + \beta_k x_k + u$ and $x_1 = z + v$, with $y, x_1, x_2, \dots, x_k$ being the observables.

Question 3

For the classical linear model

$$y = X\beta + \varepsilon$$

under the restrictions $E(\varepsilon) = 0$ and $E[\varepsilon\varepsilon'] = \sigma^2 I$ (with nonrandom X having rank $k = \dim(\beta)$), suppose you believe a set of linear restrictions $H\beta = \theta$ hold, where H is an $r \times k$ matrix of rank $r \le k$ and θ is an r-vector of known constants.

A. Let $\hat{\beta}$ be the classical (unconstrained) least squares estimator and $\tilde{\beta}$ denote the constrained least squares estimator, which minimizes the squared length of $y - Xc$ (over c) subject to the restrictions $Hc = \theta$. Show that $\tilde{\beta}$ can be written as

$$\tilde{\beta} = \hat{\beta} - (X'X)^{-1}H'[H(X'X)^{-1}H']^{-1}(H\hat{\beta} - \theta).$$

B. Suppose you are given the following classical least squares estimates and the usual estimate of the covariance matrix:

$$\hat{\beta} = \begin{bmatrix} 0.3 \\ -0.3 \end{bmatrix}, \qquad \hat{V}(\hat{\beta}) = \begin{bmatrix} 0.4 & -0.1 \\ -0.1 & 0.05 \end{bmatrix}.$$

Use these estimates to obtain a constrained estimate of β_2 subject to the restriction $\beta_1 + \beta_2 = 1$.

C. For the general estimator $\tilde{\beta}$ of part A., show that it is unbiased (provided the restrictions $H\beta = \theta$ are correct) and derive an expression for its (singular) covariance matrix.

D. Use the estimates given in part B. to derive an estimate of the covariance matrix of the constrained least squares estimate. Which of the two coefficients, β_1 or β_2, gains the most (in terms of precision of its estimate) by imposing the constraint $\beta_1 + \beta_2 = 1$?

Question 4

Consider the following two stochastic equations:

$$y_i = \beta_0 \cdot x_i + u_i \qquad \text{and}$$

$$x_i = z_i'\alpha_0 + v_i, \qquad i=1,\ldots,n,$$

where the scalar β_0 and the p-dimensional vector α_0 are unknown parameters, y_i, x_i, and z_i are observable, u_i and v_i are unobservable, and the observations are i.i.d. with $E(u_i \cdot z_i) = E(v_i \cdot z_i) = 0$ for all i, and with $E[z_i z_i'] \equiv A$, $E[u_i^2 z_i z_i'] \equiv B$, $E[u_i v_i z_i z_i'] \equiv C$, and $E[v_i^2 z_i z_i'] \equiv D$, finite.

A. Let

$$\hat{\beta}_{IV} \equiv \left[\sum_{i=1}^{n} \hat{x}_i \cdot x_i \right]^{-1} \cdot \left[\sum_{i=1}^{n} \hat{x}_i y_i \right]$$

be an estimator of β_0, where $\hat{x}_i \equiv z_i'\hat{\alpha}$ for $\hat{\alpha}$ a given consistent estimator of α_0 ($\text{plim } \hat{\alpha} = \alpha_0$). Derive the asymptotic distribution of $\hat{\beta}_{IV}$ and show that it does not depend upon the asymptotic distribution of the particular estimator $\hat{\alpha}$ chosen.

B. Now consider

$$\hat{\beta}_{IV} \equiv \left[\sum_{i=1}^{n} (\hat{x}_i)^2 \right]^{-1} \cdot \left[\sum_{i=1}^{n} \hat{x}_i y_i \right]$$

as an estimator of β_0, where $\hat{x}_i$ is defined as above. Derive the asymptotic distribution of this estimator when $\hat{\alpha} = \alpha_0$ (i.e., the true value of α_0 is known).

C. For the same estimator $\hat{\beta}_{IV}$ of part B. above, derive its limiting distribution when $\hat{\alpha}$ is the least squares estimator of α_0, i.e.,

$$\hat{\alpha} \equiv \left[\sum_{i=1}^{n} z_i z_i' \right]^{-1} \cdot \left[\sum_{i=1}^{n} z_i x_i \right].$$

Part III

Answer TWO of the following four questions (45 minutes each).

Question 5

Consider the following "stochastic trend, autoregressive measurement error" model for the generation of an observable scalar time series y_t:

$$y_t = m_t + e_t,$$

$$m_t = m_{t-1} + \eta_t, \qquad \text{and}$$

$$e_t = \rho e_{t-1} + \nu_t, \qquad |\rho| \leq 1.$$

Here η_t and ν_t are mutually independent and i.i.d. scalar error terms with zero means and variances σ_η^2 and σ_ν^2, respectively.

A. Demonstrate that y_t can be written as an ARIMA(p, d, q) process for particular values of p, d, and q, and give an expression for the autocovariance function $\gamma(s)$ of the moving average part of this representation. How do your answers change for the three special cases

(i) $\rho = 0$,

(ii) $\rho = 1$, and

(iii) $\sigma_\eta^2 = 0$ with $\rho \neq 0$ and $|\rho| < 1$?

B. For each of the three special cases of part A. above (but <u>not</u> the general case), give an expression for the projection of $P[y_{T+1}|y_T, \ldots, y_0]$, the best linear prediction of y_{T+1} on the (finite) past. Your expressions should be explicit formulae involving $y_0, \ldots, y_T$, but you need not explicitly solve for any parameters of the moving average representation in terms of the σ_η^2, σ_ν^2, and ρ; that is, you can just express the moving average part in the form

$$\theta(\mathcal{L})u_t = \sum_{k=0}^{q} \theta_k u_{t-k}, \qquad \theta_0 = 1,$$

for appropriate choice of q, without figuring out what the $\{\theta_k\}$ are.

Question 6

Data on family income y_i is obtained for a random sample $i=1,\dots,n$ of households; it is assumed that income has a Pareto distribution, with density function $f(y) = 1(y > 1)\cdot\alpha_0 y^{-\alpha_0-1}$, for α_0 in the parameter space $[\varepsilon_0, 1/\varepsilon_0]$, where ε_0 is a known positive number (near zero).

Define the kth sample moment of the data as

$$Z_n(k) \equiv 1(k \neq 0)\cdot\left[\frac{1}{n}\sum_{i=1}^{n}(y_i)^k\right] + 1(k = 0)\cdot\left[\frac{1}{n}\sum_{i=1}^{n}\ln(y_i)\right]$$

for any real number k and the estimator

$$\hat{\alpha}(k) \equiv 1(k \neq 0)\cdot[k\cdot Z_n(k)/(Z_n(k) - 1)] + 1(k = 0)\cdot[1/Z_n(k)],$$

of α_0, which is well defined for any real number k. For what values of α_0 and k is $\hat{\alpha}(k)$ strongly consistent for α_0? Given consistency, when is it asymptotically normal? Efficient? What is the asymptotic covariance of $\hat{\alpha}(0)$ and $\hat{\alpha}(k)$ for $k \neq 0$ (when both are consistent)? Cite any regularity conditions you need.

Question 7

A. Determine the orders of p and q and find the coefficients of the simplest ARMA(p,q) process which will generate the following autocovariance sequence:

$$\gamma(s) = E[y_t y_{t-s}] = \begin{cases} 2 & \text{if } s=0 \\ 1.5(.5)^{s-1} & \text{if } s=1,2,\dots \end{cases}.$$

B. Suppose $\{y_t\}$ is generated by a random walk $y_t = y_{t-1} + e_t$, $e_t \sim$ i.i.d. $(0, \sigma^2)$, y_0 fixed. An investigator is interested in testing for this hypothesis and considers the least-squares regression

$$y_t = \alpha\, y_{t-1} + u_t\,.$$

However, to guard against the possibility of first-order moving average errors he/she applies an instrumental variable procedure using y_{t-2} as an instrument. Denote this estimator by $\tilde{\alpha}_{IV}$. What is the asymptotic distribution of $T(\tilde{\alpha}_{IV} - 1)$?

C. Suppose a series of quarterly data is given by the ARMA(1,1) process

$$y_t = \alpha\, y_{t-1} + e_t + \theta\, e_{t-1}\,.$$

In an attempt to investigate the long-run properties of $\{y_t\}$ and minimize short-term fluctuations, an investigator decides to smooth the data by using a moving average of the form

$$\tilde{y}_t = (y_{t-2} + y_{t-1} + y_t + y_{t+1} + y_{t+2})/5.$$

i) What is the spectral density function of $\{\tilde{y}_t\}$?

ii) Are the spectral densities at frequency zero the same for y_t and $\tilde{y}_t$?

Question 8

Suppose you are given data from the model

$$Y = X\beta + \varepsilon ,$$

where $X'X = I_K$, $\varepsilon \sim N(0, \sigma^2 I)$, σ^2 known, and where Y is of length N. Let $\gamma > 0$ be some parameter. Let $\rho = \gamma/(1 + \gamma)$ and let $a = K + 2$.

(a) Give a formula for the MLE $\hat{\beta}$. Write down the distribution for $\hat{\beta}$ given β.

(b) Suppose you are a Bayesian with a prior given by $\beta \sim N(0, \sigma^2\gamma^{-1}I)$. Find the resulting unconditional prior distribution for $\hat{\beta}$.

(c) Using your result from (b) and the fact that $E[s^{-2}] = a$ if $s^2 \sim \chi^2_K$, show that

$$\rho = E\left[\frac{(K - 2)\sigma^2}{\hat{\beta}'\hat{\beta}}\right],$$

where the expectation is taken with respect to the prior distribution.

(d) After having seen the data, describe the posterior distribution for β. Let β^* be the Bayes estimator defined as the mean of the posterior. Show that β^* can be written as

$$\beta^* = (1 - \rho)\,\hat{\beta} .$$

(e) Suppose you are an "empirical Bayesian" in the sense that you are estimating γ or, alternatively, ρ, from the data. Thus, consider the estimator

$$\tilde{\rho} = \frac{(K - 2)\sigma^2}{\hat{\beta}'\hat{\beta}}$$

and, correspondingly,

$$\tilde{\beta} = (1 - \tilde{\rho})\,\hat{\beta} .$$

Let $\sigma^2 = 1$. Show that

$$E[(\hat{\beta} - \beta)'(\hat{\beta} - \beta)|\beta] > E[(\tilde{\beta} - \beta)'(\tilde{\beta} - \beta)|\beta] ,$$

where you may use the fact that

$$2a - 2a\beta' E[\hat{\beta}/(\hat{\beta}'\hat{\beta})|\beta] - a^2 E[1/((\hat{\beta}'\hat{\beta})|\beta] = a^2\, E[\varphi^{-1}] ,$$

where $\varphi \sim \chi^2_{(K,\ \beta'\beta/2)}$ with $E[\varphi^{-1}] > 0$.

(f) What does the inequality in (e) tell you about the maximum-likelihood estimator?

PRINCETON UNIVERSITY
Department of Economics

General Examination for the Degree of Doctor of Philosophy

Econometrics General Examination

Time: 3 hours May 22, 1991

Do not write your name on any of your examination papers, but identify them with a Code Number which you have obtained from Mrs. Alito.

Start a new paper or book for each question so that the examination can be assembled by question rather than by candidate. Be sure that your Code Number appears on each sheet or book.

Please answer 6 questions, with at least one question from each of the 3 parts. The questions are weighted equally.

PART I

QUESTION 1

Set up a model of linear simultaneous stochastic equations in econometrics.

(a) Write down the two-stage least squares estimator for the coefficients of the first structural equation.

(b) What is the covariance matrix of the asymptotic distribution of the above estimator? Sketch a proof.

(c) Write down the three-stage least squares estimator for the coefficients of all structural equations.

QUESTION 2

A logit model is defined by

$$P(y_i=1) = F(x_i'\beta_0), \qquad i = 1,\ldots,n$$

where $\{y_i\}$ is a sequence of independent binary random variables taking the value 1 or 0, x_i is a k-component vector of known constants, β_0 is a vector of unknown parameters, and $F(z) = e^z/(1+e^z)$.

(a) Write down the likelihood function for this model.

(b) Derive the first-order condition for the maximum likelihood (ML) estimator of β_0.

(c) Provide a method for computing the ML estimate.

QUESTION 3

Let y_{it} be the observation of the dependent variable for individual unit i at time t ($i = 1,2,\ldots,10$; $t = 1,\ldots,40$) which is a linear function of 5 explanatory variables (including an intercept) and a residual e_{it}, with $Ee_{it}^2 = \sigma_i^2$, $E(e_{it}e_{jt}) = \sigma_{ij}$, and $E(e_{it}e_{js}) = 0$ for $t \neq s$.

(a) If all the regression coefficients are the same for all 10 individuals, set up the model in matrix notation and derive the estimator of the coefficient vector by the method of generalized least squares. Specify the dimensions of the matrices used in defining the GLS estimator.

(b) If the intercepts are different for the 10 individuals and are treated as fixed, while the other 4 coefficients are the same for the individuals, derive the GLS estimator for the coefficient vector.

(c) If the intercepts are different but treated as random drawings from a distribution with variance σ_μ^2, set up the model in matrix notation, combining the random intercept with e_{it} in the residual vector. Find the covariance matrix of this random vector.

PART II

QUESTION 4

Briefly define and discuss the usefulness of 5 (five) of the following 7 (seven) concepts.

(1) Near-integrated process.

(2) Near observational equivalence of difference-stationary and trend-stationary processes.

(3) The spectral density function of a process evaluated at the zero frequency.

(4) The Wiener process.

(5) The autocovariance generating function.

(6) Cointegration and error correction model.

(7) Impulse response function and variance decomposition in vector autoregressive models (VAR).

QUESTION 5

Consider the continuous-time Ornstein-Uhlenbeck process

$$dy_t = \theta y_t \, dt + \sigma \, dw_t \qquad y_0 = 0, \quad 0 \le t \le S$$

where w_t is the unit Wiener process and S is the span of the data.

(a) Derive the discrete-time representation of the process $\{y_t\}$ with a sampling interval of length h.

(b) Show that the autoregressive parameter defined in (a) converges to 1 at rate T as T increases to infinity keeping the span of the data fixed (T is total number of observations).

(c) Suppose one is interested in testing $H_0: \theta = 0$ versus $H_1: \theta < 0$. Consider using a test based on a normalization of the estimated discrete time autoregressive parameter. Discuss how the power function of the test is influenced by the span of the sample (total length of the sample in units of time) and the number of observations. [You don't need to use formal theoretical derivations; give the main results and some intuition for them using your answer in (a) and (b).]

QUESTION 6

Consider a series (y_t) generated by the following model (data-generating process):

(1) $$y_t = \mu + z_t \quad ; \quad A(L)z_t = e_t$$

where $A(L) = 1 - \alpha_1 L - \dots - \alpha_k L^k$ and $e_t \sim$ i.i.d. $N(0,\sigma^2)$. A question of interest is to test whether the series is subject to changes in mean. To that effect the following statistic has been proposed (originally in the case where $\alpha_1 = \alpha_2 = \dots = \alpha_k = 0$):

(2) $$Q = T^{-2}\hat{\sigma}^{-2}\sum_{t=1}^{T-1}\left(\sum_{j=1}^{t}\hat{e}_j\right)^2$$

where $\hat{e}_j$ are the residuals from the following regression estimated by OLS:

(3) $$y_t = \hat{\mu} + \hat{e}_t$$

and $$\hat{\sigma}^2 = T^{-1}\sum_1^T \hat{e}_t^2 .$$

(a) Assuming that the roots of $A(z)=0$ all be strictly outside the unit circle, derive the limiting distribution of the test statistic Q under the null hypothesis of no structural change.

(b) Using the result in (a) briefly describe one way to have a transformed statistic whose asymptotic distribution is free of nuisance parameters and can therefore be used to carry asymptotically valid tests.

(c) Now assume that one of the roots of $A(z) = 0$ is unity and that the remaining ones are strictly outside the unit circle. Derive the limiting distribution of Q under the null hypothesis of no structural change.

PART III

QUESTION 7

Consider the linear model

$$Y = \beta_0 1_{T\times 1} + X_1\beta_1 + X_2\beta_2 + u$$

where X_1 is T×1, X_2 is T×k, k≥2, u is T×1. Assume that the u[t]'s are iid $N(0,\sigma^2)$ and that $X = [1_{T\times 1}\ X_1\ X_2]$ has full column rank. A researcher is particularly interested in estimating β_1 by OLS, but is not sure what restrictions of the type $C_2\beta_2 = 0$ to impose on β_2. In other words, for any q with $1 \le q \le k-1$ and any q×k matrix C_2 with full row rank, the researcher considers the restriction $C\beta = 0$, where

$$C = \begin{bmatrix} 0_{q\times 1} & 0_{q\times 1} & C_2. \end{bmatrix} \quad \text{and} \quad \beta = \begin{bmatrix} \beta_0 \\ \beta_1 \\ \beta_2 \end{bmatrix}.$$

(a) For given q and C, let F_C be the F-statistic for testing the restriction $C\beta = 0$. Give a formula for F_C.

(b) Let F_{max} be the F-statistic for testing $\beta_2 = 0$. Fix q, $1 \le q \le k-1$. Show that for any value F satisfying $0 \le F \le \frac{k}{q} F_{max}$, there is a full row-rank matrix C_2 of size q×k, so that $F_C = F$.

QUESTION 8

Suppose that y_0 is given (not considered random), that σ^2 is known and that

$$y_t = \rho y_{t-1} + \varepsilon_t, \qquad t = 1,\dots,T$$

where $\varepsilon_t \sim N(0,\sigma^2)$, t = 1,...,T are independent. Note that the log-likelihood function is given by

$$\log L = -\frac{T}{2}\log\left(2\pi\sigma^2\right) - \frac{1}{2\sigma^2}\sum_{t=1}^{T}\left(y_t - \rho y_{t-1}\right)^2$$

(a) Calculate $\dfrac{\partial^2 \log L}{\partial\rho^2}$.

(b) Calculate $E[y_t^2]$.

(c) Define and calculate Jeffrey's prior for ρ. How does this compare to standard BVAR methodology?

QUESTION 9

Suppose that the 4x1 vector X_t obeys

$$X_t = \gamma_0 + A(L)X_{t-1} + \eta_t$$

where A(L) is a matrix polynomial of known order p and γ_0 is nonzero. Both A(L) and γ_0 are to be estimated. Assume that the η_t's are 4x1 martingale differences with $E[\eta_t | \eta_{t-1},...] = 0$, $E[\eta_t\eta_t' | \eta_{t-1},...] = I_4$. Suppose that we can also write the regression equation as

$$\Delta X_t = \mu + \theta(L)\eta_t$$

where we assume that $\mu_1 \neq 0,...,\mu_4 \neq 0$, ΔX_t is stationary, $\theta(L)$ is invertible, and $\theta(1) \neq 0$, implying that there is at least one unit root. Note furthermore that the model can be written as

$$X_t = A^*(L)\left(\Delta X_{t-1} - \mu\right) + \left(\gamma_0 + A^*(1)\mu\right) + A(1)X_{t-1} + \eta_t$$

where $A(L) = A(1) + (1-L)A^*(L)$. Finally, assume that there are three cointegrating vectors, which can be written in matrix form as

$$\alpha = \begin{bmatrix} 1 & 0 & 0 & \alpha_1 \\ 0 & 1 & 0 & \alpha_2 \\ 0 & 0 & 1 & \alpha_3 \end{bmatrix}$$

where $\alpha_1 \neq 0$, $\alpha_2 \neq 0$, and $\alpha_3 \neq 0$.

(a) Following Sims-Stock-Watson, write the model in first-order form

$$Y_t = AY_{t-1} + G\eta_t$$

Find $Z_t^1,...,Z_t^4$ preferably by inspection of the system, where $Z_t = DY_t$ is a transformation of the system Y_t with some nonsingular matrix D, so that the first k_1 components of Z_t can be expressed as a stationary sum of current and lagged η_t's, the next k_2 components of Z_t also contain a constant, the next k_3 components of Z_t also contain a nondegenerate linear combination of the random walk $\xi_t = \sum_{s=1}^{t}\eta_s$ and the last k_4 components of Z_t also contain a time trend. Find k_1, k_2, k_3 and k_4.

(b) Is the distribution for the OLS estimators of the coefficients A(L) and γ_0 asymptotically normal? Explain why or why not.

(c) Is the distribution for the F-test for H_0:"$A_{12}(1) = 0$" asymptotically χ_1^2 ? Reason?

(d) Does your answer to (b) and (c) change if a time trend with a true coefficient of zero is included as regressor? Explain your answer.

PRINCETON UNIVERSITY
Department of Economics

General Examination for the Degree of Doctor of Philosophy

Econometrics General Examination

Time 3 hours October 1990

Do not write your name on any of your examination papers, but identify them with a code number which you have obtained from Ms. Alito.

Start a new paper or book for each question so that the examination can be assembled by question rather than by candidate. Be sure that your code number appears on each sheet or book.

Part 1

Question 1

(30 points) Define and briefly discuss SIX of the eight following concepts:

- The Gauss-Markov theorem.
- The information matrix test.
- The Lagrange Multiplier (LM) test for serial correlation.
- The Cramer-Rao lower bound.
- The effect of misspecification (omission of relevant variables or inclusion of irrelevant variables) in the standard linear model.
- Testing for a unit root in a time series of data.
- The autocovariance-generating function.
- The finite Fourier transform.

Part II

Answer TWO of the following three questions. (30 points each)

Question 2

Consider the linear model

$$Y_t = \beta_0 + X_{1t}\beta_1 + X_{2t}\beta_2 + u_t, \qquad t = 1,\dots,T$$

where X_1 is $T\times 1$, X_2 is $T\times k$, $k\geq 2$, the u_t's are i.i.d. $N(0,\sigma^2)$ and $X = \left[1_{T\times 1}\ X_1\ X_2\right]$ has full column rank. A researcher is particularly interested in estimating β_1 with OLS, but is not sure what zero restrictions to impose on β_2. In other words, for any q with $0\leq q\leq k$ and any $q\times k$ matrix C_2 with full row rank, the researcher considers the restriction $C\beta=0$, where

$$C = \begin{bmatrix} 0_{q\times 1} & 0_{q\times 1} & C_2 \end{bmatrix} \text{ and } \beta = \begin{bmatrix} \beta_0 \\ \beta_1 \\ \beta_2 \end{bmatrix}.$$

(a) Let R_C^2 be the R^2 if the restriction $C\beta=0$ is imposed. Give a formula for R_C^2.

(b) Show that the maximal R^2 is achieved when no restrictions are imposed, and the minimal R^2 is achieved when the maximal restriction $\beta_2=0$ is imposed. Call these values R^2_{max} and R^2_{min}.

(Hint: Use geometry.)

Let q satisfy $1\le q\le k-1$.

(c) Show that there is a full row-rank matrix C_2 of size $q\times k$ so that a regression with $C\beta=0$ imposed yields $R_C^2 = R^2_{max}$.

(d) Show similarly to (c) that $R_C^2 = R^2_{min}$ can be achieved.

<u>Question 3</u>

Consider the seemingly unrelated regression equations

$$y_i = X_i\beta_i + y_i, \qquad i = 1,\ldots,N$$

where y_i is $T\times 1$, X_i is $T\times k_i$, β_i is $k_i\times 1$, and u_i is $T\times 1$ with $(u_{1,t},\ldots,u_{N,t})'$ distributed as $N(0,\Sigma)$ i.i.d. across t, where Σ is positive definite and of size $N\times N$. The usual non-collinearity assumptions for X hold.

(a) Suppose Σ is known. Define the GLS estimator. (Recall that in the general GLS model the GLS estimator is given by $\hat{\beta} = (X'\Omega^{-1}X)^{-1}X'\Omega^{-1}y$.)

(b) Suppose Σ is unknown. Describe a feasible GLS estimator.

(c) Suppose Σ is diagonal. Show that the GLS estimator and the feasible GLS estimator reduce to OLS equation by equation.

(d) Suppose all equations have the same regressors $X_i=X$. Show that the GLS estimator and the feasible GLS estimator reduce to OLS equation by equation.

<u>Hint</u>: You may want to use the property of the Kronecker product, that $(A\otimes B)(C\otimes D) = (AC)\otimes(CD)$ if all products are defined, as well as the property

that $\text{diag}(A_1,\ldots,A_N)\text{diag}(B_1,\ldots,B_N) = \text{diag}(A_1B_1,\ldots,A_NB_N)$ if the A_i's and B_i's are of appropriate sizes, etc.

Question 4

Consider the following duration model:

$$y_t = x_t + u_t, \qquad t = 1,\ldots,T$$

where $y_t>x_t$ for all t, and where the u_t are i.i.d. with the exponential distribution

$$P(u_t>z) = e^{-\lambda z} \qquad \text{for } z\geq 0$$

i.e. only $z\geq 0$ (including 0) are observable and the density is continuous when restricted to $z\geq 0$. The parameter $\lambda>0$ is unknown and needs to be estimated.

(a) Give a formula for the logarithm of the likelihood function and find the maximum likelihood estimator of λ.

(b) Calculate the Cramer-Rao lower bound and make a guess for the asymptotic distribution of $\hat{\lambda}$.

(c) Define another estimator $\tilde{\lambda}$ by $\tilde{\lambda}=1$ if $|\hat{\lambda}-1| < T^{-1/4}$ and $\tilde{\lambda}=\hat{\lambda}$ if $|\hat{\lambda}-1| \geq T^{-1/4}$. Assuming that your guess in (b) is right, show that $T^{1/2}(\tilde{\lambda}-\lambda)$ is asymptotically normally distributed for $\lambda>0$ and that its asymptotic variance is 0 for $\lambda=1$. Is it true that the MLE is asymptotically of minimum variance among all consistent and asymptotically normal estimators of λ?

(d) Suppose the model is changed to

$$y_t = x_t + \beta + u_t$$

where $\beta\in\mathbb{R}$ is unknown as well. Find the MLE for (λ,β).

Part III

(45 points) Answer ONE of the following two questions.

Question 5

Consider the following data-generating process for a series $\{y_t\}$

$$y_t = \alpha y_{t-1} + u_t$$
$$u_t = e_t + \theta e_{t-1}$$

where $e_t \sim$ i.i.d. $N(0,\sigma^2)$ and $|\theta|<1$.

Suppose you estimate the following regression by ordinary least squares (OLS),

$$y_t = \alpha y_{t-1} + \varepsilon_t$$

Denote the OLS estimator of α by $\hat{\alpha}$.

(a) What is the probability limit of $\hat{\alpha}$ if $|\alpha|<1$?

(b) What is the probability limit of $\hat{\alpha}$ if $\alpha=1$?

(c) When, if at all, $\hat{\alpha}$ is a consistent estimator of α in parts (a) or (b), derive its limiting distribution.

(d) Consider now using an instrumental variable (IV) estimation method with y_{t-2} as instrument. Denote the resulting estimator by β_{IV}. Is β_{IV} consistent when $|\alpha|\leq 1$? What is its limiting distribution?

(e) Using the results in part (d) suggest a procedure to test for a unit root when it is known that the errors follow an MA(q) process. What is the crucial assumption about the order q needed for this procedure to be useful in practice?

Question 6

You have a sample of individuals who have completed a spell of unemployment. For each individual you have the number of weeks of unemployment y_i and a vector of sociodemographic characteristics (Z_i). You decide to fit an exponential model of unemployment duration

$$f(y_i,\lambda_i) = \lambda_i e^{-\lambda_i y_i} \qquad \lambda_i > 0 \qquad i = 1,\ldots,N$$

where f( ) is the density function and you set $\lambda_i = \exp(Z_i\beta)$.

(a) Write down the log likelihood function and the first order conditions. Sketch a proof of consistency.

(b) Suppose you instead decided to fit the model by nonlinear least-squares (NLS):

$$y_i = e^{Z_i\beta} + \varepsilon_i$$

What are the properties of the estimator? Calculate the asymptotic normal distribution for β.

(Hint: $Ey_i = 1/\lambda_i$, $V(y_i) = (1/\lambda_i)^2$.)

(c) Write down a specification test of the exponential model using the results of (a) and (b).

(d) Suppose we specify $\lambda_i = \exp(Z_i\beta + \eta_i)$, where $E\eta_i = 0$, $V(\eta_i) = \sigma_\eta^2$. Consider the NLS model and give an appropriate estimator. Derive its asymptotic distribution.

Part IV

(45 points) Answer ONE of the following two questions.

Question 7

Consider the general ARMA (p,q) model

$$A(L)y_t = B(L)e_t$$

with

$$A(L) = 1 + a_1L + \dots + a_pL^p$$

$$B(L) = 1 + b_1L + \dots + b_qL^q$$

where $e_t \sim$ i.i.d. $N(0,\sigma^2)$ and the roots of $A(z)=0$ and $B(z)=0$ are strictly outside the unit circle. Discuss various techniques and their relative merits to estimate the parameter vector $(a_1,\dots,a_p,b_1,\dots,b_q,\sigma^2)$ and their standard errors. Also discuss how the orders p and q can be selected.

Question 8

Individual families decide whether to purchase a portable air conditioner on the basis of its price, their incomes, and various demographic variables. Suppose for simplicity that families buy at most one portable air conditioner per season.

You have cross-section data from 1988 on family income and demographics, as well as whether the family in question bought an air conditioner (including its price if bought). Of interest to you is the price elasticity of demand at a given income level.

Describe how you would measure the elasticity using

(a) a parametric approach,

(b) a semiparametric approach,

(c) a nonparametric approach.

State a model in each case, and indicate what estimators would be appropriate for each. Contrast the large sample properties of your estimators under the three approaches.

PRINCETON UNIVERSITY
Department of Economics

General Examination for the Degree of Doctor of Philosophy

Econometrics General Examination

Time 3 hours

May 1990

Do not write your name on any of your examination papers, but identify them with a Code number which you have obtained from Ms. Alito.

Start a new paper or book for each question so that the examination can be assembled by question rather than by candidate. Be sure that your Code Number appears on each sheet or book.

For each question the number of points corresponds to a suggested time you should allocate to that question.

Part I

(30 points) Define and briefly discuss SIX of the following nine concepts:

- Wold's decomposition theorem.
- The Cramer-Rao lower bound.
- Functional weak convergence in distribution.
- Autocorrelation and heteroskedasticity consistent covariance matrix estimation.
- Sufficient statistic.
- Uniform convergence in probability.
- The incidental parameters problem.
- Testing for autocorrelation with a lagged dependent variable model.
- A general class of spectral density estimators.

PART II

(60 points) Answer TWO of the following three questions.

Question 1

For the following linear model

$$y_t = x_t'\beta + u_t \quad (t = 1,\dots,T)$$

where $X' = (x_1,\dots,x_T)$ is a matrix of observations of non-random variables and $\lim_{T\to\infty} T^{-1}X'X$ is finite non-singular and

$$u_t = \rho u_{t-1} + e_t \qquad |\rho| < 1$$

$$E(e_t) = 0, E\left(e_t^2\right) = \sigma^2 \quad \text{and} \quad E(e_te_s) = 0 \quad \text{for } t \neq s,$$

(a) Show that the probability limit of the Durbin Watson statistic is $2(1-\rho)$. (Recall $DW = \sum_{t=2}^{T}(\hat{u}_t-\hat{u}_{t-1})^2/\sum_{t=1}^{T}\hat{u}_t^2$, where $\hat{u}_t$ are the OLS residuals.)

(b) Find the limiting distribution of the suitably standardized Durbin-Watson statistic when $\rho = 0$.

Question 2

You are estimating the model

$$y = x\beta + z\gamma + \varepsilon$$

where z is a single variable. Data on z are not complete; however, z is assumed related to another variable, w, by

$$z = w\delta + \eta$$

Unfortunately, while data on w do exist, they only exist for years in which data on z DO NOT. Construct and discuss a good estimator for β and γ in this situation.

Question 3

In the model

$$y_{1t} + b_{12}y_{2t} + c_{11}x_{1t} = u_{1t}$$

$$b_{21}y_{1t} + y_{2t} + c_{22}x_{2t} = u_{2t}$$

the y_{it} are endogenous variables, the x_{it} are exogenous variables and then u_{it} are serially independent random disturbances which have the same bivariate normal distribution with zero mean and non-singular covariance matrix for each value of t.

(a) How would you obtain full information maximum likelihood (FIML) estimates of the coefficients of the above model?

(b) Prove that your procedure yields the FIML estimates.

PART III

(45 points) Answer ONE of the following two questions.

Question 1

Consider the first-order autoregressive model:

$$y_t = \alpha y_{t-1} + u_t \quad ; \quad y_0 = c$$

where c is a fixed constant and $u_t \sim$ i.i.d. $N(0,\sigma^2)$. Write an essay on the distribution of the least-squares estimator $\hat{\alpha}$ in a first-order autoregression without an intercept, i.e. $\hat{\alpha} = \sum_1^T y_t y_{t-1} / \sum_1^T y_{t-1}^2$ where T is the sample size. Your discussion could include, among other things, the following elements:

(a) The method(s) used to obtain the exact distribution;

(b) A characterization of the general feature of this exact distribution and how the parameters α and c affect it;

(c) The various limiting distributions that have been proposed (e.g. usual asymptotic distribution, near-integrated, continuous-time, small-σ asymptotic, etc.);

(d) How to compute the critical values of these limiting distributions;

(e) How good an approximation to the exact distribution each one provides.

Be as specific as you wish, but do not get lost in either details or proofs.

Question 2

Consider the model

$$y_{it} = 1(x_{it}'\beta_0 + \alpha_i + \eta_{it} > 0), \quad i = 1,\dots,n, \quad t = 1,2,$$

where y_{it} and x_{it} are observed data and α_i and η_{it} are unobserved disturbance terms. Briefly discuss the motivation for this model and write an essay on how you might estimate β_0. You could consider in your comments some or all of the following: Cases where α_i is independent of $x_i = (x_{i1}', x_{i2}')'$, cases where α_i and x_i are correlated, cases where the distribution of α_i and/or η_{it} is known, and cases where these distributions are unknown.

PART IV

(45 points) Answer ONE of the following two questions.

Question 1

Consider the model

$$y_i = f(x_i^*, \beta_0) + \varepsilon_i, \qquad E[\varepsilon_i] = 0;$$

$$x_i = x_i^* + \eta_i; \qquad E[\eta_i] = 0;$$

$$\varepsilon_i, \ \eta_i, \text{ and } x_i^* \text{ mutually independent.}$$

where x_i^* is an unobserved regressor, for which x_i is a measurement, with error η_i.

(a) Show that the nonlinear regression estimator from the regression of y_i on $f(x_i,\beta)$ will generally be inconsistent.

(b) Suppose that there are instruments z_i that are independent of both ε_i and η_i and correlated with x_i^*. Is the nonlinear two-stage least squares estimator of β with instruments z_i and residual $y_i-f(x_i,\beta)$ consistent? Why or why not ?

(c) Suppose that there is more structure on the model than in (b), with $x_i^* = z_i'\pi_0 + v_i$, where $E[v_i] = 0$ and the density of v_i has known functional form $g(v|\pi)$.

i) How could you estimate π_0 from observations on x_i and z_i?

ii) What is the form of the conditional expectation of y given z?

iii) How could you use your answers from i) and ii) to estimate β and γ by a two-step nonlinear least squares procedure ?.

iv) Suppose $g(v|\gamma)$ is the density for $N(0,\gamma^2)$. How could you modify your procedure in iii) to avoid numerical integration ?

Question 2

Consider the ARMA(1,1) model given by

$$y_t = \alpha y_{t-1} + e_t + \beta e_{t-1}$$

where $e_t \sim$ i.i.d. $N(0,\sigma^2)$.

(a) What are the conditions for this process to be stationary and invertible?

(b) Under the conditions expressed in (a) derive the autocovariance function of $\{y_t\}$.

(c) Derive the spectral density function of $\{y_t\}$ under the conditions in (a). What is the long-term effect of a unit shock e_t on the level of y_t

i) if $|\alpha| < 1$, and

ii) if $|\alpha| = 1$?

In case ii) how could you estimate a lower bound on this effect nonparametrically (i.e. without supposing you knew anything about the behavior of Δy_t)? Why is this a lower bound?

(d) Write the ARMA(1,1) in its state space form.

(e) Outline the main steps involved in estimating the parameters of this model using the Kalman filter technique.

G

University of Virginia, Department of Economics
July, 1994

Preliminary Exam
Econometrics

Instructions: Answer <u>four questions</u>, including at least one question from each of the three parts.

Part A: Statistical Methods

1. Let X,Y be bivariate normal with zero means, unit variances, and correlation ρ. Find

a. $E(X^2+Y^2)$

b. $E(Y|X)$

c. $Var(Y|X)$

d. $Cov(X^2,Y^2)$.

2. Let $U_1, \ldots, U_n$ be i.i.d. as uniform on [0,1], and let $S_n = \sum_{i=1}^{n} U_i$. You are given that, for $0 \le s \le 1$, $Pr(S_n \le s) = s^n/n!$ Let $N = \min(n: S_n > 1)$. (That is, think of drawing the U's one at a time until their sum first exceeds unity. N is the number of draws you have made.) Prove (Gnedenko's Lemma) that $E(N) = e = 2.71828\ldots$. [Hint: Show that $f(n) = Pr(N=n) = Pr(S_n > 1) - Pr(S_{n-1} > 1)$ for $n=2,3,\ldots$.]

B. Cross-section Econometrics

1. Let $y_i^* = X_i\beta + u_i$; for $i = 1,2,\ldots,n$. Assume $u_i \sim$ iid G. Let $y_i = 1$ if $y_i^* > 0$ and $y_i = 0$ otherwise. Suggest how to estimate β without assuming a specific functional form for the distribution of u_i.

2. Let the hazard rate for observation i at duration t be

$$\lambda(t|X_i,\epsilon) = \exp(X_i\beta + g(t) + \epsilon_i)$$

where ϵ_i is a measure of unobserved heterogeneity with density $h(\epsilon)$.

a) Write the density and survivor function in terms of λ and h.

b) Explain what happens to estimates of β and g if ϵ is not included.

C. Time-series Econometrics

Question 1

Let $L(\mathbf{x}, \theta)$ be the joint density of an n-vector of iid random variables $\mathbf{x} = (\mathbf{x}_1, \ldots, \mathbf{x}_n)'$ characterized by a k-vector of parameters θ. Assume that the standard conditions used to prove consistency and asymptotic normality of the (unconstrained) maximum likelihood estimator $\hat{\theta}$ apply.

Consider the hypothesis

$$\mathrm{H}_0: \quad \mathrm{h}(\theta) = 0$$

where h is a q-element vector-valued differentiable function with $q < k$. Denote the constrained estimator of θ as $\bar{\theta}$. [Formally, the constrained estimator may be obtained by solving a Lagrangean equation.]

The "Lagrange Multiplier" or LM test statistic of H_0 is defined as

$$LM = -\left.\frac{\partial \log L}{\partial \theta'}\right|_{\bar{\theta}} \left[\left.\frac{\partial^2 \log L}{\partial \theta\, \partial \theta'}\right|_{\bar{\theta}}\right]^{-1} \left.\frac{\partial \log L}{\partial \theta}\right|_{\bar{\theta}}.$$

(i) Show that $LM \to_d \chi^2(q)$ under the null. Explain each step of your reasoning carefully.

(ii) How would your arguments have to be modified if the data vector were not iid, but strictly stationary and strong mixing? (Hint: What complications are introduced if the assumption of independence is relaxed?)

Question 2

Consider a mean-zero time series $\{y_t\}_{t=1}^n$. A test of constancy of the unconditional variance of y_t, σ_t^2, is the so-called "sample split prediction test." It is defined as follows: Divide the sample into two consecutive suberas of equal length (you may assume that n is always even!) and define the sampling variances of y_t in the first and second subera, resp., as

$$\hat{\mu}_2^{(1)} = (n/2)^{-1} \sum_{t=1}^{n/2} y_t^2 \quad \text{and} \quad \hat{\mu}_2^{(2)} = (n/2)^{-1} \sum_{t=n/2+1}^{n} y_t^2.$$

The hypothesis of covariance stationarity implies the hypothesis $\mathrm{H}_0: \ \mathrm{E}\hat{\mu}_2^{(1)} = \mathrm{E}\hat{\mu}_2^{(2)}$.

Define $\hat{\tau} = \hat{\mu}_2^{(1)} - \hat{\mu}_2^{(2)}$. The "Bartlett estimate" of the long-run variance of y_t is defined as

$$\hat{v}_n^2 = \hat{\gamma}_0 + 2\sum_{j=1}^{J_n} (1 - j/(J_n + 1))\, \hat{\gamma}_j,$$

where $\hat{\gamma}_j = n^{-1} \sum_{t=1+j}^{n} (y_t^2 - \hat{\mu}_2)(y_{t-j}^2 - \hat{\mu}_2)$ and $\hat{\mu}_2 = n^{-1} \sum_1^n y_t^2$. J_n is a "lag truncation number."

Consider the test statistic $V(\tau) = (2\hat{v}_n^2)^{-1/2} (n/2)^{1/2} \hat{\tau}$.

(i) Show that $V(\tau) \to_d N(0,1)$ under the null if $\{y_t\}_{t=1}^n$ is iid and $\mathrm{E}\, y_t^4 < \infty$. (Hint: In this case, you may replace $\hat{v}_n^2$ by $\hat{\gamma}_0$. Why?)

(ii) Show that the same result also obtains under the null, i.e., $V(\tau) \to_d N(0,1)$ if $\mathrm{E}\, y_t^2 = \sigma^2 < \infty\ \forall t$ and (a) $\sup_t \mathrm{E}\,|y_t|^{4(q+\delta)} < \infty$ for some $\delta > 0$ and $q > 1$, (b) $\{y_t^2 - \sigma^2\}$ is strong mixing, with α-mixing numbers that satisfy $\sum_{m=1}^{\infty} \alpha_m^{1-2/q} < \infty$, (c) $\lim_{n\to\infty} \hat{v}_n^2 = v^2 > 0$, and (d) $J_n = O(n^{1/3})$. Explain why requirements (a)–(d) may be jointly sufficient, i.e., in which sense they serve to rule out "degeneracies" which might otherwise occur. In particular, why would q occur both in (a) and (b)?

University of Virginia
Graduate Preliminary Examination
Econometrics

Time Limit: 3 hours — January 1993

Do 4 out 6 questions.
Do at least one question from each section.
All question receive equal weight.

Section I

1. X and Y are independent Poisson variates, having p.d.f.s

$$f_X(x) = \frac{\lambda^x \cdot e^{-\lambda}}{x!}, \quad x=0,1,2,\ldots \quad \text{and} \quad f_Y(y) = \frac{\mu^y \cdot e^{-\mu}}{y!}, \quad y=0,1,2,\ldots$$

and m.g.f.s

$$M_X(t) = e^{\lambda(e^t-1)} \quad \text{and} \quad M_Y(t) = e^{\mu(e^t-1)}, \quad \text{for } t \in \mathbb{R}$$

Let n be some nonnegative integer. Show that the distribution of X conditional on the event X + Y = n is binomial, with parameters n and $\lambda/(\lambda+\mu)$.

2. Here are four statements about the sequences of random variables $\{X_n\}_{n=1}^{\infty}$ and $\{Y_n\}_{n=1}^{\infty}$:

(1) X_n converges in probability as $n \to \infty$ to the random variable Z, having distribution $F_Z(.)$.

(2) $X_n - Y_n$ converges in probability to zero an $n \to \infty$.

(3) X_n converges in distribution to $F_Z(.)$.

(4) Y_n converges in distribution to $F_Z(.)$.

True or false? (If true, give a simple proof; if false, a counterexample.)

(a) (1) => (3)

(b) (3) => (1)

(c) (3) + (4) => (2)

(d) (1) + (2) => (4)

Section II

(3) Let $y_i^* = X_i\beta + u_i$, $u_i \sim iidN(0,1)$, $i=1,2,..,n$. Let $y_i = 1$ iff $y_i^* \geq 0$ and $y_i=0$ otherwise.

(a) Show how to estimate β using maximum likelihood estimation.

(b) Show how to write the first order conditions from maximizing the log likelihood function to derive a method of moments estimator of β.

(4) Consider the model $g(y_i, X_i, \theta) = u_i$, $i=1,....,n$ where (y_i, X_i) is observed data, g is a specified function, θ is a vector of parameters to be estimated, and $u_i \sim iidF$ for some specified distribution F. Let $\hat{\theta}$ be a proposed estimator of θ. Describe in detail how to perform a Monte Carlo experiment to simulate the asymptotic distribution of $\hat{\theta}$.

Section III

(5) Consider the p_{th} order univariate autoregression $\phi(L)\,x_t = \epsilon_t$ where all the roots of $\phi(z)$ lie outside the unit circle, with the possible exception of a single root. Explain in detail how you would go about using an augmented Dicky - Fuller test to test for the existence of a unit root, being sure to discuss:

(a) Exactly what relationship would be fit to generate the test statistic.

(b) State the null and alternate hypotheses, and explain the connection between the test statistic and the presence or absence of a unit root.

(c) What is there about the distribution theory used in this test that is unusual?

(d) How would your answers to a, b, and c change if there were a constant in the AR process? A constant and a trend?

(e) Give a simple example of an ARMA model where both intuition and Monte Carlo evidence suggests that you would be likely to falsely reject the null hypothesis.

(6) Economists often write down economic models that abstract from trends, and they want to fit their models to detrended data, identifying what remains after trends are removed as the cyclical component.

(a) Explain what the Hodrick-Prescott filter is and how it is implemented.

(b) Explain the traditional method for detrending trend-stationary series.

(c) Explain the Beveridge-Nelson decomposition and how it is used to derive the cyclical component of difference-stationary processes. Be as complete as you can.

(d) Suppose trend-stationary methods are used on a difference-stationary series. What problems result?

(e) In the Beveridge-Nelson decomposition of a univariate series, are the trend and cycle correlated?

University of Virginia

Econometric Preliminary Examination
August 1992

Do 4 out of 6 questions with at least 1 question from each section.

Section A:

1.) Given the probability space $(\Omega, \mathcal{F}, P)$, let $(X,Y): \Omega \to (\mathcal{X} \times \mathcal{Y}) \subset \mathbb{R}_2$ be jointly-distributed random variables with means μ_x and μ_y, variances σ_x^2 and σ_y^2, and covariance σ_{xy}. (Obviously, $\mathcal{X}$ and $\mathcal{Y}$ are the supports of X and Y.) Suppose there is a function $g: \mathcal{X} \to \mathbb{R}$ such that $E(Y|x) = g(x)\ \forall\ x \in \mathcal{X}$.

a.) Show that $Cov[X, g(X)] = \sigma_{xy}$.

b.) Suppose X and Y are such that $g(x) = c\ \forall\ x \in \mathcal{X}$, where c is a finite constant not depending on x. Show that $\sigma_{xy} = 0$.

c.) Parts a and b have established that $E(Y|x) = c\ \forall\ x \in \mathcal{X} \Rightarrow \sigma_{xy} = 0$. Consider the converse. If $\sigma_{xy} = 0 \Rightarrow E(Y|x) =$ constant, then prove it. If not, construct a counterexample.

2.) Let T be an unbiased and efficient estimator of a parameter θ, and let Q be an unbiased estimator of θ that is not efficient. Define $U \equiv Q - T$. Let $Var(U) = \sigma^2$ and (as a normalization) $Var(T) = 1$.

a.) Prove that $Cov(U,T) = 0$.

b.) Show that $Var(Q-T) = Var(Q) - Var(T)$.

c.) Let $\{X_1, X_2, \ldots, X_n\}$ be a random sample of size n from a Poisson distribution with parameter λ, and let $\bar{X}$ and S^2 be the usual unbiased estimators of the population mean and variance--both of which in this case are equal to λ. Use the results of parts a and b to find $Var(S^2-\bar{X})$, given that

$$Var(S^2) = \frac{\lambda + 2\lambda^2}{n} + \frac{2\lambda^2}{n(n-1)}.$$

Section B:

3.) Let y_t be an $(n \times 1)$ vector that follows a first-order Gaussian VAR,

$$y_t = \phi y_{t-1} + \epsilon_t \quad .$$

Here the $(n \times 1)$ vector ϵ_t is i.i.d. $N(0,\Omega)$ and ϕ indicates an $(n \times n)$ matrix of autoregressive coefficients. The initial value y_0 taken to be fixed at 0.

a.) Under what conditions is the above process covariance-stationary?

b.) Consider a sample of T observations $(y_1, y_2, \ldots, y_T)$. Write down the expression for the log of the sample likelihood function, treating the first observation y_0 as deterministic.

c.) Write down the formulas for the maximum likelihood estimates of ϕ and Ω.

d.) Describe how you would construct a likelihood ratio test of the null hypothesis that $\phi = 0$. Be as precise as possible, giving the exact expressions that you would calculate, the degrees of freedom, and the details of how you would decide if the null hypothesis is true or false.

4.) Let y_t be an $(n \times 1)$ vector that follows a Gaussian first-order vector moving average process,

$$y_t = \mu + \epsilon_t + \Theta\epsilon_{t-1} \quad .$$

Here μ is an $(n \times 1)$ vector of parameters, Θ is an $(n \times n)$ matrix of parameters, and the $(n \times 1)$ vector ϵ_t is i.i.d. $N(0,\Omega)$.

a.) Under what conditions is the above process covariance-stationary?

b.) Assuming that y_t is covariance-stationary, calculate its mean and autocovariances.

c.) Let $\bar{y} = T^{-1} \sum_{t=1}^{T} y_t$ be the sample mean. Calculate the asymptotic variance-covariance matrix of $\bar{y}$, that is, find a matrix S such that

$$\sqrt{T} \left\{ \bar{y} - E(\bar{y}) \right\} \xrightarrow{L} N(0,S) \quad .$$

d.) Suggest an estimate of S that is positive definite for almost all realizations of $(y_1, y_2, \ldots, y_T)$.

e.) Describe how you would test the null hypothesis that the first element of μ (denoted μ_1) is zero.

Section C:

5.) Let $y_i = g(X_i, \theta) + u_i$ where X_i is a set of observed variables, $u_i \sim iidF$, and θ is an m x 1 vector of parameters to estimate. Assume $Eu_i = 0$ and $Var\ u_i = \sigma^2$. Let Z_i be a valid set of instruments for X_i, i.e.,

$$g_\theta' Z/N \rightarrow Q$$

$$u'Z/N \rightarrow 0$$

where N is the sample size and Q has rank m. Describe how to estimate θ and provide the asymptotic distribution of your estimate.

6.) Let $y_i^* = X_i\beta + u_i$, $i = 1,2,\ldots,N$ where $u_i \sim iidN(0,\sigma^2)$.
Let $y_i = 1(y_i^* > 0)$.

a.) What is the maximum likelihood estimate of β?

b.) Let β_k be the kth element of β. Construct a Lagrange Multiplier Test for $H_0: \beta_k = 0$ against

$$H_A: \beta_k \neq 0.$$

UNIVERSITY OF VIRGINIA
Department of Economics
Econometrics Graduate Preliminary Examination
August 1991

TIME LIMIT: 3 HOURS
ANSWER 4 QUESTIONS, AT LEAST 1 FROM EACH SECTION.

Section A:

1. Let $y_{ij}^* = X_{ij}\beta + u_{ij}$ $j=1,2,\ldots,m$; $i=1,2,\ldots,n$

Let $y_{ij} = \begin{cases} 1 & \text{if } y_{ij}^* \geq y_{ik}^* \ \forall k \\ 0 & \text{otherwise} \end{cases}$.

Let $u_{ij} \sim$ iidF.

a) What is the MLE of β?

b) What is the MOM estimator of β?

c) Let $y_i = [y_{i1}, y_{i2}, \ldots, y_{im}]$. What is the covariance matrix of y_i?

2. Let $y_{1i}^* = X_{1i}\beta_1 + u_{1i}$

$y_{2i}^* = X_{2i}\beta_2 + u_{2i}$.

The econometrician observes

$$y_{2i} = \begin{cases} 1 & \text{if } y_{2i}^* > 0 \\ 0 & \text{otherwise} \end{cases}$$

and y_{1i}^* iff $y_{2i} = 1$. Assume $u_i \sim N\left[\begin{pmatrix} 0 \\ 0 \end{pmatrix}, \begin{pmatrix} \sigma_{11} & \sigma_{12} \\ \sigma_{12} & \sigma_{22} \end{pmatrix}\right]$

a) What are sufficient conditions for identification of each parameter?

b) How would you estimate the identifiable parameters using MLE? Why might the estimates be different from those using Heckman's two-step procedure?

Section B:

1. if $X_1,\ldots,X_n$ are elements of a random sample from a distribution with mean μ and variance $\sigma^2 < \infty$, find the expected value and probability limit of each of the following proposed estimators of μ^2. (In parts c and d assume that n is even.)

a. $\bar{X}^2$, where $\bar{X} = n^{-1} \sum X_i$.

b. $n^{-1} \sum X_i^2$

c. $2n^{-1}(X_1X_2 + X_3X_4 + \ldots + X_{n-3}X_{n-2} + X_{n-1}X_n)$

d. $[2n^{-1}(X_1 + \ldots + X_{n/2})]\cdot[2n^{-1}(X_{n/2+1} + \ldots + X_n)]$

e. $\bar{X}^2 - S^2/n$, where $S^2 = (n-1)^{-1} \sum (X_i - \bar{X})^2$.

2. Let $X_1,X_2,\ldots,X_n$ be i.i.d. random variables with $P(X_1 > 0) = p$. For $j=1,1,\ldots,n$ define $Y_j = 1$ if $X_j > 0$ and $Y_j = 0$ otherwise.

a. Show that the maximum-likelihood estimator of p is $\hat{p} = n^{-1} \sum_{j=1}^{n} Y_j$.

b. Assuming that the regularity conditions hold (and they do), show that the asymptotic variance of $\hat{p}$ is $p(1-p)/n$. Show that this is also the *exact* variance for each n.

c. Using the asymptotic theory appropriate for m.l.e.s under the regularity conditions, build a 95% confidence interval for p, assuming that $n = 100$ and $y_1 + \ldots + y_{100} = 70.0$.

d. Use the likelihood-ratio procedure and the data given in part c to test at the .05 level H_0: $p = .05$ vs. H_1: $p \neq .05$.

Section C:

1. Consider the following linear regression model:

$$y_t = x_t'\beta + u_t \ .$$

The scalar y_t is the dependent variable, x_t is a (k × 1) vector of explanatory variables, β is a (k × 1) vector of coefficients, and u_t is an i.i.d. error term satisfying

$$E(u_t) = 0$$

$$E(u_t u_s) = \sigma^2 \quad \text{for } t = s$$

$$= 0 \quad \text{otherwise} \ .$$

Although the unconditional mean of u_t is zero, it is correlated with x_t:

$$E(u_t | x_t) \neq 0 \ .$$

Suppose that there exists a (k × 1) vector of instrumental variables z_t such that u_t is independent of z_s for all t and s.

a. Give an example of a real-world problem for which instrumental variables might be the appropriate estimation procedure. Be sure to explain intuitively why OLS would not give consistent estimates and the reason why your nominated variables would be valid instruments.

b. Write down the formula for the instrumental variables estimate of β.

c. What further assumptions do you need in order to establish that the instrumental variables estimator is consistent? Prove that the estimator is consistent under these assumptions.

d. Calculate the asymptotic distribution of the instrumental variables estimator. Again state any auxiliary assumptions you had to make in order for this derivation to be valid.

e. Use the results from part (d) to describe exactly how you would calculate a t-test of the null hypothesis that the coefficient on the first variable (the first element of β, denoted β_1) is the same as the coefficient on the second variable (the second element of β, denoted β_2).

2. Let y_t denote an (n × 1) vector of variables observed at date t.

   a. What does it mean for the elements of y_t to be cointegrated? Give both a formal definition and an intuitive description.

   b. Describe one procedure for estimating the cointegrating vector.

   c. Describe in words how you could test the null hypothesis of no cointegration.

   d. Assuming that the elements are cointegrated, describe a procedure for testing a hypothesis about the value of the cointegrating vector.

UNIVERSITY OF WASHINGTON

G

ECONOMETRICS FIELD EXAMINATION

Autumn 1994

Committee: Zivot, Chair
Nelson, Parks, Rose, Startz

Time: 4 hours
Answer all questions

Questions #1 and #2 are "warm-up", short answer questions.

1. For each of the following, indicated whether or not you agree, wholly or in part, and briefly justify your answer:

   (a) Because it provides a better fit to the sample data, generalized least squares estimation of a linear regression is better than classical least squares.

   (b) Negative autocorrelation in the disturbance term of a regression model can reduce the variance of the classical least squares estimator of the coefficient parameters below what it would be in absence of autocorrelation, and may make the variance even less than that of the generalized least squares estimator.

   (c) The classical linear regression model cannot be appropriate for the relationship $Y_t = \alpha + \beta X_{t-1} + \varepsilon_t$ because the regressor is a lagged variable.

   (d) Consider the VAR: $Y_t = \alpha + B X_{t-1} + \varepsilon_t$ where Y is a vector of k observed variables, B is a kxk matrix of coefficients, and ε is a vector of k disturbances with mean zero and covariance matrix Σ. Treat Y_0 as given. Nothing is known about the elements of the parameter matrices. Estimation of the model by single equation least squares, taking one element of Y at a time and regressing it on all the elements of the lagged vector Y, will lead to less efficient estimates than would a full ML estimation of the VAR.

   (e) Consider a regression of y on x1 and x2, all scalars. Although both x1 and x2 are positively correlated, y is not autocorrelated. It is reasonable therefore to assume that the disturbance in the model is not autocorrelated.

   (f) The instrumental variables estimator is both unbiased and efficient in samples of any size.

2. Suppose that $y = \beta x + u$ is a one right-hand side variable regression equation. You have a large number of observations and the equation meets all the usual regression assumptions. Unfortunately, you don't observe x. You do observe

$$z_1 = \gamma_1 x + \varepsilon_1$$
$$z_2 = \gamma_2 x + \varepsilon_2$$

where both ε's are i.i.d. and uncorrelated with u, x, and each other. For notational convenience, define $\sigma_1^2 = \text{var}(\varepsilon_1)$ and $\sigma_2^2 = \text{var}(\varepsilon_2)$.

(a) Assume you know ex ante that $\gamma_1 = \gamma_2 = 1$ and the values of σ_1^2 and σ_2^2. Give two instrumental variable estimators of β and explain which is better.

(b) Suppose $\gamma_1 = 1$, but γ_2 is unknown. What is the appropriate estimator?

(c) Suppose neither γ is known. In principle, is it possible to derive an estimator for β?

3. Suppose you have a panel data set containing data on i = 1 to N units over t = 1 to T time periods for a dependent variable, Y, and a vector of K independent variables, X.

(a) Describe each of the following models, and outline how each model can be estimated:

(i) Generalized Least Squares (GLS), where the error components are specified to be:

$$u_{it} = v_i + \varepsilon_{it}$$

(ii) Fixed Effects (Unit Specific).

(b) What factors would you consider in choosing among the GLS, OLS, and Fixed Effects models? Discuss characteristics of the data set and hypothesis tests which are commonly used to distinguish these models.

(c) What are the within- and between-units estimators?

(d) Show that the GLS estimator can be expressed as a matrix weighted average of the within- and between-units estimators.

4. Consider the AR(2) process

$$y_t = \alpha + \phi_1 y_{t-1} + \phi_2 y_{t-2} + \varepsilon_t, \varepsilon_t \sim i.i.d.N(0,\sigma^2)$$

(a) What does it mean for the above process to be covariance stationary? What are the necessary and sufficient conditions for the above AR(2) model to be covariance stationary?

(b) What is the unconditional mean, μ, of the process y_t? What is the unconditional variance?

(c) Determine the autocovariance function of the AR(2) model (determine an algorithm for computing $E[(y_t - \mu)(y_{t-k} - \mu)]$.

(d) Write the AR(2) model in state-space form. Using the state-space form, write an expression for y_{t+3} by starting the process at time t and then iterating out to time t+3.

(e) Determine the Wold representation of the series (MA representation) and thus the sequence of dynamic multipliers (it is sufficient to simply determine an algorithm for computing the moving average coefficients from the autoregressive coefficients).

5. Consider the problem of trying to determine if a stationary representation or a difference-stationary representation (unit root representation) is more appropriate for a particular data series, say, the real exchange rate between the US dollar and the Japanese Yen. For simplicity, the stationary and unit root models can be nested in the simple AR(1) model

$$y_t = \alpha y_{t-1} + \varepsilon_t, \varepsilon_t \sim i.i.d.(0, \sigma^2)$$

where $|\alpha| < 1$ gives a stationary model and $\alpha = 1$ gives a unit root model.

(a) Is the distinction between the two representations really that important? That is, what are the economic and statistical consequences of the two representations (you may use the exchange rate example and the simple AR(1) model above to help illustrate your answer)?

(b) Consider estimating the above AR(1) model by OLS.

(i) Under the assumption of stationarity, $|\alpha| < 1$, what is the asymptotic distribution of the OLS estimator of α?

(ii) Under the assumption of a unit root, $\alpha = 1$, what is the asymptotic distribution of the OLS estimator of α?

(iii) Briefly compare and contrast the asymptotic distributions you found in (i) and (ii).

(c) Briefly describe how you could construct a test to discriminate between the stationary and unit root models. What are the null and alternative hypotheses of the test? What statistic do you use to test the hypotheses? What is the distribution of this test statistic (you don't have to give the mathematical formula – just describe the distribution and give some intuition)?

UNIVERSITY OF WASHINGTON

ECONOMETRICS FIELD EXAMINATION

Autumn 1993

Startz, Chair
Nelson
Parks

Time: 4 hours
Answer all questions. Each question carries equal weight.

1. In specifying and estimating an econometric model, one often encounters a situation where there are more equations than unknown parameters. For example, in a method of moments approach to estimation there are usually more moment restrictions than unknown parameters. One possible estimation approach is to choose a subset of equations such that there are exactly the same number of equations as unknown parameters. Describe a "better" estimation approach that utilizes all of the equations to estimate the unknown parameters. In addition, explain the advantages and/or disadvantages of the "better" approach where you should define what is meant by the term "better".

2. Consider the model

$$y(t) = \phi\, y(t-1) + \alpha + \varepsilon(t);\ \varepsilon(t) \text{ iid } N(0,\sigma)$$

a. Derive the mean and variance of y.

b. Derive the autocorrelation function for y and its Yule-Walker equations.

c. Derive the likelihood function for the model using the prediction error decomposition method.

d. Compare the maximum likelihood estimate of ϕ with the moment estimate and the least squares estimate.

e. Use the transfer function of the model to derive the spectrum of y from the spectrum of ε.

f. For the time average of the y's defined as

$$w(t) = .5[y(t)+y(t-1)]$$

find its ARMA representation.

g. How would you attempt to address the question of whether w is more or less "smooth" than y?

h. For the y model, use the information matrix to obtain the asymptotic variance covariance matrix of the ML estimates of the parameters (ϕ,σ) assuming α is known.

i. Summarize what can be said about the small sample distribution of estimates of ϕ.

3. Suppose that we have data on the price of a financial instrument, but we do not know if a given observation is for the bid or ask or something in between. Call the "true" price x(t) and the observed price y(t). We have strong theoretical reasons to believe that x evolves as a random walk

$$x(t) = x(t-1) + u(t);\ u(t) \text{ iid } N(0,\sigma_u)$$

and we assume that the observation errors caused by the bid/ask interval are independent of the u's. Thus

$$y(t) = x(t) + \varepsilon(t);\ \varepsilon(t) \text{ iid } N(0,\sigma_\varepsilon)$$

a. Derive the ARIMA representation of y.

b. Does the price model put any testable restrictions on that representation? If so, what are they and how could they be tested?

c. Given data on observed price, how would you go about estimating the parameters of the price model. How would you estimate the width of the bid-asked spread?

c. Put the price model in state space form and show how the Kalman filter can be used to estimate the "true" price x from the observed prices y.

4. The absolute price version of the Rotterdam model of Barten and Theil results in differential demand equations of the form

$$w_i^* Dq_i = \mu_i Dq + \sum_j \pi_{ij} Dp_j + u_i \qquad \text{for goods } i=1,\ldots,n$$

where w_i^* denotes the ith share (averaged between observations t and t-1), Dqi denotes the log first difference of the quantity consumes of the tith good, Dpi denotes the log first difference of the ith price, and $Dq = \sum_i w_i Dq_i$ denotes the log first difference of a measure of real income. [i.e. $Dx_t = \ln x_t - \ln x_{t-1}$]. The symbols μ and π represent unknown parameters to be estimated; u_i is a random disturbance, normally distributed with mean zero. Observation subscripts have been suppressed.

Theoretical restrictions include:

Adding up:

$$\sum_i \mu_i = 1, \quad \sum_i \pi_{ij} = 0$$

Homogeneity:

$$\sum_j \pi_{ij} = 0$$

Symmetry:

$$\pi_{ij} = \pi_{ji}$$

You should assume that the disturbances are contemporaneously correlated. The covariance matrix for the complete system is then singular, but you can avoid this awkwardness in the context of maximum likelihood estimation by arbitrarily omitting one of the share equations from the system. (The parameter restrictions permit recovery of all of the missing parameters.)

(a) Show by adding the n demand equations that the disturbances must add to zero. Show that the nth equation is redundant by adding up the first n-1 equations and showing that the sum gives the nth.

(b) How would you impose the homogeneity condition on a typical equation? If you wanted to estimate the model with homogeneity imposed but not symmetry how would you proceed? Would GLS give more efficient estimates than single equation OLS in this context? Why or why not?

(c) Discuss the problems of estimating the model with symmetry imposed and of testing the symmetry condition. In this discussion you should treat the homogeneity and adding-up restrictions as part of the maintained hypothesis. Under the assumptions given discuss the properties of your estimates and tests.

[In discussing the approaches to estimation and testing in parts b and c, include enough detail so that your research assistant could follow the instructions.]

(d) If n, the number of commodities, is moderate to large, you may encounter practical difficulties in estimating the model as a system when symmetry is not imposed. Why? Would it be possible to test the symmetry hypothesis without estimating the unconstrained model? Sketch the approach.

5. a. Suppose that we have T independent observations $y_1,\ldots,y_T$ drawn by simple random sampling from a Pareto distribution which has the following pdf.

$$P(y|\alpha) = \frac{\alpha\, 10000^{\alpha}}{y^{\alpha+1}}$$

i. Find the ML estimator for α.
ii. What are its properties?
iii. Propose a test for $H_0{:}\alpha=2$ against the alternative that $\alpha<2$.
iv. Derive the information matrix (1x1), and use it to obtain an asymptotic variance for the ML estimator.
v. What would you use as the finite sample estimate of the variance?

b. Analyze the consequences for the least squares estimates in the classical linear regression model of the following departures from the standard assumptions:
i. One of the explanatory variables is a lagged dependent variable.
ii. In addition to i the disturbances are serially correlated.

UNIVERSITY OF WASHINGTON

ECONOMETRICS FIELD EXAMINATION

Autumn 1992

Committee: Parks (chair), Gritz, Nelson

YOU HAVE FOUR HOURS TO COMPLETE THE EXAMINATION
ANSWER ALL QUESTIONS.
THE QUESTIONS CARRY EQUAL WEIGHT

1. In specifying and estimating an econometric model one often encounters a situation where there are more equations than unknown parameters. For example, in a method of moments approach to estimation there are usually more moment restrictions than unknown parameters. One possible estimation approach is to choose a subset of equations such that there are exactly the same number of equations as unknown parameters. Describe a "better" estimation approach that utilizes all of the equations to estimate the unknown parameters. In addition, explain the advantages and/or disadvantages of the "better" approach where you should define what is meant by the term "better".

2. Consider the classical linear model with normality

Ω: $y \sim N(X\beta, \sigma^2 I)$ the unrestricted model

where y is Tx1, X is Txk, fixed and full column rank, β is kx1. The parameters β and σ^2 are unknown constants.

The information matrix is defined as

$$I(\gamma) = -E\left[\frac{\partial^2 L}{\partial\gamma\partial\gamma'}\right]$$

where L is the log-likelihood function.

Imposition of the hypothesis H_0: $R\beta = r$ results is the restricted model:

ω: $y \sim N(X\beta, \sigma^2 I)$ subject to $R\beta = r$.

Let $\gamma' = (\beta', \sigma^2)$ be the full parameter vector; let $\hat{\gamma}' = (\hat{\beta}', \hat{\sigma}^2)$ be its unconstrained MLE; and let $\tilde{\gamma}' = (\tilde{\beta}', \tilde{\sigma}^2)$ be its constrained MLE. Let $L(\hat{\gamma})$ and $L(\tilde{\gamma})$ be the value of the log-likelihood function evaluated at the unconstrained and constrained MLEs respectively.

The Lagrange multiplier (LM) test can be written generally as

$$LM = \left.\frac{\partial L}{\partial \gamma}\right|_{\tilde{\gamma}}' \left[I(\tilde{\gamma})\right]^{-1} \left.\frac{\partial L}{\partial \gamma}\right|_{\tilde{\gamma}}$$

where $\left.\frac{\partial L}{\partial \gamma}\right|_{\tilde{\gamma}}$ is the gradient of the log-likelihood function (sometimes referred to as the score vector) evaluated at $\tilde{\gamma}$, and where $I(\tilde{\gamma})$ is the information matrix evaluated at $\tilde{\gamma}$.

(a) Derive the LM test for H_0 above. What is its distribution, and what properties does it have?

(b) In applications the information matrix is sometimes consistently estimated using the observed information matrix evaluated at the constrained point, i.e. without taking expectations. The observed information evaluated at the constrained point is defined as

$$I_{ob}(\tilde{\gamma}) = -\left.\left[\frac{\partial^2 L}{\partial \gamma \partial \gamma'}\right]\right|_{\tilde{\gamma}}$$

Derive the expression for the observed information evaluated at the constrained point in the above case. Will it have the block diagonal feature of the expected information matrix? Explain. Is the resulting LM statistic based on the observed information guaranteed to be positive? Explain.

3. Consider a system of seemingly unrelated regression equations which includes the same explanatory variables in each equation.

(a) Does estimation of this SUR system by joint generalized least squares yield an efficiency gain over individual least squares estimation of each equation if parameter restrictions involve only parameters within an equation?

(b) Does the answer to part (a) change if there are cross-equation parameter restrictions? Explain.

4. Consider the model

$$y(t) = \alpha + \phi y(t-1) + u(t)$$

where $u(t) \sim i.i.d.\, N(0, \sigma^2)$.

(a) Use the prediction error decomposition to derive the likelihood function for this model.

(b) How does the MLE differ from the OLS estimator in this case?

(c) Derive the asymptotic variance of the MLE $\hat{\phi}$. Does it depend on σ^2? Why or why not?

(d) Can you evaluate $E(\hat{\phi})$? Can you evaluate plim($\hat{\phi}$)? What is known about the bias of $\hat{\phi}$?

5. Review the econometric methodology and the main empirical findings for one of the following areas of applied econometric research:

(a) models of return on risky assets in which expected return depends on conditional variance.

(b) predictability of stock returns.

(c) a topic of your choosing (the choice of topic as well as the discussion will enter into the evaluation).

6. Let $y(t)$ be output, and we are interested in the deviations of output from trend. The following model is proposed:

$$y(t) = x(t) + c(t)$$

where

$$x(t) = x(t-1) + \mu + \eta_t$$

$$c(t) = \phi c(t-1) + \varepsilon_t$$

with $|\phi| < 1$, η_t is $i.i.d\ (0, \sigma_\eta^2)$, ε_t is $i.i.d\ (0, \sigma_\varepsilon^2)$

and $\text{cov}(\eta_t, \varepsilon_{t-s}) = 0$ for all s.

(a) Is this a state space model? Why or why not?

(b) Derive the ARIMA representation of $\{y\}$.

(c) What restrictions does the model put on the parameteres of the univariate representation?

(d) What restrictions does it put on the autocorrelations of the process?

(e) Show whether the parameters of the model are identified. If the covariance between η and ε were non-zero, would the model be identified?

(f) Discuss how one would estimate the value of $x(t)$ given data on $y(t)$, $y(t-1)$,....

UNIVERSITY OF WASHINGTON

ECONOMETRICS FIELD EXAMINATION
Spring 1992
Committee: Parks (chair), Gritz, Nelson

YOU HAVE FOUR HOURS TO COMPLETE THE EXAMINATION
ANSWER ALL QUESTIONS.
THE QUESTIONS CARRY EQUAL WEIGHT

1. In specifying and estimating an econometric model one often encounters a situation where there are more equations than unknown parameters. For example, in a method of moments approach to estimation there are usually more moment restrictions than unknown parameters. One possible estimation approach is to choose a subset of equations such that there are exactly the same number of equations as unknown parameters. Describe an "better" estimation approach that utilizes all of the equations to estimate the unknown parameters. In addition, explain the advantages and/or disadvantages of the "better" approach where you should define what is meant by the term "better".

2. Consider the classical linear model with normality

Ω: $y \sim N(X\beta, \sigma^2 I)$ the unrestricted model

where y is Tx1, X is Txk, fixed and full column rank, β is kx1. The parameters β and σ^2 are unknown constants.

The information matrix is defined as

$$I(\gamma) = -E\left[\frac{\partial^2 L}{\partial\gamma\partial\gamma'}\right]$$

where L is the log-likelihood function.

Imposition of the hypothesis H_0: $R\beta = r$ results is the restricted model:

ω: $y \sim N(X\beta, \sigma^2 I)$ subject to $R\beta = r$.

Let $\gamma' = (\beta', \sigma^2)$ be the full parameter vector; let $\hat{\gamma}' = (\hat{\beta}', \hat{\sigma}^2)$ be its unconstrained MLE; and let $\tilde{\gamma}' = (\tilde{\beta}', \tilde{\sigma}^2)$ be its constrained MLE. Let $L(\hat{\gamma})$ and $L(\tilde{\gamma})$ be the value of the log-likelihood function evaluated at the unconstrained and constrained MLEs respectively.

The Lagrange multiplier (LM) test can be written generally as

$$LM = \frac{\partial L}{\partial \gamma}\bigg|_{\tilde{\gamma}}' [I(\tilde{\gamma})]^{-1} \frac{\partial L}{\partial \gamma}\bigg|_{\tilde{\gamma}}$$

where $\frac{\partial L}{\partial \gamma}\Big|_{\tilde{\gamma}}$ is the gradient of the log-likelihood function (sometimes referred to as the score vector) evaluated at $\tilde{\gamma}$, and where $I(\tilde{\gamma})$ is the information matrix evaluated at $\tilde{\gamma}$.

(a) Derive the LM test for H_0 above. What is its distribution, and what properties does it have?

(b) In applications the information matrix is sometimes consistently estimated using the observed information matrix evaluated at the constrained point, i.e. without taking expectations. The observed information evaluated at the constrained point is defined as

$$I_{ob}(\tilde{\gamma}) = -\left[\frac{\partial^2 L}{\partial \gamma \partial \gamma'}\right]\Bigg|_{\tilde{\gamma}}$$

Derive the expression for the observed information evaluated at the constrained point in the above case. Will it have the block diagonal feature of the expected information matrix? Explain. Is the resulting LM statistic based on the observed information guaranteed to be positive? Explain.

3. Consider a system of seemingly unrelated regression equations which includes the same explanatory variables in each equation.

(a) Does estimation of this SUR system by joint generalized least squares yield an efficiency gain over individual least squares estimation of each equation if parameter restrictions involve only parameters within an equation?

(b) Does the answer to part (a) change if there are cross-equation parameter restrictions? Explain.

4. Consider the model

$$y(t) = \alpha + \phi y(t-1) + u(t)$$

where $u(t) \sim i.i.d.N(0, \sigma^2)$.

(a) Use the prediction error decomposition to derive the likelihood function for this model.

(b) How does the MLE differ from the OLS estimator in this case?

(c) Derive the asymptotic variance of the MLE $\hat{\phi}$. Does it depend on σ^2? Why or why not?

(d) Can you evaluate $E(\hat{\phi})$? Can you evaluate $\text{plim}(\hat{\phi})$? What is known about the bias of $\hat{\phi}$?

5. Review the econometric methodology and the main substantive conclusions for one of the following topics in the recent literature:

(a) models of return on risky assets in which expected return depends on conditional variance.

(b) predictability of stock returns.

(c) a topic of your choosing (the choice of topic as well as the discussion will enter into the evaluation).

6. Let $y(t)$ be output, and we are interested in the deviations of output from trend. The following model is proposed:

$$y(t) = x(t) + c(t)$$

where

$$x(t) = x(t-1) + \mu + \eta_t$$

$$c(t) = \phi c(t-1) + \varepsilon_t$$

$$\text{with } |\phi| < 1, \quad \eta_t \text{ is } i.i.d\ (0, \sigma_\eta^2), \quad \varepsilon_t \text{ is } i.i.d\ (0, \sigma_\varepsilon^2)$$

$$\text{and} \quad \text{cov}(\eta_t, \varepsilon_{t-s}) = 0 \quad \text{for all } s.$$

(a) Is this a state space model? Why or why not?

(b) Derive the ARIMA representation of $\{y\}$.

(c) What restrictions does the model put on the parameteres of the univariate representation?

(d) What restrictions does it put on the autocorrelations of the process?

(e) Show whether the parameters of the model are identified. If the covariance between η and ε were non-zero, would the model be identified?

(f) Discuss how one would estimate the value of $x(t)$ given data on $y(t)$, $y(t-1)$,....

G

Ph.D. Preliminary Examination
MAJOR FIELD
Econometrics

August 10, 1990
Morning Session
9-12 a.m.

UNIVERSITY OF WISCONSIN
Department of Economics

INSTRUCTIONS: On the top of each page please write your assigned number (not your name), the date, "Major Field--Econometrics," and the Part of the exam and the number of each question being answered. Return the question sheets with your answer sheet. DO NOT write on the question sheets.

PART I. (One hour)

Suppose that each member of a population is characterized by (y,s,z,x), where $y \in \mathbb{R}^1$, $s \in \mathbb{R}^1$, $z = 0$ or 1, and $x \in \mathbb{R}^k$. In a "switching regression" problem, a researcher draws a random sample of size N, observes all the realizations of (z,x), but observes y only when $z = 1$, and observes s only when $z = 0$. Suppose that the researcher wants to learn $E(y|z)$ on the support of x. Discuss the identification of $E(y|x)$ in the following cases:

A. The researcher has no prior information about the distribution of (y,s,z,x).

B. The researcher knows that $P(y \geq s|x) = 1$.

C. The researcher knows that there exists an (unknown) $\alpha \in \mathbb{R}^1$ such that $P(y=s+\alpha|x) = 1$.

D. The researcher has the information in part C, and also knows that $E(y|x=x_0) = E(y|x=x_1)$. Here x_0 and x_1 are known, distinct values of x.

PART II. (One Hour)

A. In a certain population, $y = \alpha + \beta z + u$ and $x = z + v$, where z, u, and v are (unobserved) independent random variables, with $E(z) = \mu$, $E(u) = 0 = E(v)$.

In random sampling from that population, only x and y are observed. Let $\hat{y} = a + b x$ and $\hat{x} = c + d y$ denote the sample least-squares linear regression of y on x, and of x on y, respectively. Show that $\text{plim } b \leq \beta \leq \text{plim } (1/d)$.

Also, develop the extension of that result to a multiple regression case, where $y = \alpha + \beta_1 z + \beta_2 x_2 + \dots + \beta_k x_k + u$ and $x_1 = z + v$, with y, x_1, x_2, ..., x_k being the observables.

B. Consider the following "stochastic trend, autoregressive measurement error" model for the generation of an observable scalar time series y_t:

$$y_t = m_t + e_t,$$

$$m_t = m_{t-1} + \eta_t, \quad \text{and}$$

$$e_t = \rho e_{t-1} + \nu_t, \quad |\rho| \leq 1.$$

Here η_t and ν_t are mutually independent and i.i.d. scalar error terms with zero means and variances σ_η^2 and σ_ν^2, respectively.

Demonstrate that y_t can be written as an ARIMA(p, d, q) process for particular values of p, d, and q, and give an expression for the autocovariance function $\gamma(s)$ of the moving average part of this representation. How do your answers change for the three special cases (i) $\rho = 0$, (ii) $\rho = 1$, and (iii) $\sigma_\eta^2 = 0$ with $\rho \neq 0$ and $|\rho| < 1$?

PART III. (One hour)

For the simple linear model

$$y_t = \beta_o x_t + u_t , \qquad t = 1, \ldots, T,$$

suppose you wish to test the null hypothesis H_o: $E(x_t u_t) = 0$, under the maintained hypothesis $E(z_t u_t) = 0$, where y_t, x_t, and z_t are scalar observable random variables and β_o is an unobservable coefficient. To simplify calculations, assume that all variables have mean zero ($E(x_t) = E(z_t) = E(u_t) = 0$), and that, under the null hypothesis, the errors are homoskedastic ($E(u_t^2 | x_t, z_t) \equiv \sigma_u^2$).

Consider the following two approaches for testing this hypothesis:

(i) Estimate β_o by the IV estimator $\tilde{\beta} \equiv (z'y)/(z'x)$, where x, y, and z are T-dimensional vectors of observed variables. Then, using the residual vector $\tilde{u} \equiv y - \tilde{\beta}x$, check whether the sample covariance of x and $\tilde{u}$ is significantly different from zero using $S_1 \equiv (x'\tilde{u})/\sqrt{T}$.

(ii) Check whether the IV estimator $\tilde{\beta}$ is significantly different from the least squares estimator $\hat{\beta} \equiv (x'y)/(x'x)$, using $S_2 \equiv \sqrt{T}\ (\hat{\beta} - \tilde{\beta})$.

For either of these two approaches, a consistent estimator of the unknown variance σ_u^2 is given by $s_u^2 \equiv (\tilde{u}'\tilde{u})/T$.

A. Show that the ratio of S_1 to S_2 does not depend upon the dependent variable y_t, and that (suitably normalized) test statistics for each of these approaches are algebraically identical.

B. Derive the limiting distribution of this (suitably normalized) test statistic under the sequence of local alternative hypotheses $H_{A,T}$: $u_t = x_t(\delta_o/\sqrt{n}) + v_t$, where δ_o is an arbitrary scalar and v_t is independent of x_t.

Ph.D. Preliminary Examination
MAJOR FIELD
Econometrics

August 10, 1990
Afternoon Session
1-3 p.m

UNIVERSITY OF WISCONSIN
Department of Economics

INSTRUCTIONS: On the top of each page please write your assigned number (not your name), the date, "Major Field--Econometrics," and the Part of the exam and the number of each question being answered. Return the question sheets with your answer sheet. DO NOT write on the question sheets.

PART IV. (One hour)

Let (y_i, x_i), $i = 1,\ldots,N$, be a random sample of observations of the random variable (y,x). Here y is a binary indicator with $y = 0$ or 1, and x has support in $\mathbb{R}^1$. Suppose that one wants to learn $P(y=1|x=x_o)$, where x_o is a given value of x. Let it be known that $P(y=1|x)$ is continuously differentiable with $|\partial P(y=1|x)/\partial x| \le \alpha$ for all x, where $\alpha > 0$ is a known constant.

Characterize the asymptotic bias and variance of the following estimates of $P(y=1|x=x_o)$:

A. A K-nearest neighbor estimate, with K being a fixed integer rather than varying with N.

B. A kernel estimate, the kernel being the uniform density on $[-.5, .5]$ and the bandwidth being a fixed $h > 0$ rather than varying with N.

C. An estimate of the form

$$\exp(b_{1N}+b_{2N}x_o)/[1+\exp(b_{1N}+b_{2N}x_o)],$$

where (b_{1N}, b_{2N}) is the maximum likelihood estimate of the parameters of a logit model fit to the data.

/

<u>PART</u> <u>V</u>. (One hour)

This question considers testing for serial correlation in the presence of ARCH(1).

A. Let

$$\hat{\rho}_j = \left(\sum_{t=j+1}^{T} e_t e_{t-j} \right) / \left(\sum_{t=1}^{T} e_t^2 \right)$$

be the jth sample autocorrelation of a zero mean random variable e_t for a sample size of T. What is a 95% confidence interval for ρ_j under the null that $e_t \sim \text{iid } N(0, \sigma^2)$? (No need to derive anything - just give the usual confidence interval based on the asymptotic distribution.)

For the remainder of the problem assume that the conditional variance of e_t follows an ARCH(1) process:

$$(*) \qquad e_t | I_{t-1} \sim N(0, h_t), \quad h_t = w + \alpha e_{t-1}^2, \quad 0 < w, \quad 0 \le \alpha < (1/3)^{1/2},$$

where I_{t-1} is the information generated by past e_t, and the condition on α guarantees the existence of the unconditional fourth moment of e_t. It may be shown that if (*) is the data generating process,

$$\sqrt{T}\,(\hat{\rho}_j - \rho_j) \overset{A}{\sim} N(0, 1+[\gamma_2(j)/\sigma^4]),$$

where $\gamma_2(j) = E[(e_t^2 - \sigma^2)(e_{t-j}^2 - \sigma^2)]$ is the jth autocovariance of e_t^2 and $\sigma^2 = E[e_t^2]$ is the <u>un</u>conditional variance of e_t.

B. What is $\gamma_2(0)$ in terms of α and w? What is $\gamma_2(j)$ in terms of α, w, and $\gamma_2(0)$? [Hint: Conditional normality implies a relationship between $E_{t-1}e_t^4$ and h_t^2, which can be used to compute the unconditional fourth moment of e_t.]

(continued next page)

PART V. (continued)

C. Will tests of H_o: $\rho_j = 0$ with the confidence interval that you gave in part A above tend to reject too often or too infrequently? Also, will such tests tend to be more poorly sized for large or for small j? (Assume that T is very large so that the asymptotic approximation is accurate.)

D. The Ljung-Box statistic is

$$T(T+2) \sum_{j=1}^{m} (T-j)^{-1} \hat{\rho}_j^2 ,$$

where m is a fixed integer. How would you modify this so that it is valid whether e_t^2 ~ iid or e_t^2 ~ ARCH(1)? What is the resulting distribution of your test statistic? (You may assume, under the conditions listed in (*), that the sample correlations are asymptotically uncorrelated and that any other sample moments that you need to compute converge in probability to the corresponding population moments.)